MW00783892

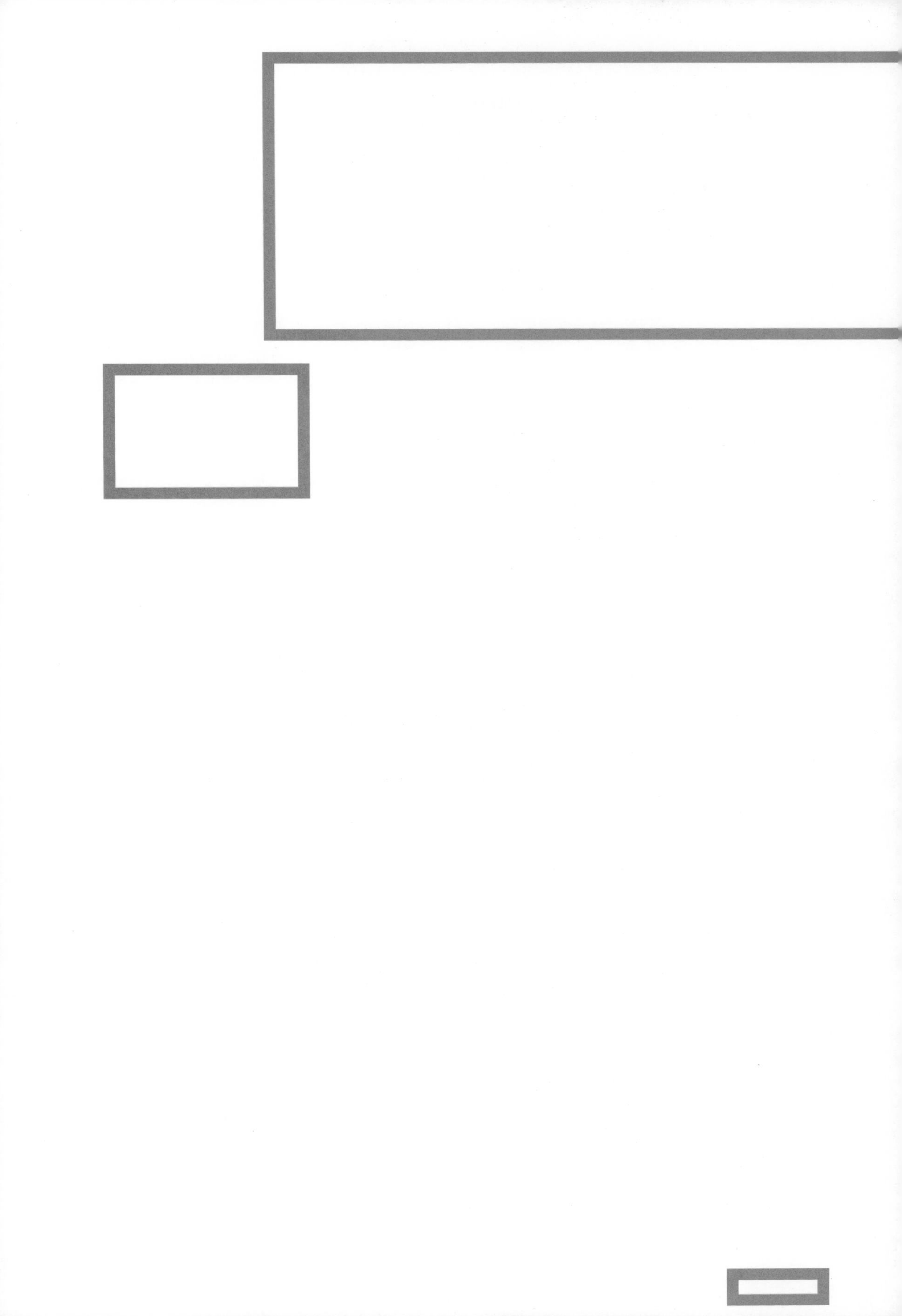

PIPE DUCT ROOM

Structuring De

Graphic Grids in
Theory and Practice

Ulysses Voelker

There are two legendary misinterpretations of the term "communication design" – the subject you are studying. The first is almost anecdotal: We contemplate the shape of telephones and smartphones. Very funny.
The second interpretation is as popular as it is wrong: Many people think that our mission is to create attractive surfaces. Closer to the truth, but not good enough.
Our actions require much more than that and are therefore much more complex. Everything we do is about the "construction" of visual communication.

Preface

"Visual communication" indicates the fact that there are people who want to communicate something nonverbally to other people. What these people want to say, to whom what is said should be addressed and in what way – are the topics we are dealing with. I must admit: Attractive surfaces are sometimes the issue, but not primarily. That depends very much on the communication intentions, the medium, and who finds what attractive at all.
I was talking about "constructing" visual communication. But what does that mean? It means that, within the framework of the creative laws inherent in every medium, we arrange, systematize and create hierarchies for content, i.e. "stage" it. These media laws make a book look like a book from afar or a magazine look like a magazine from afar. They tell us designers what to watch out for. The most important helper in constructing is "the grid". Its function and application is a topic of this book.

Furthermore, I would like to take you behind the scenes, i.e. where design is conceived and implemented. You will notice a new world opening up here, which is not only about craft instruments such as the grid, but also about cultural habits, principles of order and modes of action, technical innovations, and proven strategies. In other words, it is about visual communication in all its facets.
I would like to reveal these principles and show you that every design is embedded in communication processes, which in turn consist of diverse analyses and intellectual conclusions. This book introduces you to the principles of visual communication in four chapters. Chapter A is devoted to design practice: Where do you use which grids? What is their significance? How are they constructed?

In chapter B, I give answers to the seemingly simple questions: What is important when designing? How do you start?
In chapter C, I will deal with questions of a theoretical nature such as, for example, what is "visual rhetoric"? What are "the four sides of a message"? How do method and intuition relate to each other?
Chapter D contains a glossary. It explains various technical terms used in this book. I also recommend further reading.

So you are holding a compact mix of explanations, practical tips and background information in your hands. After reading it, you will look at the topic "structuring design" (and a bit also at the world) with different eyes. You will then be able to design more precisely and responsibly, I am sure.

SOMON
KG
12
UPRA
KG
12

A Graphic Grids in Everyday Design

Behind the scenes of design — Which grids are used where and how — The medium is the message: from the novel to the website, from the baseline grid to the responsive layout — The invisible grid always sends signals — Some things sound complicated, but actually everything is quite simple

A
A1
A2
A3
A4
A5
A6
A7
A8
B
B1
C
C1
C2
C3
D
D1
D2
D3
D4

Well, what is a grid anyway? It's never consciously perceived, yet it's everywhere: A grid organizes graphic elements on a surface – images, text columns, colored areas, and so on. It defines their positions and sizes as well as the edge distances, and in this way structures the entire graphic design with a "blueprint" consisting of a grid of lines.

Introduction
A — 1

The grid can be simple or multi-part – depending on the requirements. A novel 1 consists of not much more than a long text block, while the page of a newspaper 2 consists of a large number of articles, which in turn are divided into headings, texts, images and captions. It follows logically that the grid of a book is rather simple, the grid of a newspaper rather multi-part. The "construction style" of the grid is determined by the content requirements.

Before the grid can divide content (simple or multi-part), it must be decided how large the area in which the content is organized should be on a page: You have to define a type area. This is surrounded by margins – the result is an area within the area. The edge distances are handled differently from medium to medium. Divisions are made within the type area surrounded by edge distances. The area is divided into vertical columns. The number of columns is freely selectable and depends on the content and the medium. The columns are separated by so-called column spacing. The area is also – a necessity for some media – divided in the vertical: This results in equal-sized modules, which are formed from a multiple of the line spacing. Possible image sizes can be derived from them. In addition, images and/or texts can be aligned with them. There. That defines a grid. It doesn't get much more complicated from here on. Yet it gets more detailed. Because there are very different contents. They each require an obvious medium, which the designer then chooses (in coordination with the sender) – this can be a novel in book form, a magazine, an encyclopedia, a website, a newspaper or an atlas, to name just a few examples.

Each medium awakens a certain reading expectation through its design. Each reading expectation is followed by a certain reading behavior. The grid is partly responsible for ensuring that content; expectation and behavior correspond with each other. This is absolutely necessary because we are all rather conservative when it comes to reading: A newspaper

→ D1
Line spacing

"Grün ist die Hoffnung"
T. C. Boyle
(German edition of "Budding Prospects")

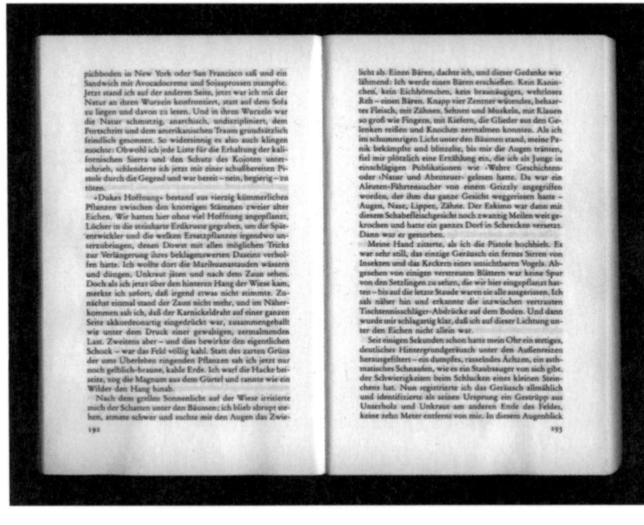

pichboden in New York oder San Francisco saß und ein Sandwich mit Avocadocreme und Sojasprossen mampfte. Jetzt stand ich auf der anderen Seite, jetzt war ich mit der Natur an ihren Wurzeln konfrontiert, statt auf dem Sofa zu liegen und davon zu lesen. Und in ihren Wurzeln war die Natur schmutzig, anarchisch, undiszipliniert, dem Fortschritt und dem amerikanischen Traum grundsätzlich feindlich gesonnen. So widersinnig es also auch klingen mochte: Obwohl ich jede Liste für die Erhaltung der kalifornischen Sierra und den Schutz des Kojoten unterschrieb, schlenderte ich jetzt mit einer schußbereiten Pistole durch die Gegend und war bereit – nein, begierig – zu töten.

»Dukes Hoffnung« bestand aus vierzig kümmerlichen Pflanzen zwischen den knorrigen Stämmen zweier alter Eichen. Wir hatten hier ohne viel Hoffnung angepflanzt, Löcher in die steinharte Erdkruste gegraben, um die Spätentwickler und die welken Ersatzpflanzen irgendwo unterzubringen, denen Dowst mit allen möglichen Tricks zur Verlängerung ihres beklagenswerten Daseins verholfen hatte. Ich wollte dort die Marihuanastauden wässern und düngen, Unkraut jäten und nach dem Zaun sehen. Doch als ich jetzt über den hinteren Hang der Wiese kam, merkte ich sofort, daß irgend etwas nicht stimmte. Zunächst einmal stand der Zaun nicht mehr, und im Näherkommen sah ich, daß der Karnickeldraht auf einer ganzen Seite akkordeonartig eingedrückt war, zusammengeballt wie unter dem Druck einer gewaltigen, zermalmenden Last. Zweitens aber – und dies bewirkte den eigentlichen Schock – war das Feld völlig kahl. Statt des zarten Grüns der ums Überleben ringenden Pflanzen sah ich jetzt nur noch gelblich-braune, kahle Erde. Ich warf die Hacke beiseite, zog die Magnum aus dem Gürtel und rannte wie ein Wilder den Hang hinab.

Nach dem grellen Sonnenlicht auf der Wiese irritierte mich der Schatten unter den Bäumen; ich blieb abrupt stehen, atmete schwer und suchte mit den Augen das Zwie-

192

licht ab. Einen Bären, dachte ich, und dieser Gedanke war lähmend: Ich werde einen Bären erschießen. Kein Kaninchen, kein Eichhörnchen, kein braunäugiges, wehrloses Reh – einen Bären. Knapp vier Zentner wütendes, behaartes Fleisch, mit Zähnen, Sehnen und Muskeln, mit Klauen so groß wie Fingern, mit Kiefern, die Glieder aus den Gelenken reißen und Knochen zermalmen konnten. Als ich im schummrigen Licht unter den Bäumen stand, meine Panik bekämpfte und blinzelte, bis mir die Augen tränten, fiel mir plötzlich eine Erzählung ein, die ich als Junge in einschlägigen Publikationen wie ›Wahre Geschichten‹ oder ›Natur und Abenteuer‹ gelesen hatte. Da war ein Aleuten-Fährtensucher von einem Grizzly angegriffen worden, der ihm das ganze Gesicht weggerissen hatte – Augen, Nase, Lippen, Zähne. Der Eskimo war dann mit diesem Schabefleischgesicht noch zwanzig Meilen weit gekrochen und hatte ein ganzes Dorf in Schrecken versetzt. Dann war er gestorben.

Meine Hand zitterte, als ich die Pistole hochhielt. Es war sehr still, das einzige Geräusch ein fernes Sirren von Insekten und das Keckern eines unsichtbaren Vogels. Abgesehen von einigen verstreuten Blättern war keine Spur von den Setzlingen zu sehen, die wir hier eingepflanzt hatten – bis auf die letzte Staude waren sie alle ausgerissen. Ich sah näher hin und erkannte die inzwischen vertrauten Tischtennisschläger-Abdrücke auf dem Boden. Und dann wurde mir schlagartig klar, daß ich auf dieser Lichtung unter den Eichen nicht allein war.

Seit einigen Sekunden schon hatte mein Ohr ein stetiges, deutliches Hintergrundgeräusch unter den Außenreizen herausgefiltert – ein dumpfes, rasselndes Ächzen, ein asthmatisches Schnaufen, wie es ein Staubsauger von sich gibt, der Schwierigkeiten beim Schlucken eines kleinen Steinchens hat. Nun registrierte ich das Geräusch allmählich und identifizierte als seinen Ursprung ein Gestrüpp aus Unterholz und Unkraut am anderen Ende des Feldes, keine zehn Meter entfernt von mir. In diesem Augenblick

193

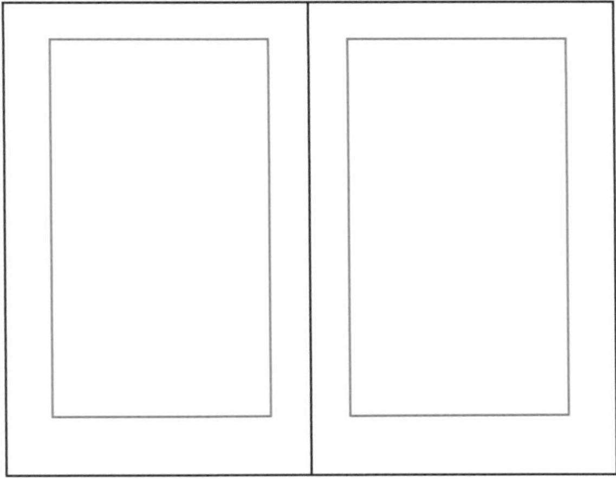

1 The grid of a novel is simple. The red lines in the drawing indicate the type area – and at the same time the different distances to the edge.

that doesn't look like one is not even taken at hand; a novel that has four columns on each page annoys us and is put aside.

I take a closer look at the following media: novel P. 14, non-fiction book P. 32, art catalog P. 46, magazine P. 58, newspaper P. 74, website P. 86. In the chapter "Further applications" the role of grids in signage, business stationery and in posters is addressed. For various reasons, this is done somewhat more briefly on P. 102.

I don't want to limit myself to showing what grids do in each case, but I also have to consider what influences their design and what has to be considered before they can be applied. Before we jump headlong into the media, I would like to address a few basic matters of course (conventions) that underlie all shown media regarding the reading direction. In European culture the following applies: A line is read from left to right, a text column is captured from top left to bottom right, and the pages of a publication are (usually) turned from front left to back right. This is what we are used to. I know that stating these conventions sounds banal in its obviousness. But there are regions in the world where things are quite different: In Japan, a line of text does not run from left to right, but from top to bottom. In the Arabic-speaking world or in Israel, the line runs from right to left. In this book I will refer to the cultural conventions that are customary in large parts of Europe. This also includes: Large fonts seem loud and important to us, while small fonts seem quieter and less important. Less text reads quickly and can be designed "rougher" than long texts that require care. And so on. Typography as we know it addresses such sensitivities and habits down to the smallest detail. All the examples I will be discussing here will have to deal with them. Further information, especially on micro-typography, can be found in the book "Detail in typography"*.

*
Detail in typography, Jost Hochuli
→ Further reading p. 162

"Süddeutsche Zeitung"
Issue of February 21, 2017

THEMA DES TAGES

Vorwärts – und ja nicht streiten

Agenda für Ältere

Kapitalstarke Marktverhältnisse

DIE SEITE DREI

Wir leben

War was?

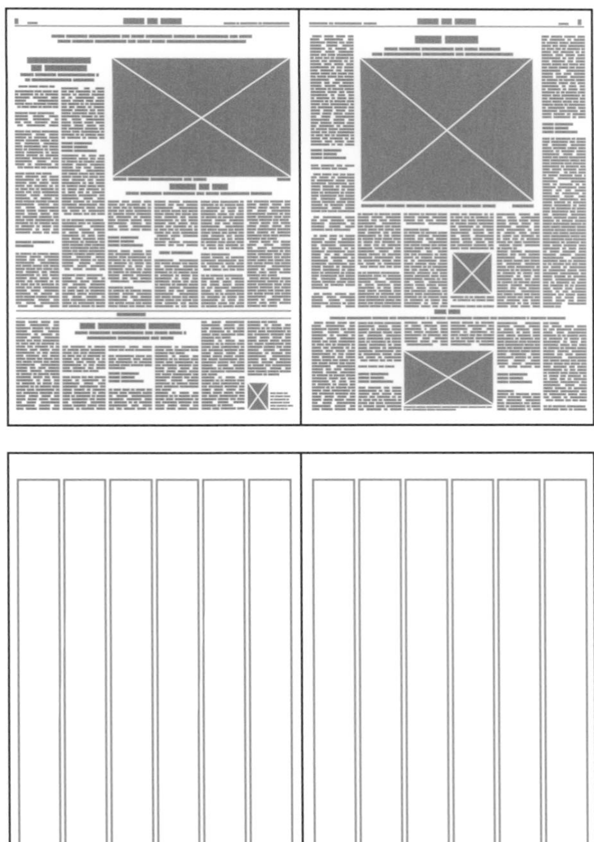

A
A1
A2
A3
A4
A5
A6
A7
A8

B
B1

C
C1
C2
C3

D
D1
D2
D3
D4

2 The lower drawing of the underlying grid shows: A large number of columns provide greater flexibility for text and image widths.

Now let us look at the grids in the mentioned media. For a better understanding, I would first like to explain what has to be considered when handling a grid that only structures text. The best way to do this is with the "book" example. Books come in different forms. From a grid perspective, the simplest form is a novel. It has a single-column grid that consistently structures the text body over many pages. In this way, the design corresponds to the reading expectation one has of a novel 1.
The readers' willingness to engage in "linear reading" is accordingly high: They know that they must read the entire text from beginning to end (i.e. "linearly") in order to fully understand it.

The grid in novels A—2

An initial question in the design of novels (besides the type of binding, the size, the paper, etc.) is certainly that of the format. It is common to choose an upright format because of a number of practical considerations (for example, the book must fit on a bookshelf and you must be able to hold it well in your hand when reading).
It is also important how the book comes across and functions when opened. Since the eyes of the readers look at the entire surface presented to them, the design of books is a double-page spread design. For the upright book there are a number of suggestions regarding the proportions of width to height. Many well-known typographers (from Tschichold to Hochuli) have in the past hundred years thought about a harmonious relationship between these proportions.

The approach to the "golden ratio", which is regarded as the epitome of harmonious side relationships, has always played a role. These considerations concerned not only the book format as a single page (e.g. when the book lies closed on the table), but also the double-page spread with its symmetrically placed type areas on the left and right, i.e. the grid 2. Type areas can be designed in many ways, as the examples on the following pages show 3–6.

→ D1

Reading expectation
Linear reading
Binding types
Paper
Golden ratio
Book formats
Symmetry

"Ulysses"
James Joyce

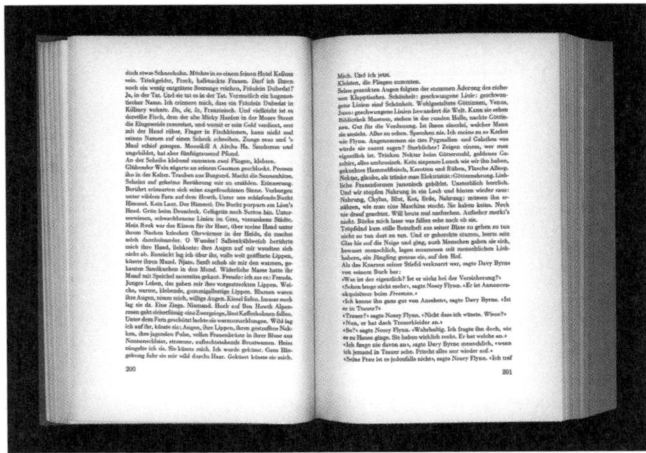

"Tropic of Capricorn"
Henry Miller

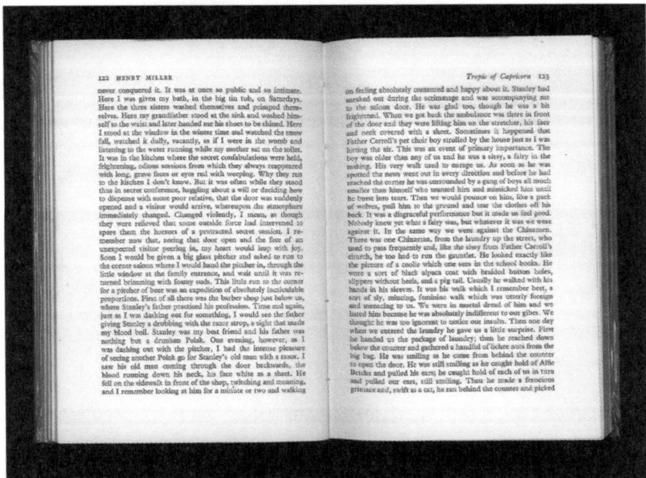

"Kritik der Macht"
Axel Honneth

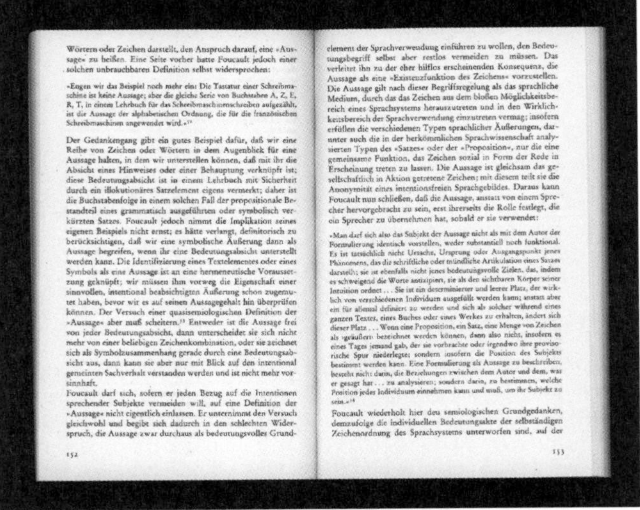

1 All examples shown serve the reading expectation of a novel, although the type area and the width of the margin differ from case to case.

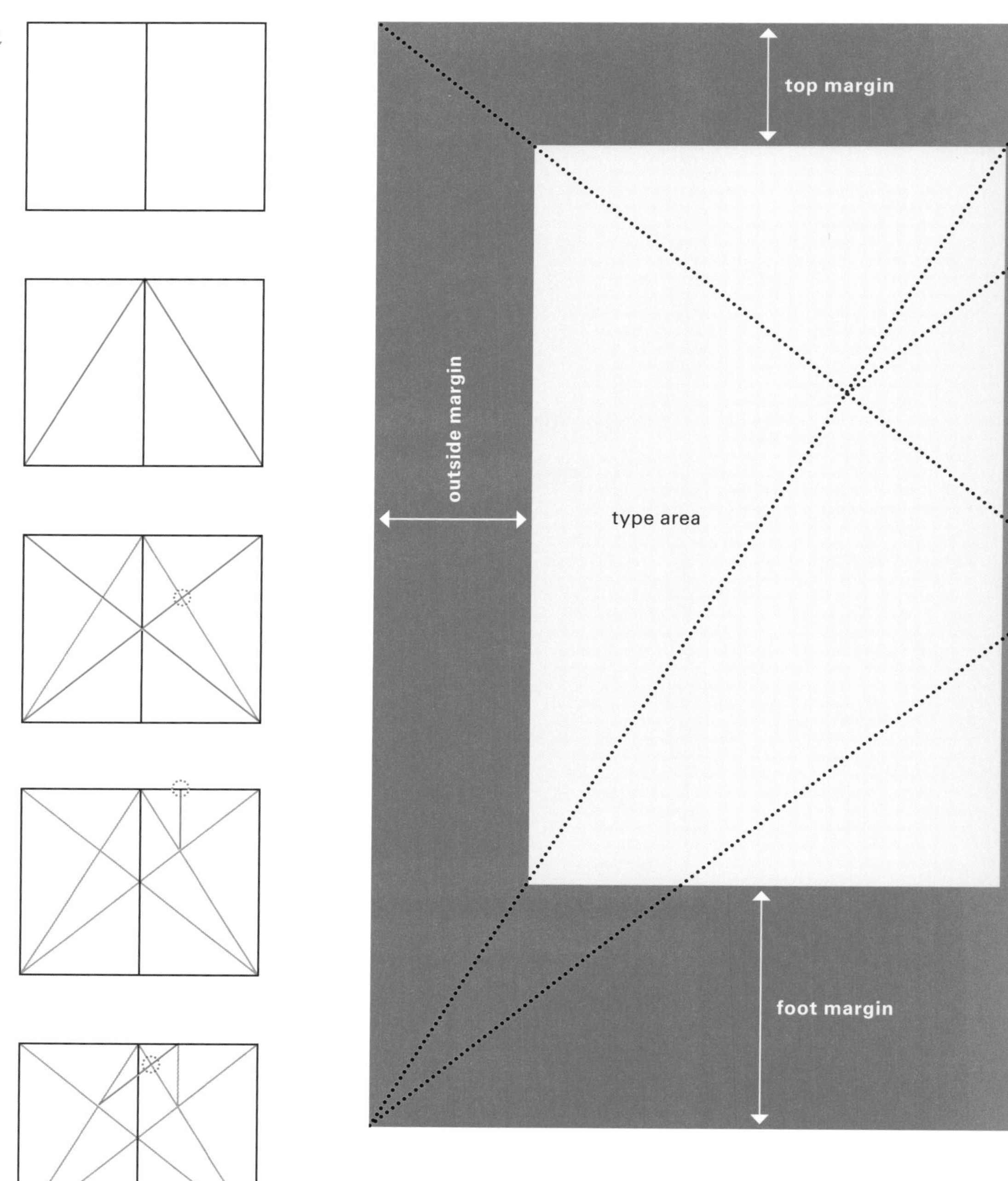

2 The large illustration shows a type area constructed according to the principle of the golden ratio (see the black dotted lines). The margins are created automatically here. The ten small illustrations show step by step how the type area was constructed as a double-page spread format. The type area design according to the golden ratio is rare nowadays, as it produces very large margins, which means an uneconomical use of space. Nevertheless, the margin proportions (narrowest in the gutter and then dynamically widening above, outside and below) are still applied.

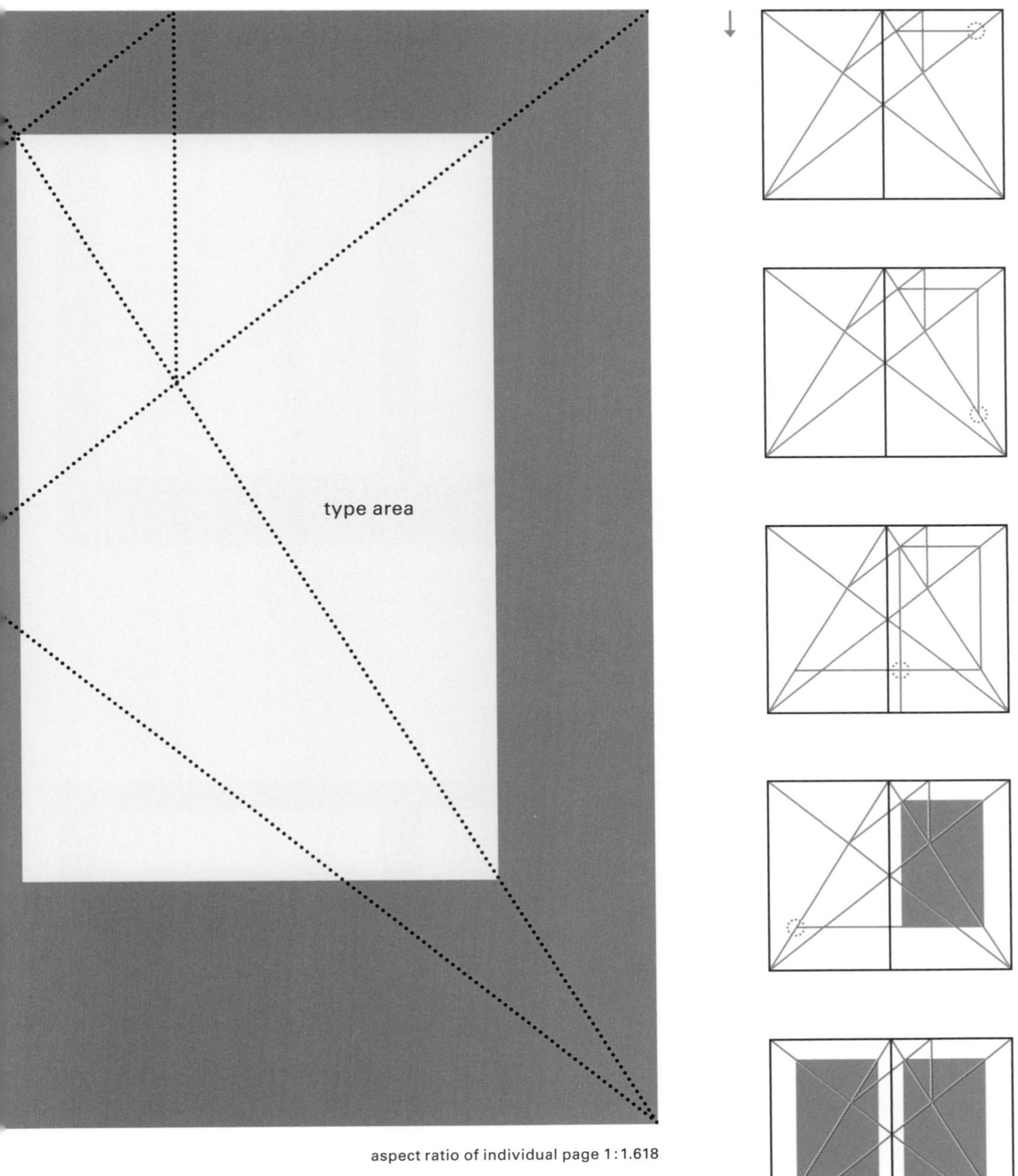

aspect ratio of individual page 1:1.618

A

A1

A2

A3

A4

A5

A6

A7

A8

B

B1

C

C1

C2

C3

D

D1

D2

D3

D4

16—17

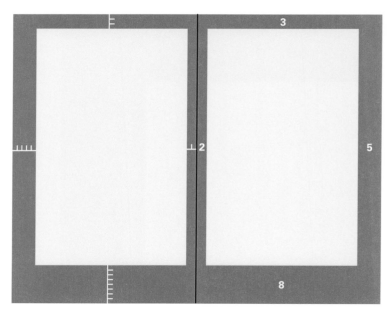

3 The type area design based on the Fibonacci sequence: 2 to 3 to 5 to 8. The formats of the individual book pages shown here are each based on a ratio of 1:1.618 (width:height).

4 A type area design that is often chosen for space-saving reasons: It is the principle 2 to 3 to 4 to 5 (and is thus roughly guided by the ratios of the Fibonacci sequence).

→ D1

Fibonacci sequence
Margins

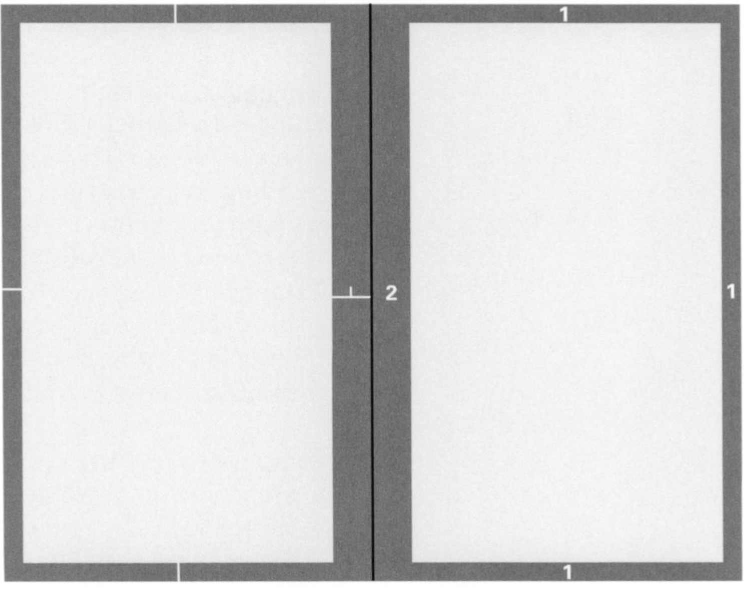

A
A1
A2
A3
A4
A5
A6
A7
A8

5 There are contemporary trends that produce unusually narrow margins (here: 2 to 1 to 1 to 1). Whether this type of design works depends on various aspects (sender's intention, content, target group expectations).

B
B1

C
C1
C2
C3

D
D1
D2
D3
D4

6 As a general rule, the use and nature of the medium determine the width of the margins. In relation to this illustration example, this could mean that a 300-page hardcover book will receive an adhesive binding, so the inside margin (A) must be wide enough so that the contents remain clearly visible when the book is opened. Since the book has to be held with both hands due to its weight and size, the outside margin (B) was given an approximate thumb width.

The basic design of a novel's type area is based on "inner" and "outer" criteria: The decisions on a font, its font size, line length and line spacing are, so to speak, "internal" matters of the type area. The length of a line is perceived as pleasantly readable if it comprises about ten medium-length words [7]. Depending on the size of the book, this results in an ideal type area width that meets this requirement. The width of the type area can be controlled by selecting an easily readable font size (usually between 8 and 12 pt, depending on the font selected and the line spacing). The "outer" criteria involve the placement of the type area in the format. This is where the edge distance comes into play.

To complete the picture of a novel double-page spread, the page numbers (so-called "dead" running titles) and any information such as chapter titles (so-called "living" running titles) must be placed. This is done outside the type area, usually at the top, outside or foot margin of the page. If one considers the "inner" and "outer" criteria together, then a novel layout is successful if the left and right type area are harmoniously embedded in the double-page spread and a pleasantly readable text (ideally justified) is presented.
It can then be said that the content requirement, the reading expectation and the reading process – "linear reading" – ideally correspond with each other.

→ D1

Font size
Line length
Line spacing
Justified typesetting

Dear King, the news about you state that you are the smartest of all wise men and the bravest of all brave men. Be so gracious as to present me a thousandth of your knowledge by answering a question. The king was already a little drunk when he replied: Gladly, noble lord, I will do that.

8 pt/10 pt
ø 72 characters per line

Dear King, the news about you state that you are the smartest of all wise men and the bravest of all brave men. Be so gracious as to present me a thousandth of your knowledge by answering a question. The king was already a little drunk when he replied: Gladly, noble lord, I will do that.

8.5 pt/10.5 pt
ø 66 characters per line

Dear King, the news about you state that you are the smartest of all wise men and the bravest of all brave men. Be so gracious as to present me a thousandth of your knowledge by answering a question. The king was already a little drunk when he replied: Gladly, noble lord, I will do that.

9.2 pt/11.2 pt
ø 64 characters per line
12 words per line

Dear King, the news about you state that you are the smartest of all wise men and the bravest of all brave men. Be so gracious as to present me a thousandth of your knowledge by answering a question. The king was already a little drunk when he replied: Gladly, noble lord, I will do that.

9.5 pt/11.5 pt
ø 60 characters per line

Dear King, the news about you state that you are the smartest of all wise men and the bravest of all brave men. Be so gracious as to present me a thousandth of your knowledge by answering a question. The king was already a little drunk when he replied: Gladly, noble lord, I will do that.

10 pt/12 pt
ø 59 characters per line

A
A1
A2
A3
A4
A5
A6
A7
A8
B
B1
C
C1
C2
C3
D
D1
D2
D3
D4

7 The illustration shows a right paperback page with a scale of 1 : 1. The margins are defined in a ratio of 2 to 3 to 4 to 5. The different sizes and line spacing of the text blocks in Times Ten typeface show paragraphs that have different readability. Of the five text groups – all set justified – the middle one is the most balanced typographically.

Back to the page number (technical term: folio) and the running title. Both items of information serve help the orientation in the book. While there is no book without folios, the necessity of a running title is based on the complexity of the content (as is the case with a textbook divided into many chapters, for example). Such an editorial complexity is naturally rather small for the long texts of a novel. Sometimes – when a novel consists of several chapters – they are also required, as the example novel "Water Music" below shows 8.

"Water Music"
T. C. Boyle

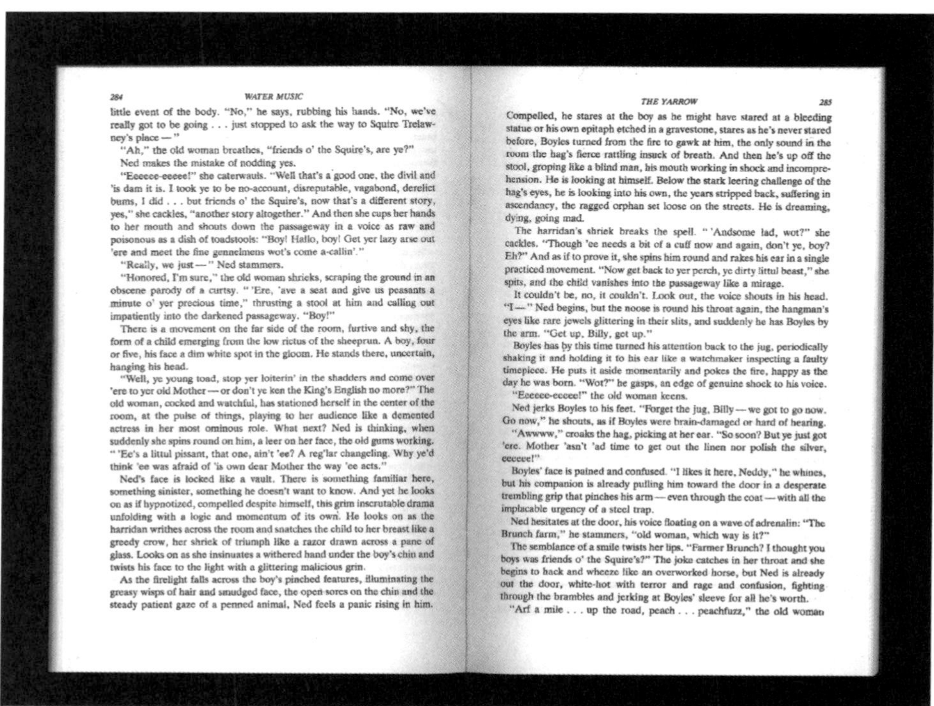

284 *WATER MUSIC*

little event of the body. "No," he says, rubbing his hands. "No, we've really got to be going . . . just stopped to ask the way to Squire Trelawney's place — "

"Ah," the old woman breathes, "friends o' the Squire's, are ye?"

Ned makes the mistake of nodding yes.

"Eeeeee-eeeee!" she caterwauls. "Well that's a good one, the divil and 'is dam it is. I took ye to be no-account, disreputable, vagabond, derelict bums, I did . . . but friends o' the Squire's, now that's a different story, yes," she cackles, "another story altogether." And then she cups her hands to her mouth and shouts down the passageway in a voice as raw and poisonous as a dish of toadstools: "Boy! Hallo, boy! Get yer lazy arse out 'ere and meet the fine gennelmens wot's come a-callin'."

"Really, we just — " Ned stammers.

"Honored, I'm sure," the old woman shrieks, scraping the ground in an obscene parody of a curtsy. " 'Ere, 'ave a seat and give us peasants a minute o' yer precious time," thrusting a stool at him and calling out impatiently into the darkened passageway. "Boy!"

There is a movement on the far side of the room, furtive and shy, the form of a child emerging from the low rictus of the sheeprun. A boy, four or five, his face a dim white spot in the gloom. He stands there, uncertain, hanging his head.

"Well, ye young toad, stop yer loiterin' in the shadders and come over 'ere to yer old Mother — or don't ye ken the King's English no more?" The old woman, cocked and watchful, has stationed herself in the center of the room, at the pulse of things, playing to her audience like a demented actress in her most ominous role. What next? Ned is thinking, when suddenly she spins round on him, a leer on her face, the old gums working. " 'Ee's a littul pissant, that one, ain't 'ee? A reg'lar changeling. Why ye'd think 'ee was afraid of 'is own dear Mother the way 'ee acts."

Ned's face is locked like a vault. There is something familiar here, something sinister, something he doesn't want to know. And yet he looks on as if hypnotized, compelled despite himself, this grim inscrutable drama unfolding with a logic and momentum of its own. He looks on as the harridan writhes across the room and snatches the child to her breast like a greedy crow, her shriek of triumph like a razor drawn across a pane of glass. Looks on as she insinuates a withered hand under the boy's chin and twists his face to the light with a glittering malicious grin.

As the firelight falls across the boy's pinched features, illuminating the greasy wisps of hair and smudged face, the open sores on the chin and the steady patient gaze of a penned animal, Ned feels a panic rising in him.

THE YARROW 285

Compelled, he stares at the boy as he might have stared at a bleeding statue or his own epitaph etched in a gravestone, stares as he's never stared before, Boyles turned from the fire to gawk at him, the only sound in the room the hag's fierce rattling insuck of breath. And then he's up off the stool, groping like a blind man, his mouth working in shock and incomprehension. He is looking at himself. Below the stark leering challenge of the hag's eyes, he is looking into his own, the years stripped back, suffering in ascendancy, the ragged orphan set loose on the streets. He is dreaming, dying, going mad.

The harridan's shriek breaks the spell. " 'Andsome lad, wot?" she cackles. "Though 'ee needs a bit of a cuff now and again, don't ye, boy? Eh?" And as if to prove it, she spins him round and rakes his ear in a single practiced movement. "Now get back to yer perch, ye dirty littul beast," she spits, and the child vanishes into the passageway like a mirage.

It couldn't be, no, it couldn't. Look out, the voice shouts in his head. "I — " Ned begins, but the noose is round his throat again, the hangman's eyes like rare jewels glittering in their slits, and suddenly he has Boyles by the arm. "Get up, Billy, get up."

Boyles has by this time turned his attention back to the jug, periodically shaking it and holding it to his ear like a watchmaker inspecting a faulty timepiece. He puts it aside momentarily and pokes the fire, happy as the day he was born. "Wot?" he gasps, an edge of genuine shock to his voice.

"Eeeeee-eeeee!" the old woman keens.

Ned jerks Boyles to his feet. "Forget the jug, Billy — we got to go now. Go now," he shouts, as if Boyles were brain-damaged or hard of hearing.

"Awwww," croaks the hag, picking at her ear. "So soon? But ye just got 'ere. Mother 'asn't 'ad time to get out the linen nor polish the silver, eeeeee!"

Boyles' face is pained and confused. "I likes it here, Neddy," he whines, but his companion is already pulling him toward the door in a desperate trembling grip that pinches his arm — even through the coat — with all the implacable urgency of a steel trap.

Ned hesitates at the door, his voice floating on a wave of adrenalin: "The Brunch farm," he stammers, "old woman, which way is it?"

The semblance of a smile twists her lips. "Farmer Brunch? I thought you boys was friends o' the Squire's?" The joke catches in her throat and she begins to hack and wheeze like an overworked horse, but Ned is already out the door, white-hot with terror and rage and confusion, fighting through the brambles and jerking at Boyles' sleeve for all he's worth.

"Arf a mile . . . up the road, peach . . . peachfuzz," the old woman

8 The folios are aligned with the upper outer edges of the type area. Left above the type area: the "dead" running title "Water Music" (book title). Right: the "living" running title "The Yarrow" (chapter title).

The technical jargon distinguishes between "living" and "dead" running titles. A living running title in our example "Water Music" is the naming of the chapter "The Yarrow" to which the opened double-page spread belongs ("living" because the chapter titles change in the course of the book). Dead running titles are the single folios, but also the book title appearing on every left page of the book (i.e. information that does not change).

Folios and running titles are placed in the margins and therefore do not belong to the type area. There are no fixed rules for their placement except perhaps that the information should facilitate orientation and therefore be clearly visible 9.

9 The possibilities to place pagination and running titles are manifold. However, they are always located outside the type area in the margins.

The basic design parameters described in this chapter naturally differ from book to book, because this medium is not only used by novels. The following pages illustrate this.

However much the design may change, the basic triad "content requirement – reading expectation – reading process" does not change.

A glossary shows this very clearly. Although it is rare to find it in a novel, it also appears in many media as an information appendix. I would like to present the glossary at this point, as the single-column type area now becomes multi-column 10.

A glossary consists of a large number of small "information tidbits", which are arranged in alphabetical order. The "information tidbits" are so numerous that they have to be very small. The expectation of reading is quite different from that of a novel. You don't want to read a reference book from front to back, you want to "consult" it. The reading behavior corresponds to this: One picks out the "information tidbit" one was looking for and gladly accepts that it is represented in small letters and in a limited number of lines. Narrow margins provide a space-filling type area. The small texts must not have too long lines, so there are many columns in which they are structured. The indications "full page, small font, small text groups arranged alphabetically and a multi-part grid" indicate that the publication should be read "consultatively".

The examples "novel" and "glossary" have shown that a type area must necessarily be divided into one or more columns. Such a horizontal division can be found in all media – whether newspapers, magazines, websites or e-books. The following chapters "non-fiction book", "magazine" and "newspaper" will show what to look out for when creating a grid when text and image are to be combined.

→ D1

Consultative reading

"Detailtypografie"
Friedrich Forssman,
Ralf de Jong

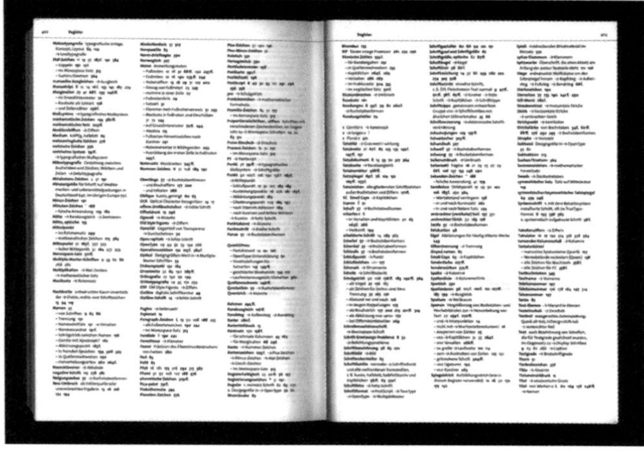

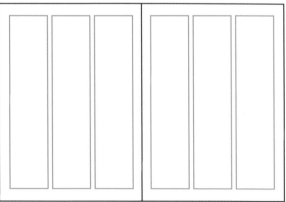

10 An example double-page spread of the glossary from the book "Detailtypografie" shows a multi-column type area. It organizes a lot of information in a clear way.

A A1 A2 A3 A4 A5 A6 A7 A8 B B1 C C1 C2 C3 D D1 D2 D3 D4

Finally, the illustrations on the following pages present once again the manifold possibilities of a novel design. But they also show that single-column type area – despite all differences in terms of expression and additive textual explanations – is an essential feature of linearly readable novel texts.

doch etwas Schneehuhn. Möchte in so einem feinen Hotel Kellner sein. Trinkgelder, Frack, halbnackte Frauen. Darf ich Ihnen noch ein wenig entgrätete Seezunge reichen, Fräulein Dubedat? Ja, in der Tat. Und sie tat es in der Tat. Vermutlich ein hugenottischer Name. Ich erinnere mich, dass ein Fräulein Dubedat in Killiney wohnte. *Du, de, la*, Französisch. Und vielleicht ist es derselbe Fisch, dem der alte Micky Hanlon in der Moore Street die Eingeweide rausreisst, und womit er sein Geld verdient, erst mit der Hand rüber, Finger in Fischkiemen, kann nicht mal seinen Namen auf einen Scheck schreiben. Zunge raus und 's Maul schief gezogen. Moooikill A Aitcha Ha. Saudumm und ungebildet, hat aber fünfzigtausend Pfund.

An der Scheibe klebend summten zwei Fliegen, klebten.

Glühender Wein zögerte an seinem Gaumen geschluckt. Pressen ihn in der Kelter. Trauben aus Burgund. Macht die Sonnenhitze. Scheint auf geheime Berührung mir zu erzählen. Erinnerung. Berührt erinnerten sich seine angefeuchteten Sinne. Verborgen unter wildem Farn auf dem Howth. Unter uns schlafende Bucht Himmel. Kein Laut. Der Himmel. Die Bucht purpurn am Lion's Head. Grün beim Drumleck. Gelbgrün nach Sutton hin. Unterseewiesen, schwachbraune Linien im Gras, versunkene Städte. Mein Rock war das Kissen für ihr Haar, über meine Hand unter ihrem Nacken kriechen Ohrwürmer in der Heide, du machst mich durcheinander. O Wunder! Salbenkühlweich berührte mich ihre Hand, liebkoste: ihre Augen auf mir wandten sich nicht ab. Entzückt lag ich über ihr, volle weit geöffnete Lippen, küsste ihren Mund. Njam. Sanft schob sie mir den warmen, gekauten Sandkuchen in den Mund. Widerliche Masse hatte ihr Mund mit Speichel sauersüss gekaut. Freude: ich ass es: Freude. Junges Leben, das gaben mir ihre vorgestreckten Lippen. Weiche, warme, klebende, gummigallertige Lippen. Blumen waren ihre Augen, nimm mich, willige Augen. Kiesel fielen. Immer noch lag sie da. Eine Ziege. Niemand. Hoch auf Ben Howth Alpenrosen geht sicherfüssig eine Zwergziege, lässt Kaffeebohnen fallen. Unter dem Farn geschützt lachte sie warmumschlungen. Wild lag ich auf ihr, küsste sie; Augen, ihre Lippen, ihren gestrafften Nakken, ihre jagenden Pulse, vollen Frauenbrüste in ihrer Bluse aus Nonnenschleier, stramme, aufrechtstehende Brustwarzen. Heiss züngelte ich sie. Sie küsste mich. Ich wurde geküsst. Ganz Hingebung fuhr sie mir wild durchs Haar. Geküsst küsste sie mich.

Mich. Und ich jetzt.

Klebten, die Fliegen summten.

Seine gesenkten Augen folgten der stummen Äderung des eichenen Klapptisches. Schönheit: geschwungene Linie: geschwungene Linien sind Schönheit. Wohlgestaltete Göttinnen, Venus, Juno: geschwungene Linien bewundert die Welt. Kann sie sehen Bibliothek Museum, stehen in der runden Halle, nackte Göttinnen. Gut für die Verdauung. Ist ihnen einerlei, welcher Mann sie ansieht. Alles zu sehen. Sprechen nie. Ich meine zu so Kerlen wie Flynn. Angenommen sie täte Pygmalion und Galathea was würde sie zuerst sagen? Sterblicher! Zeigen einem, wer man eigentlich ist. Trinken Nektar beim Göttermahl, goldenes Geschirr, alles ambrosisch. Kein sixpence Lunch wie wir ihn haben, gekochtes Hammelfleisch, Karotten und Rüben, Flasche Allsop. Nektar, glaube, als tränke man Elektrizität: Götternahrung. Liebliche Frauenformen junonisch gebildet. Unsterblich herrlich. Und wir stopfen Nahrung in ein Loch und hinten wieder raus: Nahrung, Chylus, Blut, Kot, Erde, Nahrung: müssen ihn ernähren, wie man eine Maschine stocht. Sie haben keins. Noch nie drauf geachtet. Will heute mal nachsehen. Aufseher merkt's nicht. Bücke mich lasse was fallen sehe nach ob sie.

Tröpfelnd kam stille Botschaft aus seiner Blase zu gehen zu tun nicht zu tun dort zu tun. Und er gehorchte stumm, leerte sein Glas bis auf die Neige und ging, auch Menschen gaben sie sich, bewusst menschlich, lagen zusammen mit menschlichen Liebhabern, ein Jüngling genoss sie, auf den Hof.

Als das Knarren seiner Stiefel verknarrt war, sagte Davy Byrne von seinem Buch her:

«Was ist der eigentlich? Ist er nicht bei der Versicherung?»

«Schon lange nicht mehr», sagte Nosey Flynn. «Er ist Annoncenakquisiteur beim *Freeman*.»

«Ich kenne ihn ganz gut von Ansehen», sagte Davy Byrne. «Ist er in Trauer?»

«Trauer?» sagte Nosey Flynn. «Nicht dass ich wüsste. Wieso?»

«Nun, er hat doch Trauerkleider an.»

«So?» sagte Nosey Flynn. «Wahrhaftig. Ich fragte ihn doch, wie es zu Hause ginge. Sie haben wirklich recht. Er hat welche an.»

«Ich fange nie davon an», sagte Davy Byrne menschlich, «wenn ich jemand in Trauer sehe. Frischt alles nur wieder auf.»

«Seine Frau ist es jedenfalls nicht», sagte Nosey Flynn. «Ich traf

little event of the body. "No," he says, rubbing his hands. "No, we've really got to be going . . . just stopped to ask the way to Squire Trelawney's place — "

"Ah," the old woman breathes, "friends o' the Squire's, are ye?"

Ned makes the mistake of nodding yes.

"Eeeeee-eeeee!" she caterwauls. "Well that's a good one, the divil and 'is dam it is. I took ye to be no-account, disreputable, vagabond, derelict bums, I did . . . but friends o' the Squire's, now that's a different story, yes," she cackles, "another story altogether." And then she cups her hands to her mouth and shouts down the passageway in a voice as raw and poisonous as a dish of toadstools: "Boy! Hallo, boy! Get yer lazy arse out 'ere and meet the fine gennelmens wot's come a-callin'."

"Really, we just — " Ned stammers.

"Honored, I'm sure," the old woman shrieks, scraping the ground in an obscene parody of a curtsy. " 'Ere, 'ave a seat and give us peasants a minute o' yer precious time," thrusting a stool at him and calling out impatiently into the darkened passageway. "Boy!"

There is a movement on the far side of the room, furtive and shy, the form of a child emerging from the low rictus of the sheeprun. A boy, four or five, his face a dim white spot in the gloom. He stands there, uncertain, hanging his head.

"Well, ye young toad, stop yer loiterin' in the shadders and come over 'ere to yer old Mother — or don't ye ken the King's English no more?" The old woman, cocked and watchful, has stationed herself in the center of the room, at the pulse of things, playing to her audience like a demented actress in her most ominous role. What next? Ned is thinking, when suddenly she spins round on him, a leer on her face, the old gums working. " 'Ee's a littul pissant, that one, ain't 'ee? A reg'lar changeling. Why ye'd think 'ee was afraid of 'is own dear Mother the way 'ee acts."

Ned's face is locked like a vault. There is something familiar here, something sinister, something he doesn't want to know. And yet he looks on as if hypnotized, compelled despite himself, this grim inscrutable drama unfolding with a logic and momentum of its own. He looks on as the harridan writhes across the room and snatches the child to her breast like a greedy crow, her shriek of triumph like a razor drawn across a pane of glass. Looks on as she insinuates a withered hand under the boy's chin and twists his face to the light with a glittering malicious grin.

As the firelight falls across the boy's pinched features, illuminating the greasy wisps of hair and smudged face, the open sores on the chin and the steady patient gaze of a penned animal, Ned feels a panic rising in him.

Compelled, he stares at the boy as he might have stared at a bleeding statue or his own epitaph etched in a gravestone, stares as he's never stared before, Boyles turned from the fire to gawk at him, the only sound in the room the hag's fierce rattling insuck of breath. And then he's up off the stool, groping like a blind man, his mouth working in shock and incomprehension. He is looking at himself. Below the stark leering challenge of the hag's eyes, he is looking into his own, the years stripped back, suffering in ascendancy, the ragged orphan set loose on the streets. He is dreaming, dying, going mad.

The harridan's shriek breaks the spell. " 'Andsome lad, wot?" she cackles. "Though 'ee needs a bit of a cuff now and again, don't ye, boy? Eh?" And as if to prove it, she spins him round and rakes his ear in a single practiced movement. "Now get back to yer perch, ye dirty littul beast," she spits, and the child vanishes into the passageway like a mirage.

It couldn't be, no, it couldn't. Look out, the voice shouts in his head. "I — " Ned begins, but the noose is round his throat again, the hangman's eyes like rare jewels glittering in their slits, and suddenly he has Boyles by the arm. "Get up, Billy, get up."

Boyles has by this time turned his attention back to the jug, periodically shaking it and holding it to his ear like a watchmaker inspecting a faulty timepiece. He puts it aside momentarily and pokes the fire, happy as the day he was born. "Wot?" he gasps, an edge of genuine shock to his voice.

"Eeeeee-eeeee!" the old woman keens.

Ned jerks Boyles to his feet. "Forget the jug, Billy — we got to go now. Go now," he shouts, as if Boyles were brain-damaged or hard of hearing.

"Awwww," croaks the hag, picking at her ear. "So soon? But ye just got 'ere. Mother 'asn't 'ad time to get out the linen nor polish the silver, eeeeee!"

Boyles' face is pained and confused. "I likes it here, Neddy," he whines, but his companion is already pulling him toward the door in a desperate trembling grip that pinches his arm — even through the coat — with all the implacable urgency of a steel trap.

Ned hesitates at the door, his voice floating on a wave of adrenalin: "The Brunch farm," he stammers, "old woman, which way is it?"

The semblance of a smile twists her lips. "Farmer Brunch? I thought you boys was friends o' the Squire's?" The joke catches in her throat and she begins to hack and wheeze like an overworked horse, but Ned is already out the door, white-hot with terror and rage and confusion, fighting through the brambles and jerking at Boyles' sleeve for all he's worth.

"Arf a mile . . . up the road, peach . . . peachfuzz," the old woman never conquered it. It was at once so public and so intimate. Here I was given my bath, in the big tin tub, on Saturdays. Here the three sisters washed themselves and primped themselves. Here my grandfather stood at the sink and washed himself to the waist and later handed me his shoes to be shined. Here I stood at the window in the winter time and watched the snow fall, watched it dully, vacantly, as if I were in the womb and listening to the water running while my mother sat on the toilet. It was in the kitchen where the secret confabulations were held, frightening, odious sessions from which they always reappeared with long, grave faces or eyes red with weeping. Why they ran to the kitchen I don't know. But it was often while they stood thus in secret conference, haggling about a will or deciding how to dispense with some poor relative, that the door was suddenly opened and a visitor would arrive, whereupon the atmosphere immediately changed. Changed violently, I mean, as though they were relieved that some outside force had intervened to spare them the horrors of a protracted secret session. I remember now that, seeing that door open and the face of an unexpected visitor peering in, my heart would leap with joy. Soon I would be given a big glass pitcher and asked to run to the corner saloon where I would hand the pitcher in, through the little window at the family entrance, and wait until it was returned brimming with foamy suds. This little run to the corner for a pitcher of beer was an expedition of absolutely incalculable proportions. First of all there was the barber shop just below us, where Stanley's father practised his profession. Time and again, just as I was dashing out for something, I would see the father giving Stanley a drubbing with the razor strop, a sight that made my blood boil. Stanley was my best friend and his father was nothing but a drunken Polak. One evening, however, as I was dashing out with the pitcher, I had the intense pleasure of seeing another Polak go for Stanley's old man with a razor. I saw his old man coming through the door backwards, the blood running down his neck, his face white as a sheet. He fell on the sidewalk in front of the shop, twitching and moaning, and I remember looking at him for a minute or two and walking

on feeling absolutely contented and happy about it. Stanley had sneaked out during the scrimmage and was accompanying me to the saloon door. He was glad too, though he was a bit frightened. When we got back the ambulance was there in front of the door and they were lifting him on the stretcher, his face and neck covered with a sheet. Sometimes it happened that Father Carroll's pet choir boy strolled by the house just as I was hitting the air. This was an event of primary importance. The boy was older than any of us and he was a sissy, a fairy in the making. His very walk used to enrage us. As soon as he was spotted the news went out in every direction and before he had reached the corner he was surrounded by a gang of boys all much smaller than himself who taunted him and mimicked him until he burst into tears. Then we would pounce on him, like a pack of wolves, pull him to the ground and tear the clothes off his back. It was a disgraceful performance but it made us feel good. Nobody knew yet what a fairy was, but whatever it was we were against it. In the same way we were against the Chinamen. There was one Chinaman, from the laundry up the street, who used to pass frequently and, like the sissy from Father Carroll's church, he too had to run the gauntlet. He looked exactly like the picture of a coolie which one sees in the school books. He wore a sort of black alpaca coat with braided button holes, slippers without heels, and a pig tail. Usually he walked with his hands in his sleeves. It was his walk which I remember best, a sort of sly, mincing, feminine walk which was utterly foreign and menacing to us. We were in mortal dread of him and we hated him because he was absolutely indifferent to our gibes. We thought he was too ignorant to notice our insults. Then one day when we entered the laundry he gave us a little surprise. First he handed us the package of laundry; then he reached down below the counter and gathered a handful of lichee nuts from the big bag. He was smiling as he came from behind the counter to open the door. He was still smiling as he caught hold of Alfie Betcha and pulled his ears; he caught hold of each of us in turn and pulled our ears, still smiling. Then he made a ferocious grimace and, swift as a cat, he ran behind the counter and picked

Wörtern oder Zeichen darstellt, den Anspruch darauf, eine »Aussage« zu heißen. Eine Seite vorher hatte Foucault jedoch einer solchen unbrauchbaren Definition selbst widersprochen:

»Engen wir das Beispiel noch mehr ein: Die Tastatur einer Schreibmaschine ist keine Aussage; aber die gleiche Serie von Buchstaben A, Z, E, R, T, in einem Lehrbuch für das Schreibmaschinenschreiben aufgezählt, ist die Aussage der alphabetischen Ordnung, die für die französischen Schreibmaschinen angewendet wird.«[52]

Der Gedankengang gibt ein gutes Beispiel dafür, daß wir eine Reihe von Zeichen oder Wörtern in dem Augenblick für eine Aussage halten, in dem wir unterstellen können, daß mit ihr die Absicht eines Hinweises oder einer Behauptung verknüpft ist; diese Bedeutungsabsicht ist in einem Lehrbuch mit Sicherheit durch ein illokutionäres Satzelement eigens vermerkt; daher ist die Buchstabenfolge in einem solchen Fall der propositionale Bestandteil eines grammatisch ausgeführten oder symbolisch verkürzten Satzes. Foucault jedoch nimmt die Implikation seines eigenen Beispiels nicht ernst; es hätte verlangt, definitorisch zu berücksichtigen, daß wir eine symbolische Äußerung dann als Aussage begreifen, wenn ihr eine Bedeutungsabsicht unterstellt werden kann. Die Identifizierung eines Textelementes oder eines Symbols als eine Aussage ist an eine hermeneutische Voraussetzung geknüpft; wir müssen ihm vorweg die Eigenschaft einer sinnvollen, intentional beabsichtigten Äußerung schon zugemutet haben, bevor wir es auf seinen Aussagegehalt hin überprüfen können. Der Versuch einer quasisemiologischen Definition der »Aussage« aber muß scheitern.[53] Entweder ist die Aussage frei von jeder Bedeutungsabsicht, dann unterscheidet sie sich nicht mehr von einer beliebigen Zeichenkombination, oder sie zeichnet sich als Symbolzusammenhang gerade durch eine Bedeutungsabsicht aus, dann kann sie aber nur mit Blick auf den intentional gemeinten Sachverhalt verstanden werden und ist nicht mehr vorsinnhaft.

Foucault darf sich, sofern er jeden Bezug auf die Intentionen sprechender Subjekte vermeiden will, auf eine Definition der »Aussage« nicht eigentlich einlassen. Er unternimmt den Versuch gleichwohl und begibt sich dadurch in den schlechten Widerspruch, die Aussage zwar durchaus als bedeutungsvolles Grundelement der Sprachverwendung einführen zu wollen, den Bedeutungsbegriff selbst aber restlos vermeiden zu müssen. Das verleitet ihn zu der eher hilflos erscheinenden Konsequenz, die Aussage als eine »Existenzfunktion des Zeichens« vorzustellen. Die Aussage gilt nach dieser Begriffsregelung als das sprachliche Medium, durch das das Zeichen aus dem bloßen Möglichkeitsbereich eines Sprachsystems herauszutreten und in den Wirklichkeitsbereich der Sprachverwendung einzutreten vermag; insofern erfüllen die verschiedenen Typen sprachlicher Äußerungen, darunter auch die in der herkömmlichen Sprachwissenschaft analysierten Typen des »Satzes« oder der »Proposition«, nur die eine gemeinsame Funktion, das Zeichen sozial in Form der Rede in Erscheinung treten zu lassen. Die Aussage ist gleichsam das gesellschaftlich in Aktion getretene Zeichen; mit diesem teilt sie die Anonymität eines intentionsfreien Sprachgebildes. Daraus kann Foucault nun schließen, daß die Aussage, anstatt von einem Sprecher hervorgebracht zu sein, erst ihrerseits die Rolle festlegt, die ein Sprecher zu übernehmen hat, sobald er sie verwendet:

»Man darf sich also das Subjekt der Aussage nicht als mit dem Autor der Formulierung identisch vorstellen, weder substantiell noch funktional. Es ist tatsächlich nicht Ursache, Ursprung oder Ausgangspunkt jenes Phänomens, das die schriftliche oder mündliche Artikulation eines Satzes darstellt; sie ist ebenfalls nicht jenes bedeutungsvolle Zielen, das, indem es schweigend die Worte antizipiert, sie als den sichtbaren Körper seiner Intuition ordnet ... Sie ist ein determinierter und leerer Platz, der wirklich von verschiedenen Individuen ausgefüllt werden kann; anstatt aber ein für allemal definiert zu werden und sich als solcher während eines ganzen Textes, eines Buches oder eines Werkes zu erhalten, ändert sich dieser Platz ... Wenn eine Proposition, ein Satz, eine Menge von Zeichen als ›geäußert‹ bezeichnet werden können, dann also nicht, insofern es eines Tages jemand gab, der sie vorbrachte oder irgendwo ihre provisorische Spur niederlegte; sondern insofern die Position des Subjekts bestimmt werden kann. Eine Formulierung als Aussage zu beschreiben, besteht nicht darin, die Beziehungen zwischen dem Autor und dem, was er gesagt hat ... zu analysieren; sondern darin, zu bestimmen, welche Position jedes Individuum einnehmen kann und muß, um ihr Subjekt zu sein.«[54]

Foucault wiederholt hier den semiologischen Grundgedanken, demzufolge die individuellen Bedeutungsakte der selbständigen Zeichenordnung des Sprachsystems unterworfen sind, auf der

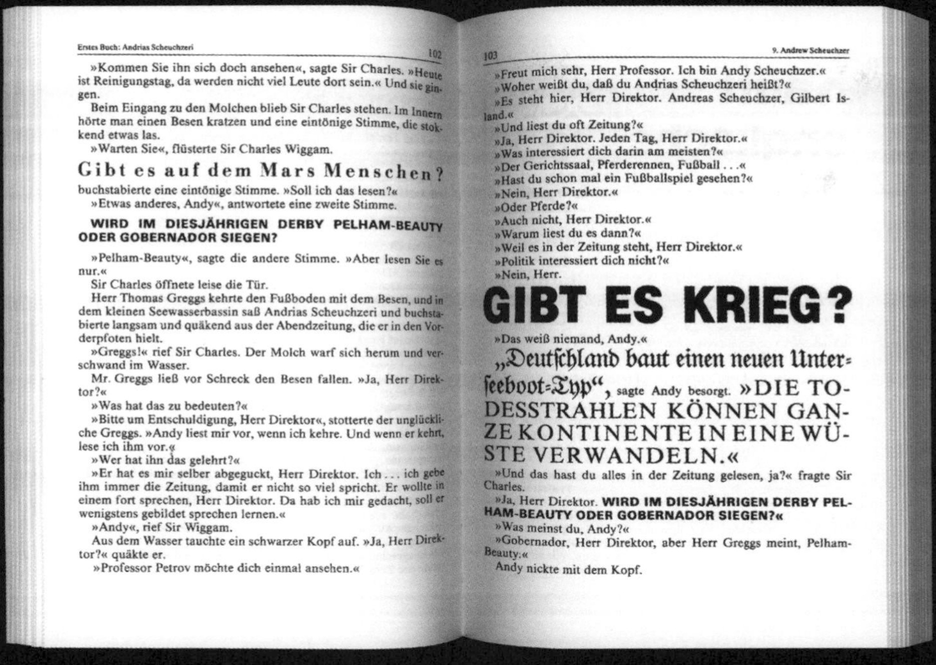

Erstes Buch: Andrias Scheuchzeri 102

»Kommen Sie ihn sich doch ansehen«, sagte Sir Charles. »Heute ist Reinigungstag, da werden nicht viel Leute dort sein.« Und sie gingen.

Beim Eingang zu den Molchen blieb Sir Charles stehen. Im Innern hörte man einen Besen kratzen und eine eintönige Stimme, die stokkend etwas las.

»Warten Sie«, flüsterte Sir Charles Wiggam.

Gibt es auf dem Mars Menschen?

buchstabierte eine eintönige Stimme. »Soll ich das lesen?«

»Etwas anderes, Andy«, antwortete eine zweite Stimme.

WIRD IM DIESJÄHRIGEN DERBY PELHAM-BEAUTY ODER GOBERNADOR SIEGEN?

»Pelham-Beauty«, sagte die andere Stimme. »Aber lesen Sie es nur.«

Sir Charles öffnete leise die Tür.

Herr Thomas Greggs kehrte den Fußboden mit dem Besen, und in dem kleinen Seewasserbassin saß Andrias Scheuchzeri und buchstabierte langsam und quäkend aus der Abendzeitung, die er in den Vorderpfoten hielt.

»Greggs!« rief Sir Charles. Der Molch warf sich herum und verschwand im Wasser.

Mr. Greggs ließ vor Schreck den Besen fallen. »Ja, Herr Direktor?«

»Was hat das zu bedeuten?«

»Bitte um Entschuldigung, Herr Direktor«, stotterte der unglückliche Greggs. »Andy liest mir vor, wenn ich kehre. Und wenn er kehrt, lese ich ihm vor.«

»Wer hat ihn das gelehrt?«

»Er hat es mir selber abgeguckt, Herr Direktor. Ich ... ich gebe ihm immer die Zeitung, damit er nicht so viel spricht. Er wollte in einem fort sprechen, Herr Direktor. Da hab ich mir gedacht, soll er wenigstens gebildet sprechen lernen.«

»Andy«, rief Sir Wiggam.

Aus dem Wasser tauchte ein schwarzer Kopf auf. »Ja, Herr Direktor?« quäkte er.

»Professor Petrov möchte dich einmal ansehen.«

103 9. Andrew Scheuchzer

»Freut mich sehr, Herr Professor. Ich bin Andy Scheuchzer.«

»Woher weißt du, daß du Andrias Scheuchzeri heißt?«

»Es steht hier, Herr Direktor. Andreas Scheuchzer, Gilbert Island.«

»Und liest du oft Zeitung?«

»Ja, Herr Direktor. Jeden Tag, Herr Direktor.«

»Was interessiert dich darin am meisten?«

»Der Gerichtssaal, Pferderennen, Fußball . . .«

»Hast du schon mal ein Fußballspiel gesehen?«

»Nein, Herr Direktor.«

»Oder Pferde?«

»Auch nicht, Herr Direktor.«

»Warum liest du es dann?«

»Weil es in der Zeitung steht, Herr Direktor.«

»Politik interessiert dich nicht?«

»Nein, Herr.

GIBT ES KRIEG?

»Das weiß niemand, Andy.«

„Deutschland baut einen neuen Unterseeboot-Typ", sagte Andy besorgt. »DIE TODESSTRAHLEN KÖNNEN GANZE KONTINENTE IN EINE WÜSTE VERWANDELN.«

»Und das hast du alles in der Zeitung gelesen, ja?« fragte Sir Charles.

»Ja, Herr Direktor. **WIRD IM DIESJÄHRIGEN DERBY PELHAM-BEAUTY ODER GOBERNADOR SIEGEN?**«

»Was meinst du, Andy?«

»Gobernador, Herr Direktor, aber Herr Greggs meint, Pelham-Beauty.«

Andy nickte mit dem Kopf.

5

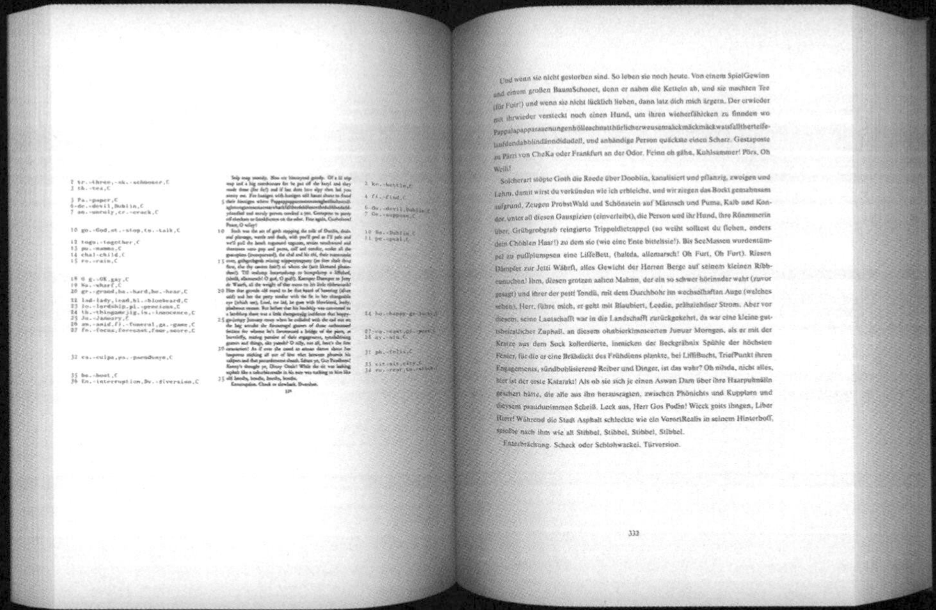

6

Dann schwang er sich wieder auf seinen Panzer. Ich war zwar entschlossen, so schnell wie möglich die Spritze fertigzumachen, aber drei Tage, das war knapp. Und blaumachen wollte ich nicht. Ich wollte nicht noch im letzten Moment ein Risiko eingehen durch Blaumachen. Zaremba wäre doch glatt nach vierundzwanzig Stunden aufgetaucht und hätte nach dem Rechten geschnüffelt. Oder Addi. Ich war immerhin sein größter Erziehungserfolg. Ich wollte die Spritze fertigmachen, sie Addi auf den Tisch knallen und dann abdampfen nach Mittenberg und von mir aus die Lehre zu Ende machen. So weit war ich. Ich weiß nicht, ob das einer versteht, Leute. Wahrscheinlich war mir einfach bloß mulmig wegen Weihnachten. Ich stand zwar nie besonders auf diesen Weihnachtsklimbim und das. »O du fröhliche« und Bäumchen und Kuchen. Aber mulmig war mir doch irgendwie. Wahrscheinlich ging ich auch deswegen *gleich* zur Post, um zu sehen, ob im Schließfach was von Willi war. Sonst ging ich immer erst nach Feierabend.

Mir wurde sofort komisch, als im Schließfach ein Eilbrief von Willi war. Ich riß ihn auf. Ich wurde nicht wieder.
Der wichtigste Satz war...
mach mit mir, was du willst. Ich hab es nicht ausgehalten. Ich hab deiner Mutter gesagt,

wo du bist. Das du dich nicht wunderst, wenn sie auftaucht.

Der Brief war zwei Tage gegangen. Ich wußte, was ich zu tun hatte. Ich machte sofort kehrt. Wenn sie den Frühzug in Mittenberg nahm, hätte sie schon dasein müssen, Wegezeit eingerechnet. Folglich hatte ich noch eine Chance bis zum Abendzug. Ich kaufte einen Armvoll Milchtüten, weil Milch am einfachsten satt macht, und schloß mich in der Laube ein. Ich verhängte alle Fenster. Vorher machte ich draußen noch einen Zettel an: Bin gleich wieder da!
Im Fall aller Fälle. Das konnte auch für den nächsten blöden Bulldozer gut sein, dachte ich. Dann stürzte ich mich auf meine Spritze. Ich fing an zu schuften wie irr, ich Idiot.

»Am Montag, einen Tag vor Weihnachten, kam er nicht zur Arbeit. Wir waren nicht besonders sauer deswegen. Es war unwahrscheinlich mild, und wir konnten den Tag gut nutzen, aber wir hatten den Jahresplan

---

Solomonski
Eigentlich Albert Salomonski (1839–1915), legendärer Zirkusartist und -direktor, eröffnete 1880 in Moskau einen eigenen Zirkus am Zwetnoi Boulevard.

Jussems
Eine von Juri S. Rjabinin gegründete vierköpfige Akrobatentruppe.

Nikitin
Dmitri (1835–1918), Akim (1843–1917) und Pjotr (1846–1921) Nikitin, gründeten in Moskau verschiedene Zirkusse, gemeint ist offenbar der Zirkus auf der Großen Gartenstraße, der ab 1919 verstaatlicht wurde und dann der »2. Staatszirkus« hieß. Der konservative Preobraschenski nennt den Zirkus also noch bei seinem alten Namen. Das Gebäude auf der Großen Gartenstraße greift Bulgakow in seinem Roman *Meister und Margarita* wieder auf, indem er das Theater *Varieté* dort ansiedelt.

Filippowitsch trank den Kaffee aus, sah auf die Uhr, betätigte den Repetierknopf, und sie schlug sanft ein Viertel 9. Seiner guten alten Gewohnheit gemäß sank der Professor auf die gotische Lehne zurück und nahm sich die Zeitung vom Beistelltischchen.
– Doktor, tun Sie mir den Gefallen und fahren Sie mit ihm in den Zirkus. Nur überprüfen Sie bitte vorher anhand des Programms, ob Kater mitwirken.
– Das Pack würd ich nie in den Zirkus reinlassen –, murrte Lumpikow und schüttelte mit dem Kopf.
– Ach, dort wird so mancher hereingelassen –, versetzte Filipp Filippowitsch mehrdeutig, – nun, was läuft denn heute?
– Bei *Solomonski*[*] –, las Bormenthal, – 4 irgendwelche ... Jussems[*] sowie »Ein Mann am toten Punkt«.
– Was sind denn Jussems? –, rätselte Filipp Filippowitsch, Schlimmes ahnend.
– Weiß der Himmel, ich höre das Wort zum ersten Mal.
– Dann schauen Sie doch lieber bei *Nikitin*. Wir können uns keine Überraschungen leisten.
– Bei *Nikitin*[*] ... Bei *Nikitin* ... Hmmm ... Elefanten und »Der menschliche Höhenflug«.
– Nun, was halten Sie von Elefanten, mein lieber Lumpikow? –, fragte Filipp Filippowitsch misstrauisch.
Jener reagierte gekränkt.
– Na ist doch eh klar. Elefanten sind keine Kater. 's sind nützliche Tiere.
– Fein. Wenn sie nützlich sind, fahren Sie hin und schauen sie sich an. Und in allen Dingen sollten Sie unbedingt auf Iwan Arnoldowitsch hören. Am Büfett bitte keine großen Reden. Und, Iwan Arnoldowitsch, ich verlasse mich auf Sie: Kein Bier für Lumpikow.
10 Minuten später fuhren Iwan Arnoldowitsch und Lumpikow in den Zirkus, Lumpikow trug eine Schiebermütze mit Entenschnabel und einen Mantel aus steifem Stoff mit hochgeklapptem Kragen. Nun wurde es in der Wohnung still. Filipp Filippowitsch begab sich in sein

Kabinett. Das Licht unter dem grünen Schirm machte den riesigen Raum noch ruhiger. Der Professor ging auf und ab.
Die Zigarre leuchtete lange und heiß mit einem blässlich grünen Glimmen. Während er die Hände in die Hosentaschen steckte, brütete seine Gelehrtenstirn mit Hofratsecken einen trüben Gedanken aus. Seine Lippen schmatzten leicht, durch die Zähne sang er:

Zu des Niles heil'gem Ufer ...

und murmelte etwas vor sich hin.
Endlich tat er die Zigarre in den Aschenbecher, marschierte zum Schrank, welcher ganz und gar aus Glas bestand, und ließ das gesamte Zimmer sogleich von drei stärksten Deckenstrahlern erglühen. Er griff in den Glasschrank ins dritte Fach nach einer glatten schmalen Flasche und begann, sie grübelnd im Glanz der blendenden Lampen zu begutachten. In der klaren und dickflüssigen Brühe schwamm oben ein weißes Knubbelchen, entfernt aus Lumpis gehirnlichen Tiefen. Filipp Filippowitsch zuckte die Schultern, krümmte den Mund, machte »hmmm-hmmm« und verschlang das Knubbelchen mit den Augen, als wollte er in ihm, dem Unversenkbaren, den Grund für all die absonderlichen Episoden entdecken, die das Leben in der Pretschistenka-Wohnung so komplett umgekrempelt haben.
Mag schon sein, dass der hochgebildete Mensch ihn dann auch tatsächlich entdeckte. Auf jeden Fall, nachdem er die Hirnanhangsdrüse nun zur Genüge studiert hatte, stellte er die Flasche zurück in den Schrank, sperrte ihn zu, steckte den Schlüssel in die Westentasche und stürzte sich rücklings, den Kopf eingezogen, die Hände im Jackett vergraben, auf das Sofaleder. Er schmauchte noch lange die zweite Zigarre, kaute ihr Ende vollkommen durch, bevor er, getaucht in Einsamkeit, grün gefärbt, wie der greise Faust, ausrief:
– Bei Gott, ich glaube, ich tue es!
Keiner erwiderte etwas darauf. Keine Geräusche mehr in der Wohnung. (In der Obuchow-Gasse wird ja bekanntlich der Verkehr gegen

THE GRID IN NOVELS

1 Ulysses
James Joyce

2 Water Music
T. C. Boyle

3 Tropic of Capricorn
Henry Miller

4 Kritik der Macht
Axel Honneth

5 Der Krieg mit den Molchen
Karel Capek

6 Finnegans Wake
James Joyce

7 Die neuen Leiden des jungen W.
Ulrich Plenzdorf

8 Das hündische Herz
Michail Bulgakow

A

A1

A2

A3

A4

A5

A6

A7

A8

B

B1

C

C1

C2

C3

D

D1

D2

D3

D4

We are all familiar with non-fiction books, because we went to school. And sometimes I still ask myself today whether my lack of affection for one subject or another had something to do with the confusing non-fiction books I had to plough through. But it's not that simple: A non-fiction book confronts us designers with the task of combining texts and images, but we are expected do so with the greatest possible reading comfort and optimal reading guidance.

The grid in non-fiction books A–3

Primarily, of course, a sensible reading guidance is also required for non-fiction books: Headlines refer to the corresponding columns, marginal columns supplement the text, and picture captions assist comprehension. In other words: The content is presented in a comprehensible way, creating a harmonious overall picture. Such creative harmony also requires recurring image sizes. They stand in a (invisible) relationship to one another – for example, in that their formats behave proportionally to one another. And it is also part of creative harmony that pictures, when they stand next to (or in) the text, refer to row lines (i.e. to the baseline grid). Thus, images should not float in space "somehow" without reference to each other 1.

In the following I would like to explain what this means in detail. First, to clarify the term: A baseline grid defines the vertical distance between lines of text, it is the manifested line spacing. It can be used to align incoming text (in principle, this applies to all media). The aim is for texts to "hold registers" (i.e. stand on the same font lines) if, for example, they are distributed next to each other in several columns.

This system "baseline grid" is now combined with the system "module". The latter is the vertical division of the type area into modules of the same size, which are separated from each other by a vertical distance. A module also aligns its width with a column that the grid has already defined horizontally. Why is it necessary to harmonize the two systems? Because when an image is placed next to a text, it becomes related to the text. The following double-page spread shows step by step how such a structure can be created 2–5.

"Alvar Aalto"
Alvar Aalto, Karl Fleig

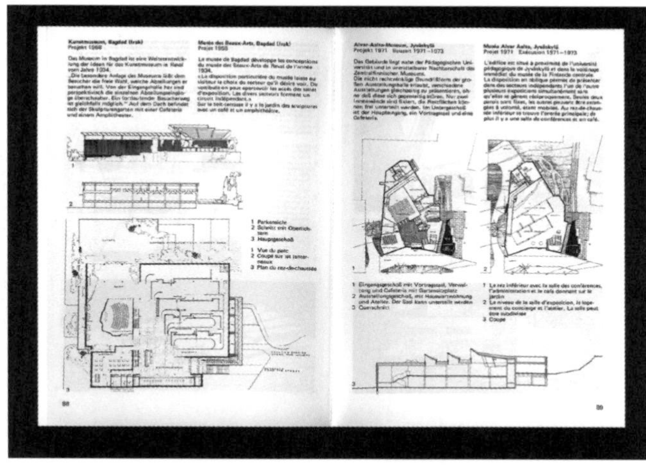

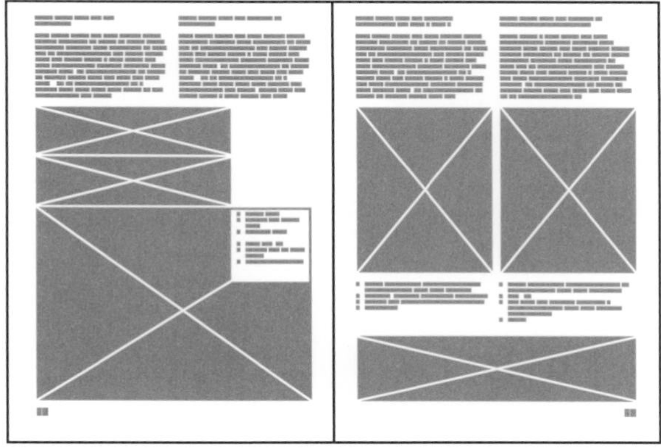

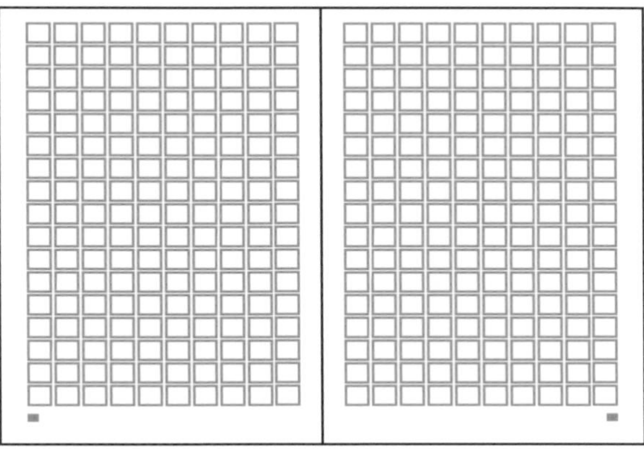

A
A1
A2
A3
A4
A5
A6
A7
A8
B
B1
C
C1
C2
C3
D
D1
D2
D3
D4

1 The example double-page spread from a non-fiction book shows that a lot of information has to be organized here – easily comprehensible for the reader. This is why the grid is divided not only horizontally but also vertically. This vertical division into modules enables unifying reference edges and image proportionality.

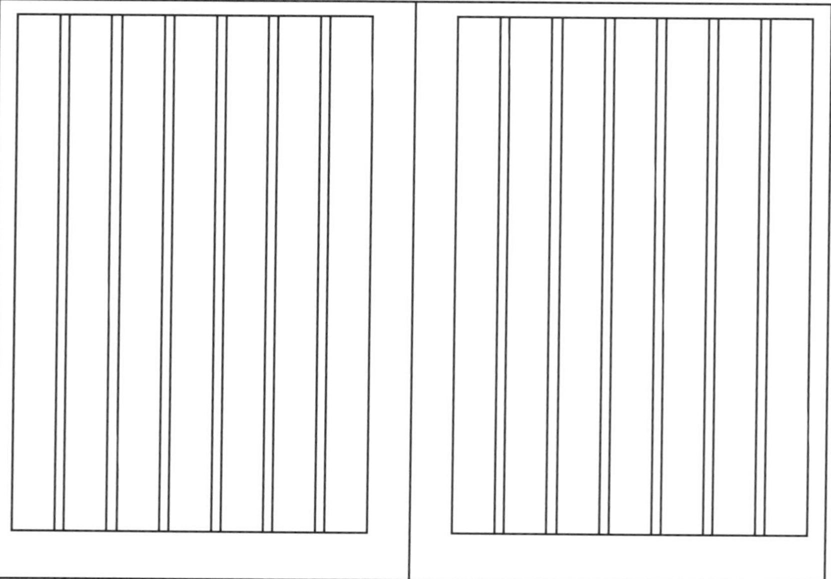

2 How do you combine the horizontal and vertical grid and the baseline grid? Here is the step-by-step structure: First you determine the size of the type area (as described in the chapter "The grid in the novel") and divide it by a self-selected number of columns.

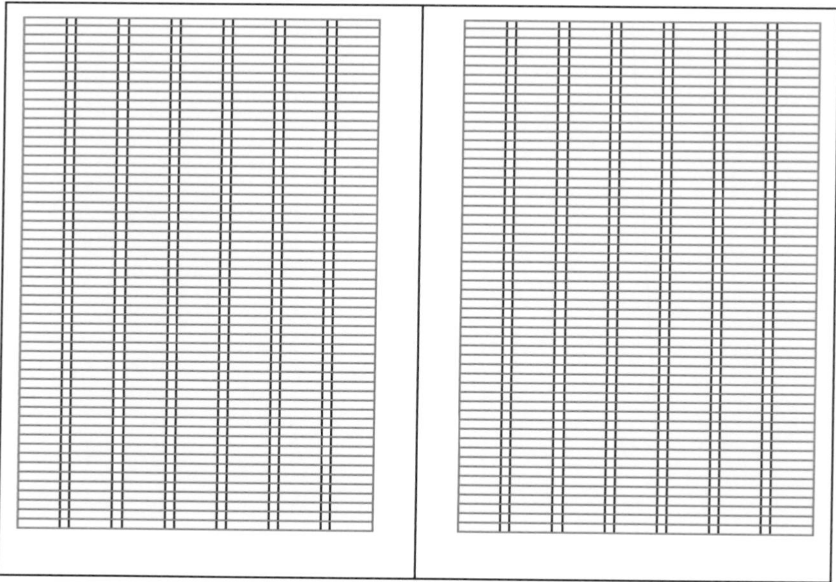

3 Then you set up the baseline grid. Before you create it, however, you have to decide on a font, a font size and thus also on a line spacing – and that for the most extensive text layer. This is usually the running text.

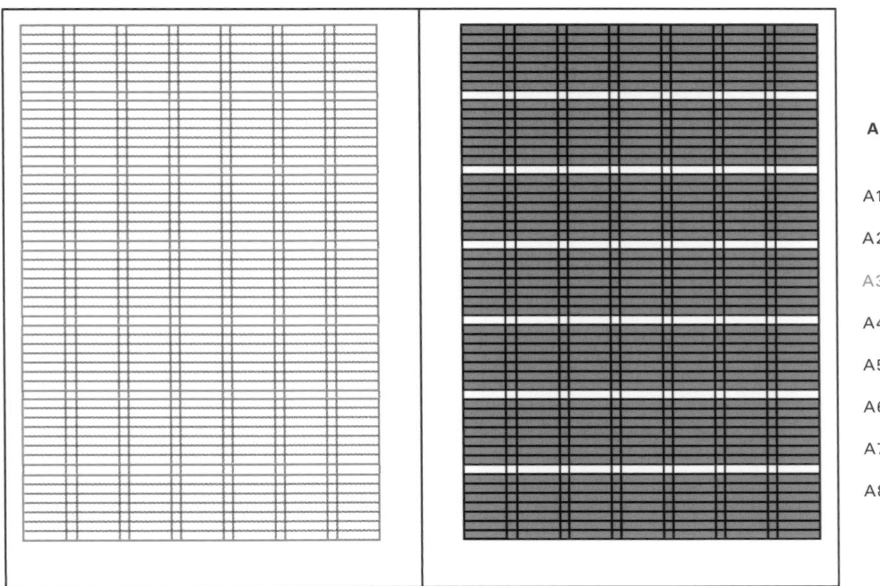

4 Now the type area is divided vertically into modules of equal size. On the left side you can see the division into lines, on the right side the resulting modules are colored for better visibility (for more information about the interplay of text and image grids see the chapter "The grid in magazines").

Officias velecest, Cor Simenditio. Ed qui te sime nobitatia invelitatem dolupta quiscius il mo estiber citaquaecto offic tet que quisciae es pella ium que pariam fugia consed moluptatquo esequi odi blabo. Aci sus.Ro consedis ipsum quaspicid molorro ribusci endaere ab int. Ed qui te sime nobitatia invelitatem dolupta quiscius il mo.

Aci sus.Ro consedis ipsum quaspicid. Ed qui te sime nobitatia invelitatem dolupta quiscius il mo.

Officias velecest, Cor Simenditio. Ed qui te sime nobitatia invelitatem dolupta quiscius il offic tet que quisciae es pella ium que parim fugia consed moluptatquo esequi odi blabo.

Consetetur sadipscing elitr, sed diam nonumy eirmod tempor invidunt ut labore et dolore magna aliquyam erat, sed diam voluptua. At vero eos et accusam et justo duo dolores et ea rebum. Stet clita kasd gubergren, no sea takimata sanctus est. Nam liber tempor cum soluta nobis eleifen.

Officiasu kelecest, Cor Sime

Duis autem vel eum iriure dolor in hendre.

5 If you now fill the finished grid with text and images, it looks like this. Here is a zoomed section. The running text font is located in the baseline grid, the heading as well. The image sizes are based on the modules and can be placed anywhere as long as they are aligned with the baseline grid.

Doesn't really look that complicated, does it? As you can see, other text layers can also be found in the baseline grid, e.g. headlines or sub-headlines (then with a multiple of the selected line spacing). If this is not possible, position at least the first line of a larger or smaller font, for example, on one line of the baseline grid (A4, FIG. 6 shows what this can look like with marginal texts). The images have module dimensions or a multiple thereof 6.

The module grid may look stricter than it is. But the aim of the grid is not to develop a technical life of its own and to determine the design. The vertical division of the columns should above all offer possibilities. There is no humorless "right" or "wrong" here. The vertical division into modules can be used in different ways: for example, when it comes to aligning images and texts to recurring heights in the format; or when it comes to establishing so-called "clotheslines" 7; or when it comes to forcing images and texts into a strict grid. Sometimes, however, the vertical division into modules causes more problems than benefits, and then you can neglect them.

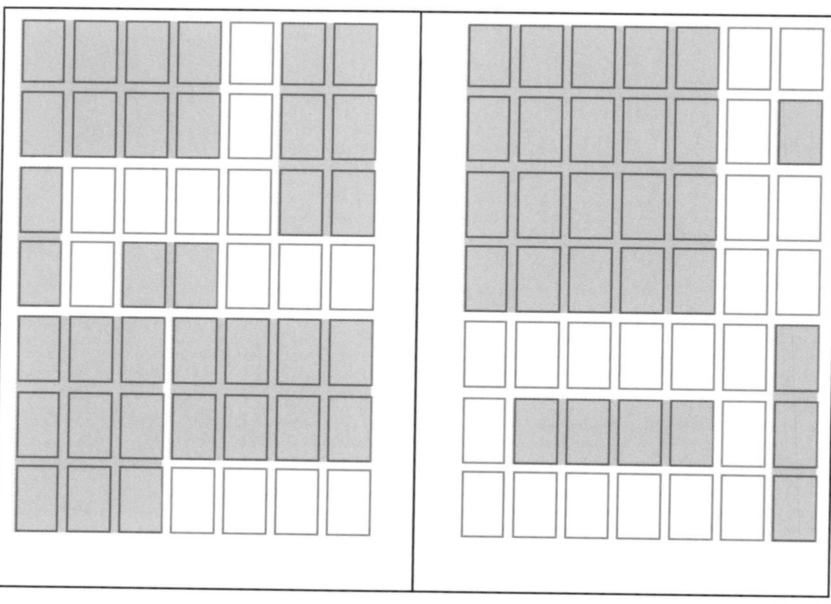

6 A module can function as a single image size. Combinations of several modules result in further image sizes that have one thing in common: They are based on one and the same module system and therefore have an invisible proportionality to each other. It is up to the designer to decide how many modules the grid is divided into vertically and how many image sizes are defined.

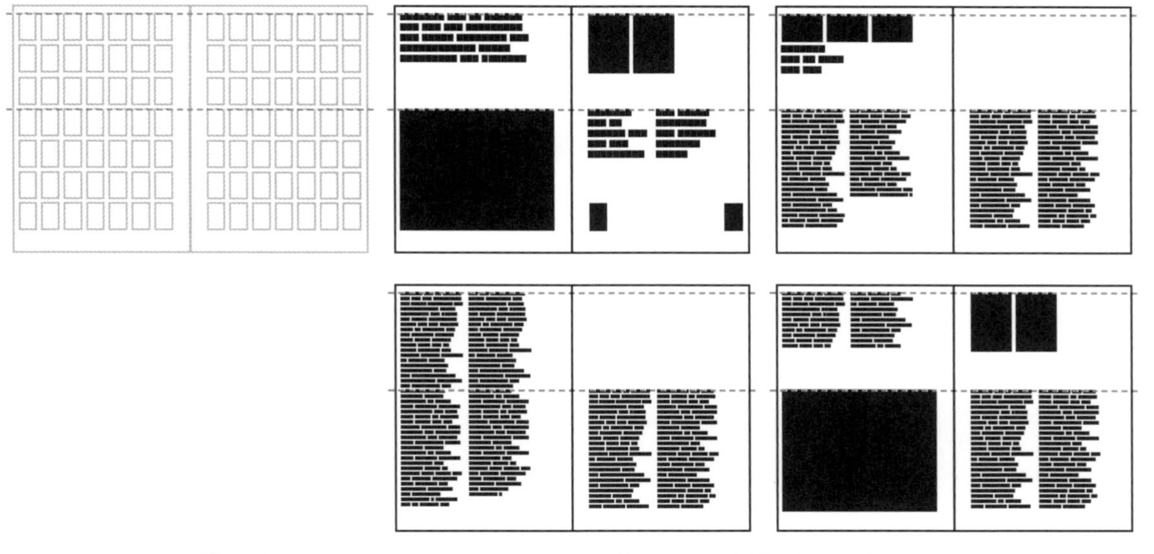

7 The illustrations show the possible combinations within the modular system. The “connectedness” of the different layouts with each other is unmistakable. Horizontal lines, on which pictures and texts “hang”, are called casually “clotheslines”.

The procedure presented here describes the functions of grid components and is therefore of an exemplary nature. The illustrations show how reliable and recognizable structures and relationships can be created. This becomes all the more important the more complex the contents and the more pages are to be designed.

But, let’s remind you once again: The creation of grids comes in second place. Before they can be developed and used, the design comes first. More on this in chapter B.

A
A1
A2
A3
A4
A5
A6
A7
A8
B
B1
C
C1
C2
C3
D
D1
D2
D3
D4

The selection of the examples shown here suggests that the contents of non-fiction books can be quite complex. This makes it all the more important for the design to be clear and concise. Recurring reference edges are an important instrument for this.

gegen als gescheitert und ersetzte es durch das der »Postmoderne«, die auf Pluralismus, auf Vielfältigkeit unterschiedlicher Sprachspiele, Handlungsformen, Lebensweisen und Wissenskonzepte zielt. Dementsprechend kennzeichnet »postmodernes Design«, dass es kein »Entweder/Oder« gibt, kein »falsches« oder »richtiges« Design im Sinne einer endgültigen und perfekten Lösung → 136, sondern ein Tolerieren verschiedener Ausdrucksweisen.

Postmoderne

Postmodernes Design. Die weitgehend theoretisch geführten funktionalismus- und gesellschaftskritischen Diskurse wurden seit den späten Siebzigerjahren von immer mehr speziell für diesen Zweck ins Leben gerufenen Designergruppen weitergeführt. Sie entwickelten provokante gestalterische Statements, die mit besonderer Vorliebe historische Formen neu kombinierten oder/und metaphorische Zeichen manipulierten, um das Verhältnis von »Hoch«- und »Niedrigkultur« weiter in Frage zu stellen. → 310 Inszeniert in oftmals eigens gegründeten Design-Galerien, erreichten die experimentellen Objekte ein zunächst irritiertes, dann aber zusehends fasziniertes Publikum.

Studio Alchimia. 1976 gründeten Alessandro und Adriana Guerriero in Mailand das Studio Alchimia, das schnell avantgardistische Designerinnen und Designer wie Alessandro Mendini, Andrea Branzi, Ettore Sottsass, Michele De Lucchi, Franco Raggi und Paolo Navone versammelte. Als experimentelles Labor mischte diese Designergruppe alle Disziplinen und konzipierte nicht nur Möbel,

sondern auch Kleidung, Dekorationsgegenstände, Architekturprojekte oder Bühnenbilder, die sie in einer eigenen Galerie ausstellte. Aus seiner These, klassisches Industriedesign sei in seinem hohen kulturellen Anspruch gescheitert, entwickelte Alessandro Mendini die Theorie des »banalen Designs«, das auf der Überzeugung basiert, das gewöhnliche Gestaltungsverständnis eines Durchschnittsbürgers präge unsere Gesellschaft weitaus stärker als idealistische Designvorstellungen einer gesellschaftlichen Elite. Entsprechend überarbeitete die »Alchimisten-Werkstatt« banale Alltagsgegenstände durch Zugabe von Farbe oder dekorative Elemente und erarbeitete aus dem derart ironisch Überbetonten neue ästhetische Qualitäten, die international Vorbildcharakter erlangen sollten. → 286

Memphis. Im Winter 1980/81 formierte sich in Mailand die Gruppe Memphis. Die Doppeldeutigkeit des Begriffs – altägyptische Hauptstadt und Grabstätte von Elvis Presley in Tennessee/USA – ist zugleich Stil und Programm: Sie verweist auf ein von der Pop-Art geprägtes Re-Design des Vorhandenen, nun allerdings in einer modischen Variante. 1981 stellten etwa 20 internationale Designer ihre Memphis-Entwürfe vor, bei denen praktische Funktionen zugunsten symbolhafter Deutungsmöglichkeiten in den Hintergrund traten. Jetzt rückten Material und Dekor der Oberfläche in den Vordergrund. Grelle Pop- und sanfte Neonfarben, kleine Bacterio- und grobe Schwarzweiß-Oberflächenmuster ergaben zusammen mit den neuen, am Computer konstruierten bunten Ornamenten von Nathalie du Pasquier eine aufregende Mischung, die nicht mehr eindeutig zuzuordnen war. → 294 Eben diese semantische

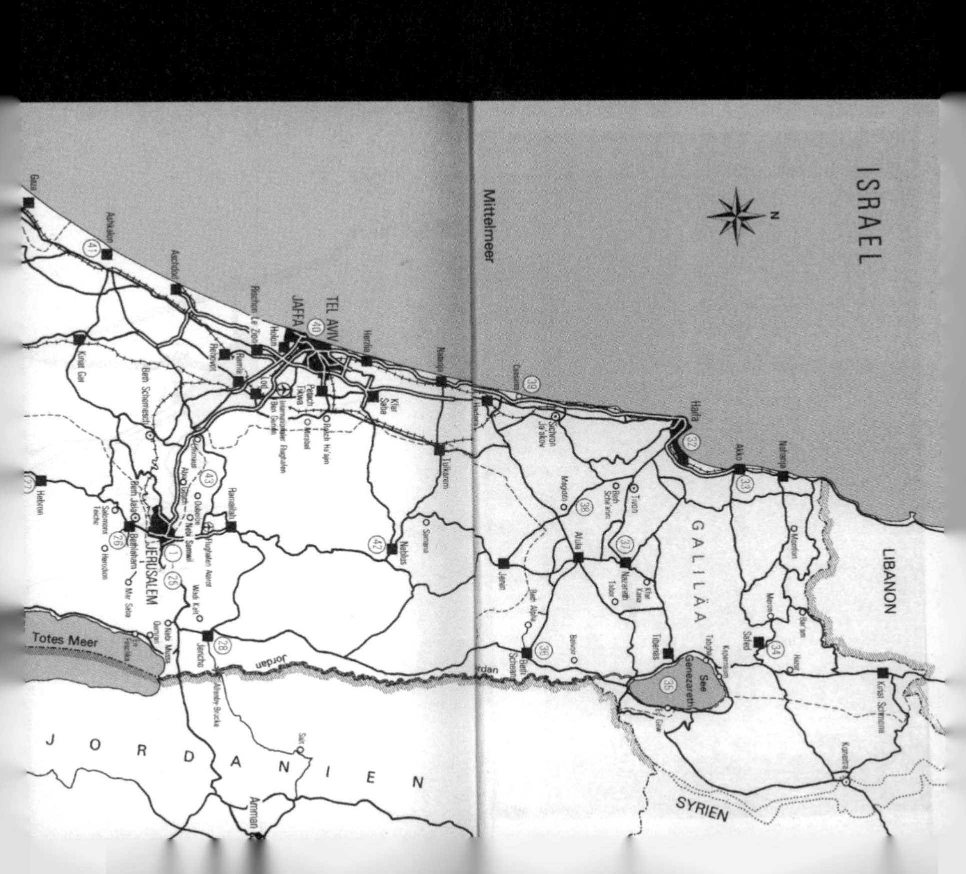

ONTSPANNEN 650 ONTVANGEN

ONTVANGENIS 651 ONTWERP

3

Das Sefiroth-System als die zentrale Glyphe der Kabbala: 10 Sefiroth als Manifestationen Gottes, 22 »wahre« Wege und 32 Pfade der Weisheit insgesamt. Diagramm aus Athanasius Kircher, Oedipus Aegyptiacus, Rom 1652.

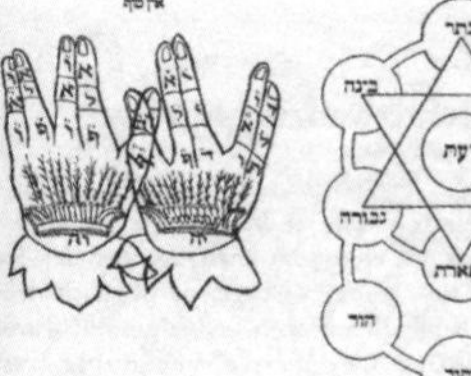

Rechts: moderner »kabbalistischer Baum«. Links: zwei Hände, auf denen die 32 verbindenden Pfade aufgezeichnet sind.

Die Zweiundzwanzig ist auch von christlichen Exegeten untersucht worden, und Sabas von Tales (st. 532) fand die Zweiundzwanzig die Zahl der Schöpfungswerke, der Bücher des Alten Testamentes und der Tugenden Christi. Doch kennt auch das Avesta zweiundzwanzig Gebete.
In merkwürdiger Vervielfachung erscheint die Zahl bei den 22000 Rindern Salomos.

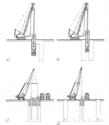

the cloud's central model of data storage and management, which is handled and owned by a handful of corporations.

The coming of the cloud is best described by Aaron Levie, the founder and CEO of Box, one of Silicon Valley's fastest growing cloud storage providers. As Levie states, the biggest driver of the cloud is the ever-expanding spectrum of mobile devices—iPhones, iPads, Androids, and so forth—that enable users to tap into the cloud: "If you think about the market that we're in, and more broadly just the enterprise software market, the kind of transition that's happening now from legacy systems to the cloud is literally, by definition, a once-in-a-lifetime opportunity. This is probably going to happen at a larger scale than any other technology transition we've seen in the enterprise. Larger than client servers. Larger than mainframes."[8] Google, one of the world's seven largest cloud companies, has recently compared itself to a bank.[9] That comparison is apt. If data in the cloud is like money in the bank, what happens to that data while it resides in the cloud?

THE UNITED STATES CLOUD AND THE PATRIOT ACT

The amount of access and control over online data is partially determined by who has registered the site, and where it is hosted. For example, all data stored by US companies (or their subsidiaries) in non-US data centers falls under the jurisdiction of the USA Patriot Act, an antiterrorism law introduced in 2001.[10] This emphatically includes the entire US cloud—Facebook, Apple, Twitter, Dropbox, Google, Amazon, Rackspace, Box, Microsoft, and many others. Jeffrey Rosen, a law professor at George Washington University, has established that the Patriot Act, rather than investigating potential terrorists, is mostly used to spy on innocent Americans.[11] But the people being watched are not necessarily Americans. Via the cloud, people across the world are subject to the same Patriot Act powers, which are often misused by authorities. Matthew Waxman of the Council on Foreign Relations outlines the situation:

Bild 6.1. Herstellung am Beispiel einer gefrästen Schlitzwand
a, b) Herstellung eines dreiteiligen Primärschlitzes
c) Betonieren eines langen Primärschlitzes
d) Betonieren eines kurzen Sekundärschlitzes

Bild 6.2. Schlitzwandherstellung

schlitzlängen groß gewählt werden; sie liegen in der Regel zwischen 2,50 m und 7,50 m.

Leitwände

Die Leitwände sind eine Bauhilfsmaßnahme. Sie werden vor dem Aushub aus Ortbeton oder Fertigteilen hergestellt und haben folgende Hauptfunktionen:
- Führung des Schlitzgreifers
- Stützung des obersten Bodenbereiches
- Vorrat für die Stützflüssigkeit
- Auflager für Einbauteile wie Bewehrungskörbe
- Auflager für hydraulische Pressen zum Ziehen der Abschalrohre

Die Leitwände können verschiedene Querschnittsformen erhalten, s. BK 1991. Bei Ortbetonausführungen in standfestem Boden ist zur Herstellung meist nur eine Innenschalung erforderlich; nach außen wird gegen das Erdreich betoniert. Eine andere Form stellt der Winkelquerschnitt dar.

Bei schwierigen Bodenverhältnissen und gespanntem Grundwasser kann es erforderlich werden, die Leitwand über das Arbeitsniveau zu betonieren, um einen höheren Suspensionsspiegel zu ermöglichen.

Bild 6.3. Schlitzwandfräse

Die Höhe der Leitwände ist von den örtlichen Gegebenheiten abhängig und beträgt in der Regel 0,80 m bis 1,50 m.

Kreuzen Leitungen die Schlitzwandtrasse, so sind besondere Vorkehrungen zu treffen. Können die Leitungen nicht verlegt werden, so werden sie unterschlitzt. Dazu werden die Leitungen in Leerrohre verlegt und in einen Schutzriegel einbetoniert.

Die Dimensionierung erfolgt nach Erfahrung und konstruktiven Gesichtspunkten.

Herstellung von Schlitzwänden

Zur Schlitzwandherstellung werden einzelne Aushub- und Betonierabschnitte, die sogenannten Schlitzwandlamellen aneinandergereiht. Einzelheiten s. Kap. 6.2.

Die rechnerische Ermittlung der Abschnitte wird in Kapitel 9.4.2 behandelt.

Nach der Leitwandherstellung kommen folgende Arbeitsgänge:
- Schlitzaushub
  Zunächst erfolgt der Aushub einer Schlitzwandlamelle mit einem Schlitzwandgreifer. Zur Stützung der Schlitzwandungen wird eine Bentonitsuspension verwendet.
  Bodenaushub und Verluste an Stützflüssigkeit müssen laufend durch Zupumpen neuer Suspension ausgeglichen werden. Der Flüssigkeitsspiegel darf eine bestimmte Mindesthöhe innerhalb der Leitwand bei den verfahrensbedingten Schwankungen nicht unterschreiten.

Bild 6.4. Schlitzwandfräse neuer Bauart: Kompaktanlage

Bild 6.5. Fräsräder zum Lösen des Bodens bei der Schlitzwandfräse

- Einbau der Abschalelemente
  Zur stirnseitigen Begrenzung der Vorläuferlamelle gegen das Erdreich werden meist Stahlrohre eingebaut. Diese sog. Abschalrohre können in einzelnen Schüssen zur gewünschten Länge entsprechend der Schlitztiefe zusammengesetzt werden.
- Einbau der Bewehrung
  Die Bewehrungskörbe werden vormontiert und in den Schlitz abgelassen. Bei größeren Schlitztiefen kann der Einbau in einzelnen Schüssen notwendig werden. Diese werden z. B. mit Seilklemmen verbunden.
  Zur Sicherung der Betondeckung werden großflächige Abstandshalter angebunden oder Profilstähle beidseitig des Korbes in den Schlitz eingehängt. Einbauten wie z. B. Ankeraussparungen werden vor dem Absenken am Korb angebracht.
- Betonieren
  Der Beton wird nach den Regeln des Unterwasserbetonierens im Kontraktorverfahren eingebracht. Die verdrängte Stützflüssigkeit wird zur Wiederaufbereitung und -verwendung abgepumpt.
- Ziehen der Abschalelemente
  Nach dem Erstarren des Betons werden die Abschalrohre mit hydraulischen Ziehpressen gezogen. Der Zeitpunkt des Ziehens muß so gewählt werden, daß der angesteifte Beton

Register – Index

D Die Verzeichnisse machen den Katalog zum Nachschlagewerk. Hier sind alle Beteiligten genannt, die zum Gelingen eines »schönsten Buches« beigetragen haben: Autoren, Verlage, Gestalter, Künstler, Fotografen, Hersteller, Setzereien, Druckereien, Buchbindereien, Lithoanstalten, Papier- und Einbandhersteller sowie –lieferanten und Veredler. Auch die verwendeten Schriften werden aufgeführt.

E The appendices make the catalogue a reference work. Everyone involved in any of the successful or specially commended books is mentioned here by name: authors, publishers, designers, artists, photographers, producers, typesetters, printers, bookbinders, lithographers, paper manufacturers and suppliers, cover material manufacturers and suppliers, finishers. The names of typefaces used are also listed.

Autoren und Herausgeber – Authors and Editors

Gestalter – Designers

Illustratoren – Illustrators

Satz – Typesetting

Fotografen – Photgraphers

[H] Herausgeber – Editor [P] Preis der Stiftung Buchkunst – Award of the Stiftung Buchkunst
[F] Förderpreis für junge Buchgestaltung – Sponsorship Prize for Young Book Design

TOPOGRAPHIE DES KRIEGES

Im Rahmen der 8. ← ISTANBUL BIENNALE 2003 schuf die Künstlerin Doris Salcedo eine Installation, die sie selbst als »Topographie des Krieges« beschrieb.[59] Mit einem Geflecht aus ungefähr 1.550 Holzstühlen füllte sie eine Baulücke zwischen zwei Häusern im Istanbuler Stadtteil Karaköy so aus, dass sie bündig mit den Fassaden der Nachbarhäuser abschlossen. Die Arbeit setzte sich mit Krieg und seinen Folgen auseinander, ohne auf ein konkretes geschichtliches Ereignis zu fokussieren. Es ging ihr nicht um Schuldzuweisungen, nicht um »Opfer« und »Täter«, sondern um Erfahrungen, die sich auf das alltägliche Leben der Menschen auswirken.[60] Lange Zeit wurde die politische Kultur in der Türkei von Gewalt geprägt – nicht zuletzt durch den »unerklärten Bürgerkrieg« der 1970er Jahre, den politischen Gestaltungsanspruch des Militärs, der sich in drei Militärputschen äußerte, und den seit 1984 andauernden türkisch-kurdischen Konflikt.

Die Aktualität von Gewalt in den politischen Auseinandersetzungen wurde am Ende der Biennale deutlich: Am 15. und am 20. November 2003 explodierten mehrere Autobomben – vor zwei Synagogen, vor der Filiale einer britischen Bank und vor dem britischen Konsulat –, die über 60 Menschen töteten und über 700 verletzten.[61]

59
Doris Salcedo selbst über ihre Arbeit in Istanbul: www.youtube.com/watch?v=ZjYuDKFvsjY

60
Ebd.

61
Vgl. zu den unterschiedlichen Opferzahlen: www.arsiv.ntvmsnbc.com/news/249515.asp; www4.cnnturk.com/2005/turkiye/11/20/20.kasim.istanbul.saldirilari.anildi/140525.0/index.html; www.milliyet.com.tr/istanbul-bombaci-si-irak-tan-getirildi/gundem/gundemdetay/11.10.2012/1609807/default.htm

GECEKONDU FOR SALE

»Gecekondu zu verkaufen! Das […] Gecekondu ist ein Haus mit einem oder zwei Zimmern – eingebettet in eine komplexe Stadtstruktur. Bei Bedarf kann es umgebaut, abgerissen und neu gebaut oder nach einer Nacht wieder verlassen werden. Schaffe dir selbst deinen eigenen Raum«, plakatierte die Künstlerinnengruppe Oda Projesi[62] im Rahmen der 8. Istanbul Biennale 2003 auf Werbetafeln [← PLAKATWAND] im öffentlichen Raum. Das zum Kauf angebotene Gecekondu war Teil des Kunstprojektes »Ada«, für das direkt neben der zentralen Ausstellungshalle der Biennale ein ← GECEKONDU nach einem Vorbild aus den 1980er Jahren gebaut worden war. Diese nach dem ursprünglichen Bauherren »Mustafa Tetik Model« benannte Installation konnte von den Besucher_innen begangen werden.

Mit »Ada« versuchte Oda Projesi, »mögliche Räume zum Denken« und »mögliche Räume zum Träumen« zu öffnen.[63] Denn Gecekondus – die noch immer die Lebenswirklichkeit vieler türkischer Stadtbewohner_innen sind – werden in der öffentlichen Meinung (zunehmend) als Bedrohung der Stadt, von Ordnung und Sicherheit betrachtet. Die stereotypen Bilder wollten die Künstlerinnen hinterfragen. Das Projekt sollte eine Diskussion über die Idee des Gecekondus, über divergierende Bedeutungszuschreibungen und die Nutzung von Stadtraum in Istanbul anregen [← SOLIDARITÄT IN GÜLSUYU-GÜLENSU].

Seit den späten 1990er Jahren arbeitet Oda Projesi mit »räumlichen Interventionen«, wobei das alltägliche Leben, seine Funktionen und Bedeutungen, den Ausgangspunkt ihrer Projekte bilden.[64] Für sie sind die Räume des Alltags »in all ihrer Unzulänglichkeit […] ein[e] schöpferische Situation«, die dort anfängt, »wo die Vorstellungswelt der hegemonialen Raumordnung aufhört«.[65] Viele ihrer bisherigen Arbeiten entstanden in enger Zusammenarbeit mit von Marginalisierung betroffenen Bevölkerungsgruppen. Dabei stand nicht die Produktion von ästhetischen, als Kunst interpretierbaren Objekten im Vordergrund, sondern ein schöpferischer Prozess zwischen Menschen, die sich normalerweise nicht begegnen würden.[66]

62
Oda Projesi (Raum Projekt) besteht aus den Künstlerinnen Özge Açıkkol, Güneş Savaş und Seçil Yersel, vgl. www.odaprojesi.blogspot.de

63
www.odaprojesi.blogspot.de/2008/01/annex-to-knowledge.html

64
Vgl. hierzu: Özkan, Derya: »Oda Projesi produces new spaces«, in: *Iki Yilda Bir newspaper, 9th Istanbul Biennale*, 2005, zit.n. Yersel, Seçil: »Willkommen in Istanbul. Porträt einer ›gastfreundlichen‹ Stadt«, in: Haustein, Lydia/Sartorius, Joachim/Bertrams, Christoph (Hg.): *Modell Türkei? Ein Land im Spannungsfeld zwischen Religion, Militär und Demokratie*, Göttingen: Wallstein 2006, S. 99-194, hier S. 103.

65
Ebd.

66
»Es ist wichtig, dass sie [Oda Projesi] den Raum öffnen für nicht-objektbasierte Kunstpraxis in der Türkei, einem Land, dessen Kunstakademien und -markt immer noch weitgehend auf Gemälde und Skulpturen beschränkt sind.« Bishop, Claire: *Artifical Hells. Participatory Art and the Politics of Spectatorship*, London u. a.: Verso Books 2012, S. 21.

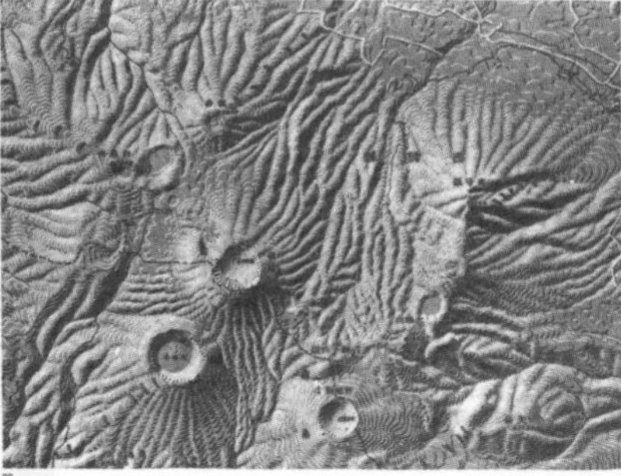

9

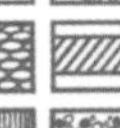

10

Drehpunkte und Schraubenlöcher müssen vorher auf der Werkzeichnung festgelegt und genau auf das Möbel übertragen werden

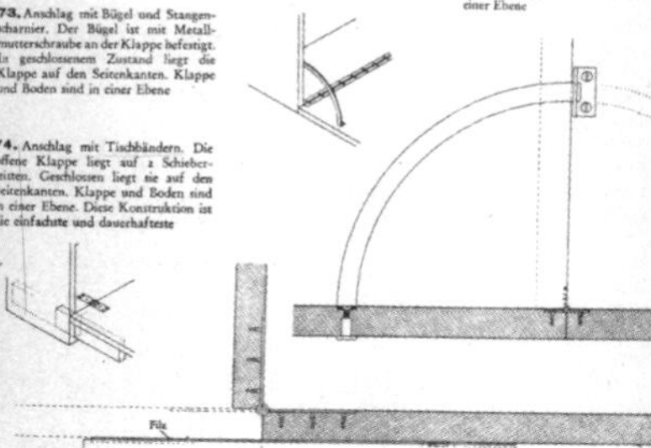

72. Anschlag mit Pultschere und einfachem Zapfenband. Die Schere ist mit Metallmutterschrauben an der Klappe befestigt, weil einfache Holzschrauben der Beanspruchung nicht genügen; in geschlossenem Zustand steht die Klappe zwischen den Seiten zurück. Klappe und Boden sind in einer Ebene

73. Anschlag mit Bügel und Stangenscharnier. Der Bügel ist mit Metallmutterschraube an der Klappe befestigt. In geschlossenem Zustand liegt die Klappe auf den Seitenkanten. Klappe und Boden sind in einer Ebene

74. Anschlag mit Tischbändern. Die offene Klappe liegt auf 2 Schieberleisten. Geschlossen liegt sie auf den Seitenkanten. Klappe und Boden sind in einer Ebene. Diese Konstruktion ist die einfachste und dauerhafteste

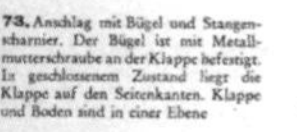

75. Türen auf Hartholzlaufschienen. Zur Verkleinerung der Reibungsflächen sind die Schienen abgerundet bzw. wellenförmig. Durch Hochheben kann die Türe ausgehängt werden

76. Türen auf Kugelschienen. Durch ihre besondere Lagerung macht die Kugel bei großer Schiebebewegung der Türe einen verhältnismäßig kleinen Weg. Mit Schrauben befestigte Hartholzstücke dienen zur oberen Führung, sie müssen beim Aushängen der Türe losgeschraubt werden

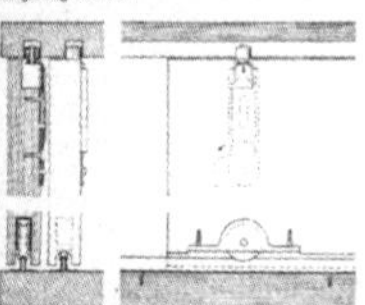

77. Türen auf Kugellagerrollen. Die Türe kann ausgehängt werden, wenn die obere Rollenführung ausgeschaltet ist

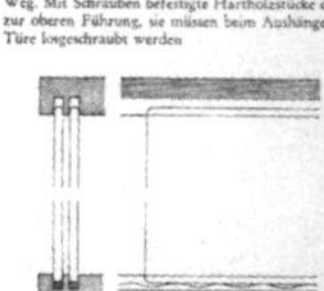

78. Scheiben auf Hartholzleisten gelagert, die zur Verkleinerung der Reibungsfläche wellenförmig sind

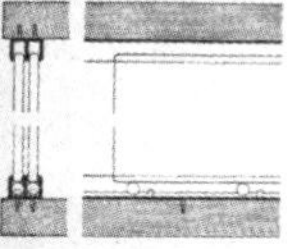

79. Scheiben auf Kugeln beweglich. Beim Schieben legen die Kugeln durch ihre besondere Lagerung einen kleinen Weg zurück

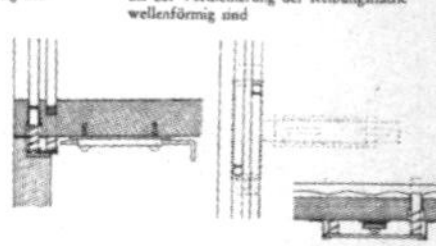

80. Beispiel eines einfachen Verschlusses für die Glasschiebetüren. Die Platte mit den beiden Schließstiften wird erst mit der Hand hochgedrückt, dann wird der Riegel darunter geschoben. Der Verschluß ist erst hergestellt, wenn der untere Teil des Schrankes geschlossen ist

Tab. 10-30 Darstellung des Berechnungsablaufs für das MULTI-Modell (Berechnungsbeispiel 10-7)

	1	2	3	4	5	6	Σ	Q_i	q_i	b_i	$\|q_i-1\|$	EQ_i	fq_i
1. Schritt (Ausgangsschritt): $v_{ij}(1) = BW_{ij}$													
1	0,000	0,915	0,902	0,823	0,612	0,763	4,016	3400	846,58	1003,87	845,58	0,0043	26,1320
2	0,915	0,000	0,763	0,763	0,524	0,741	3,707	3100	836,36	960,83	835,36	0,0045	26,9730
3	0,902	0,763	0,000	0,784	0,583	0,763	3,796	2950	777,06	1003,84	776,06	0,0046	23,9867
4	0,823	0,763	0,784	0,000	0,858	0,432	3,661	5600	1529,79	815,76	1528,79	0,0033	58,1089
5	0,612	0,524	0,583	0,858	0,000	0,187	2,763	2400	868,49	1061,21	867,49	0,0051	25,3599
6	0,763	0,741	0,763	0,432	0,187	0,000	2,886	2550	883,67	927,74	882,67	0,0050	29,5154
Σ	4,016	3,707	3,796	3,661	2,763	2,886	20,829	–	–				190,076
Z_j	3000	3500	2800	5900	2200	2600	–	20000	–				
z_j	745,98	944,28	737,55	1611,75	796,12	901,00	–	–	$f = 960,21$				
b_j	979,08	983,46	996,52	839,06	1044,55	939,23							
$\|z_j-1\|$	745,98	943,28	736,55	1610,25	795,12	900,00							
EZ_j	0,0046	0,0042	0,0047	0,0033	0,0053	0,0049							
fz_j	23,6414	29,7529	22,9344	59,5231	23,6175	30,0456	189,5148						
2. Schritt: $v_{ij}(2)$													
1	0,00	711,74	540,71	1280,64	377,72	599,25	3519,05	3400	0,9686	0,9915	0,0314	0,0043	25,3171
2	583,75	0,00	472,14	1225,38	333,68	600,40	3215,54	3100	0,9641	0,9919	0,0359	0,0045	25,9999
3	511,62	544,30	0,00	1119,97	330,44	550,05	3056,78	2950	0,9651	0,9915	0,0349	0,0046	23,1532
4	1131,06	1319,55	1045,40	0,00	1177,20	354,01	5427,22	5600	1,0318	0,9597	0,0318	0,0033	61,9570
5	366,93	395,22	339,25	1294,82	0,00	142,12	2538,34	2400	0,9455	1,0025	0,0545	0,0051	23,7186
6	532,57	650,59	516,64	758,74	130,02	0,00	2588,55	2550	0,9851	0,9836	0,0149	0,0050	29,3142
Σ	3125,91	3621,80	2914,14	5879,54	2349,06	2645,83	20336,28	–	–				189,4599
Z_j	3000	3500	2800	5900	2200	2600	–	20000	–				
z_j	0,9597	0,9664	0,9608	1,0388	0,9365	0,9827	–	–	$f = 0,9835$				
b_j	0,9992	0,9916	0,9906	0,9639	1,0001	0,9836							
$\|z_j-1\|$	0,0403	0,0336	0,0392	0,0388	0,0635	0,0173							
EZ_j	0,0046	0,0042	0,0047	0,0033	0,0053	0,0049							
fz_j	22,7241	28,7563	22,0539	63,6175	21,9335	29,7669	188,8543						
3. Schritt: $v_{ij}(3)$													
1	0,00	666,45	503,78	1326,05	339,84	575,18	3411,30	3400	0,9967	1,0011	0,0033	0,0043	25,1998
2	540,85	0,00	437,68	1262,42	298,71	573,37	3113,02	3100	0,9958	1,0015	0,0042	0,0045	25,8475
3	474,68	508,16	0,00	1155,42	296,21	526,04	2960,48	2950	0,9965	1,0012	0,0035	0,0046	23,0395
4	1159,17	1359,81	1071,93	0,00	1165,86	796,49	5553,06	5600	1,0085	0,9951	0,0085	0,0033	62,7726
5	329,86	357,26	305,14	1294,32	0,00	131,69	2418,27	2400	0,9924	1,0053	0,0076	0,0051	23,4573
6	508,42	624,51	493,47	805,40	119,93	0,00	2551,71	2550	0,9993	0,9998	0,0007	0,0050	29,2944
Σ	3012,98	3516,18	2812,00	5843,60	2220,35	2602,74	20007,85	–	–				189,6160
Z_j	3000	3500	2800	5900	2200	2600	–	20000	–				
z_j	0,9957	0,9954	0,9957	1,0097	0,9908	0,9989	–	–	$f = 0,9996$				
b_j	1,0010	1,0012	1,0010	0,9959	1,0029	0,9998							
$\|z_j-1\|$	0,0043	0,0046	0,0043	0,0097	0,0092	0,0011							
EZ_j	0,0046	0,0042	0,0047	0,0033	0,0053	0,0049							
fz_j	22,9991	28,5828	21,9347	64,4847	21,6662	29,7346	189,0022						

Die Genauigkeitsanforderung und ihre Überprüfung ergibt für den Quellverkehr des Bezirks 1:

$$EQ_1 = \frac{1}{4 \cdot \sqrt{3400}} = 0,0043 \quad |q_1(2) - 1| = |0,9686 - 1| = 0,0314 > EQ_1 = 0,0043 \, .$$

Der Verkehrsbezirk 1 erfüllt noch nicht die Genauigkeitsanforderungen. Aus Tab. 10-30 ist zu sehen, daß der Genauigkeitstest im 2. Schritt noch bei allen Verkehrsbezirken negativ ausfällt. Der Iterationsprozeß muß fortgesetzt werden. Nach der erneuten Anwendung des MULTI-Modells fällt im 4. Schritt der Genauigkeitstest für alle Verkehrsbezirke (Quell- und Zielverkehr) positiv aus. Die im vierten Iterationsschritt erzeugte Verkehrsstrommatrix erfüllt die Bedingungen des Gleichungssystems. Sie ist in Tab. 10-31 mit einigen weiteren Ergebnissen aufgeschrieben.

Tab. 10-31 Verkehrsstrommatrix $v_{ij}(4)$ nach dem 4. Schritt (Berechnungsbeispiel 10-7)

$v_{ij}(4)$	1	2	3	4	5	6	$\Sigma = Q_i(4)$	Q_i	fq_i	$P(A_i)$	$P(A_i/W)$	kq_i
1	0,00	659,36	498,60	1337,89	334,15	571,89	3401,98	3400	25,1779	0,1328	0,1700	0,7809
2	534,73	0,00	432,72	1272,12	293,34	569,39	3102,30	3100	25,8189	0,1361	0,1550	0,8783
3	469,75	502,61	0,00	1165,41	291,17	522,86	2951,80	2950	23,0185	0,1214	0,1475	0,8229
4	1168,06	1369,50	1080,16	0,00	1166,71	806,16	5590,60	5600	62,9386	0,3319	0,2800	1,1852
5	324,43	351,19	300,12	1297,51	0,00	130,10	2403,35	2400	23,4080	0,1234	0,1200	1,0285
6	505,28	620,32	490,42	815,83	118,38	0,00	2550,24	2550	29,2906	0,1544	0,1275	1,2113
$\Sigma = Z_j(4)$	3002,25	3502,99	2802,11	5888,77	2203,75	2600,41	20000,27	–	189,6525	1,0000	1,0000	–
Z_j	3000	3500	2800	5900	2200	2600	–	20000				
fz_j	22,5762	28,5495	21,9122	64,8547	21,6159	29,7286	189,0372					
$P(E_j)$	0,1194	0,1510	0,1159	0,3420	0,1143	0,1573	1,0000					
$P(E_j/W)$	0,1500	0,1750	0,1400	0,2950	0,1100	0,1300	1,0000					
kz_j	0,7962	0,8630	0,8280	1,1594	1,0395	1,2097	–					

Die Faktoren fq_i und fz_j in den einzelnen Iterationsschritten entstehen aus dem Produkt aller Einzelfaktoren bis zum jeweiligen Iterationsschritt; im dritten Schritt ergibt sich z. B.:

$$fq_1 = \frac{846,58}{1003,87} \cdot \frac{0,9686}{0,9915} \cdot \frac{0,9967}{1,0011} \cdot \sqrt{960,21 \cdot 0,9835 \cdot 0,9996} = 25,1998$$

$$fz_2 = \frac{944,28}{983,46} \cdot \frac{0,9664}{0,9916} \cdot \frac{0,9954}{1,0012} \cdot \sqrt{960,21 \cdot 0,9835 \cdot 0,9996} = 28,5828 \, .$$

Zur Demonstration der Wirkung des Lösungsansatzes wird mit den Daten des 3. Schritts der Verkehrsstrom $v_{12}(4)$ berechnet:

$$v_{12}(4) = BW_{12} \cdot fq_1(3) \cdot fz_2(3) = 0,915 \cdot 25,1998 \cdot 28,5828 = 659,36$$

1 Klassiker des Produktdesigns
Petra Eisele

2 Israel. Mit dem Westjordanland
Hermann Teifer

3 Nieuw Handwoordenboek der Nederlandse Taal

4 Das Mysterium der Zahl
Franz Carl Endres, Annemarie Schimmel

5 Black Transparency. The right to know in the age of mass surveillance
Metahaven

6 Grundbau
Arz, Schmidt, Seitz, Semprich

7 Die schönsten deutschen Bücher, The best german book design 2013

8 Urbane Interventionen Istanbul
Friedrich von Borries

9 Zeichensysteme der visuellen Kommunikation
Otl Aicher

10 Zeichensysteme der visuellen Kommunikation
Otl Aicher

11 Konstruktion einfacher Möbel
Adolf G. Schneck

12 Grundlagen der Straßen-Verkehrstechnik und der Verkehrsplanung
Werner Schnabel, Dieter Lohse

A

A1

A2

A3

A4

A5

A6

A7

A8

B

B1

C

C1

C2

C3

D

D1

D2

D3

D4

When I described in the last chapter how pictures can be placed next to texts in a non-fiction book, I concealed something so as not to complicate things at that point. The text passage is about aligning images with the column widths on the one hand and the font baselines A3, Fig. 5 on the other. This recommendation is only correct if images can be cropped: After all, it would be pure coincidence if the column widths and the line spacing were congruent with the proportions of the image, so that one could dispense with the cropping.

The grid in art catalogs A—4

Imagine you are creating an illustrated book with photographs by the artist Andreas Gursky. And imagine that you now have the glorious idea of adapting his photographs to the layout by cropping them. No, don't imagine that. Because it's obvious: Many images are "untouchable" for designers because the composition of a surface – whether it is a photograph, a painting or a drawing – includes every millimeter. In this case you have to proceed differently: You either define the height of the picture and let the width "follow suit" or you are guided by the column widths and let the height "follow suit". Another special feature: In both cases you either align the picture with a font line – or to the top edge of a line of the adjacent text. You do this if you want to create an equal height between the image and the text (at the top *or* bottom edge). The principle presented in the non-fiction book, according to which the image is guided by the top *and* bottom of the baseline grid, is therefore only partially applied here 2,3,4.

In art books, a "text right next to image" situation will not occur too often, but there are directories, catalogs, historical books, etc., where you may be confronted with such a problem. As a matter of principle, special care must be taken when dealing with images in art-related and documentary publications 1.

On the next double pages some text-picture combinations are shown 5–8.

→ D1

Images
Top edge of text, see
Letter top edge

"Jean-Michel Basquiat"
Leonhard Emmerling

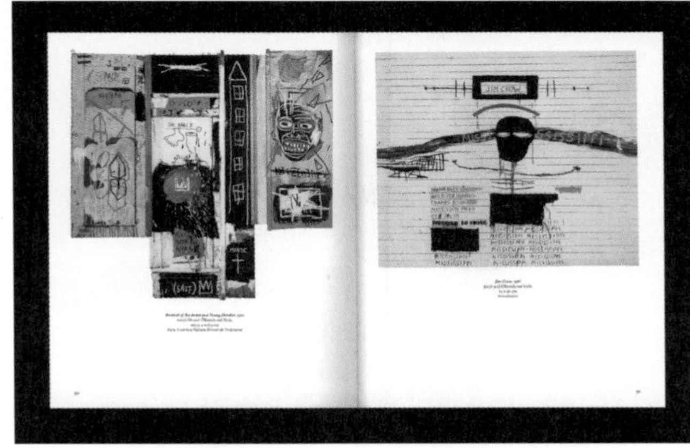

"Local Wind, Aroch. Catalogs and books published by Israeli artists in the 70s and 80s"
Yonatan Vinitsky a.o. (eds.)

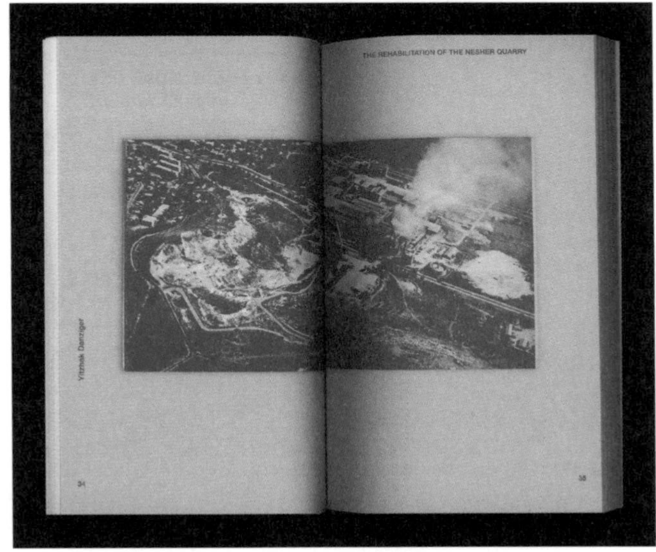

"Die schönsten deutschen Bücher, The best German book design 2013"
Stiftung Buchkunst

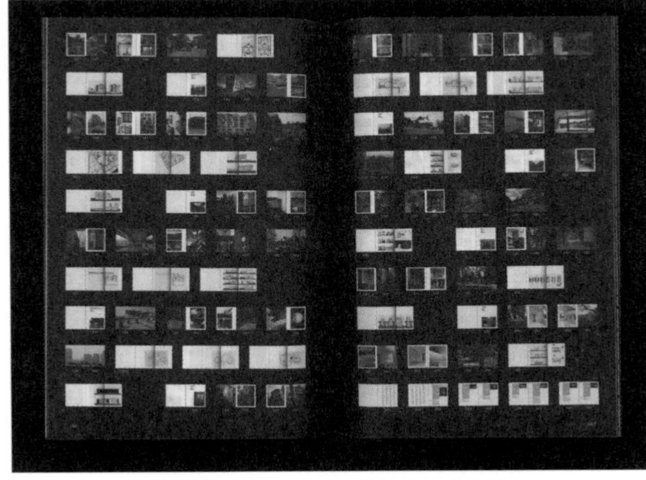

1 In art catalogs and documentary publications, the illustrations usually have constant length-width ratios. The layout must be adjusted accordingly.

A
A1
A2
A3
A4
A5
A6
A7
A8
B
B1
C
C1
C2
C3
D
D1
D2
D3
D4

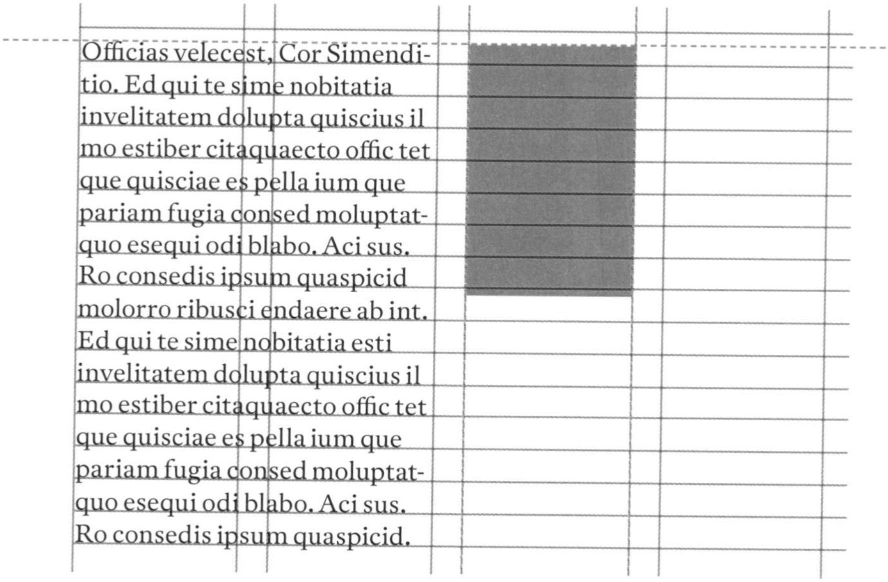

Officias velecest, Cor Simenditio. Ed qui te sime nobitatia
invelitatem dolupta quiscius il
mo estiber citaquaecto offic tet
que quisciae es pella ium que
pariam fugia consed moluptatquo esequi odi blabo. Aci sus.
Ro consedis ipsum quaspicid
molorro ribusci endaere ab int.
Ed qui te sime nobitatia esti
invelitatem dolupta quiscius il
mo estiber citaquaecto offic tet
que quisciae es pella ium que
pariam fugia consed moluptatquo esequi odi blabo. Aci sus.
Ro consedis ipsum quaspicid.

2 In this example, the image cannot be cropped, because otherwise the image content would not be reproduced correctly (just think of the image of a painting). The image is aligned to the column width.
The height of the image "runs along": Its bottom edge cannot align itself with row lines. The upper edge of the image is guided by the ascender of the adjacent font.

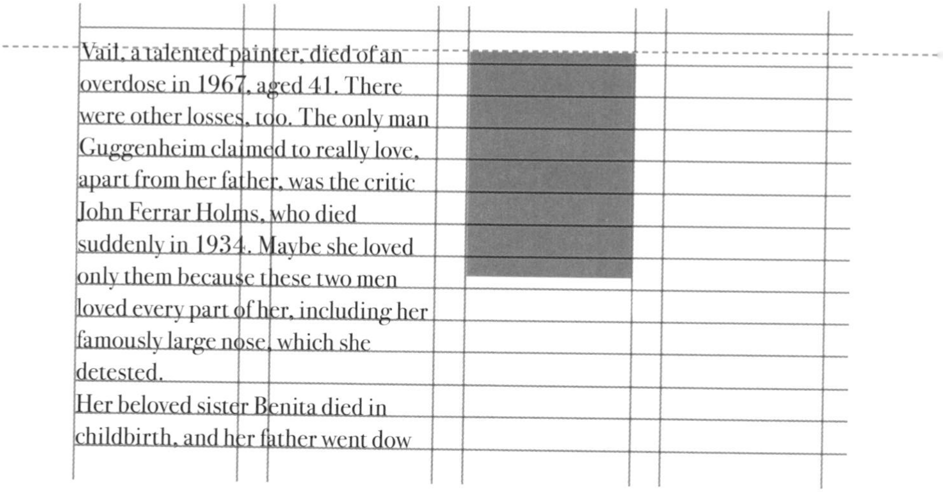

Vail, a talented painter, died of an
overdose in 1967, aged 41. There
were other losses, too. The only man
Guggenheim claimed to really love,
apart from her father, was the critic
John Ferrar Holms, who died
suddenly in 1934. Maybe she loved
only them because these two men
loved every part of her, including her
famously large nose, which she
detested.
Her beloved sister Benita died in
childbirth, and her father went dow

3 In this variant of Fig. 2, the image is also aligned with the column width; here, too, the height "follows". Different in this case: The upper edge of the image is guided by the x-height of the adjacent font. This can be useful, e.g. for English texts with only a few capitals. Or if a font has limited ascenders. The aim is to achieve the same optical height. So it depends on the typefaces and on the language whether the ascender or the x-height are the measure of things (see Fig. 5).

Officias velecest, Cor Simenditio. Ed qui te sime nobitatia
invelitatem dolupta quiscius il
mo estiber citaquaecto offic tet
que quisciae es pella ium que
pariam fugia consed moluptatquo esequi odi blabo. Aci sus.
Ro consedis ipsum quaspicid
molorro ribusci endaere ab int.
Ed qui te sime nobitatia esti
invelitatem dolupta quiscius il
mo estiber citaquaecto offic tet
que quisciae es pella ium que
pariam fugia consed moluptatquo esequi odi blabo. Aci sus.
Ro consedis ipsum quaspicid.

A
A1
A2
A3
A4
A5
A6
A7
A8

4 This image that may not be cropped is aligned with the upper edge of the adjacent font and with the font lines of the text. In contrast to the examples on the left, "the width follows" here. In this case, the image is not guided by the columns.

B
B1

C
C1
C2
C3

Vail, a talented painter, died of an overdose in 1967, aged 41. There were other losses, too. The only man
Bodoni book

D
D1
D2
D3
D4

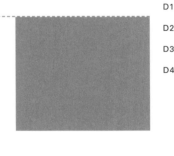

Der König war schon ein wenig trunken, als er sich schlafen legte. Der Mond schien helle und die vielen Sterne funkelten über der
Helvetica light

5 Here you can see the relationship between the upper edge of the image and the x-height of the text (as in Fig. 3) more precisely: one time with English text (Bodoni) and the other time with Helvetica, a font with a short ascender.

Officias velecest, Cor Simenditio. Ed qui te sime nobitatia invelitatem dolupta quiscius il mo estiber citaquaecto offic tet que quisciae es pella ium que pariam fugia consed moluptatquo esequi odi blabo. Aci sus. Ro consedis ipsum quaspicid molorro ribusci endaere ab int. Ed qui te sime nobitatia esti invelitatem dolupta quiscius il mo estiber citaquaecto offic tet que quisciae es pella ium que pariam fugia consed moluptatquo esequi odi blabo. Aci sus. Ro consedis ipsum quaspicid.

Duis autem vel eum iriure dolor in hendrerit in vulputate velit esse molestie consequat, vel illum dolore eu feugiat nulla facilisis at vero eros et accumsan et iusto odio dignissim qui blandit praesent luptatum zzril delenit augue duis dolore te feugait nulla facilisi.

6 In this example there is a marginal text next to the running text. With the first line, it takes up the font line of the running text, but otherwise has a life of its own – logically, because the font size is smaller and needs a smaller line spacing.

Vail, a talented painter, died of an overdose in 1967, aged 41. There were other losses, too. The only Bodoni book

Officias velecest, cor simenditio. Ed qui te sime nobitatia invelitatem. Mus debitas sum, num si officim aut inihictias aut vendam sitas eicto.

Der König war schon ein wenig trunken, als er sich schlafen legte. Der Mond schien helle und die vielen Sterne funkelten über der Helvetica light

Officias velecest, cor simenditio. Ed qui te sime nobitatia invelitatem. Mus debitas sum, num si officim aut inihictias aut vendam sitas eicto.

7 Here, too, there are various ways in which the marginal text can be guided by the running text: It can refer to the font line (as in Fig. 6), the upper edge of its ascender can take up the x-height of the running text or align itself with its ascender, for example. In all cases, the marginal text ignores a baseline grid tailored to the running text.

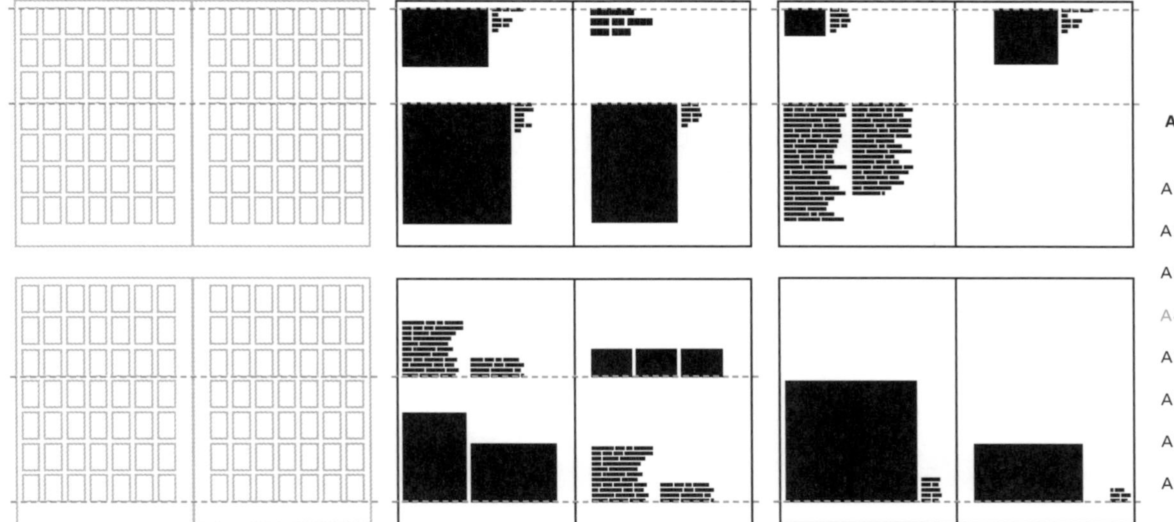

8 The decisive difference between the art catalog and the non-fiction book is that the module heights, which are responsible for the placement of the images, also determine where the corresponding texts are located: They reflect (in different ways) the upper edges of the pictures, thus deviating from a baseline grid. In the overview you can see that the pictures "hang" on reference lines from the module grid (of course it is also possible to construct them from bottom to top, quasi "standing on a stage").

B

B1

C

C1

C2

C3

D

D1

D2

D3

D4

Whether images and texts are combined according to the "art catalog principle" or the "non-fiction book principle" is up to the designer and depends on the character of the medium. Both possibilities (they do not exist as categorical "principles", I only call them that for the sake of clarity) pursue the goal of creating harmonious relationships, i.e. a calm and undisturbed reading process.
Of course, they also show what one would have to do to create restlessness and disturbances – if the concept demands it. More about this in the following chapter.

There is no prototype of an art catalog. Despite all their differences, such publications have one thing in common: They place the depicted works in the center of attention – and do without superficial gestures that could distract from the content.

10

01/2013

190 x 200 cm

Beggars Banquet

1

Amidov: BC-AD

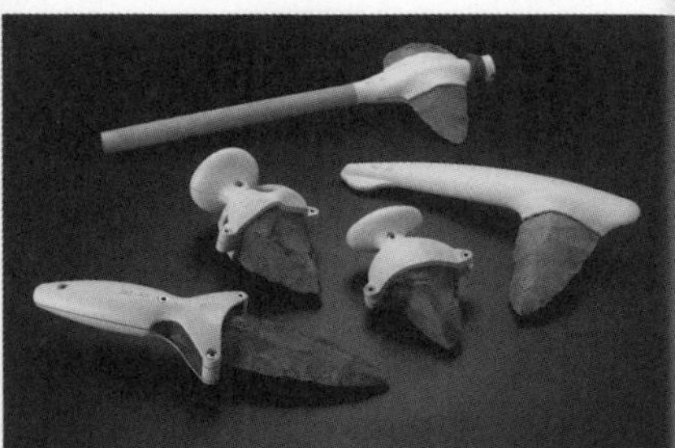

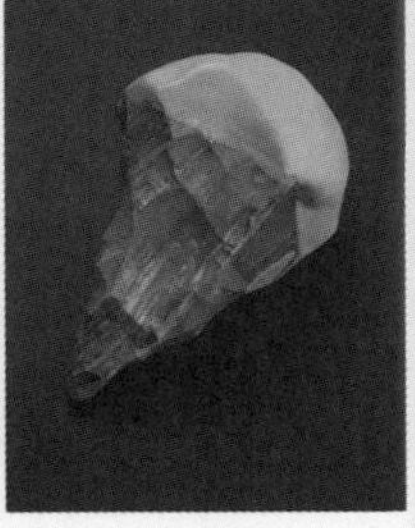

2011 – 2012

Judith Seng: Patches Tables

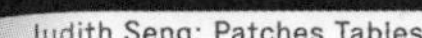

2006

2

46 29 . 04 . 2011

02 . 05 . 2011 / Egbert / Mas Malakoff (FR)

Fell at roundabout near Carrière
passed out for a moment: onlookers told
me not to move.
Ambulance - 2 police cars. Taken to
Perpignan Hospital (made jokes)
(P.S. lots of onlookers,) (I was worried about
my bike).

Didn't like the doctor, walked out

started 1st kitchen roll

Osama Bin laden killed
09.30 Saw hoopoe again.

full moon

2 small mice ate some of the poison

mouse in trap

3

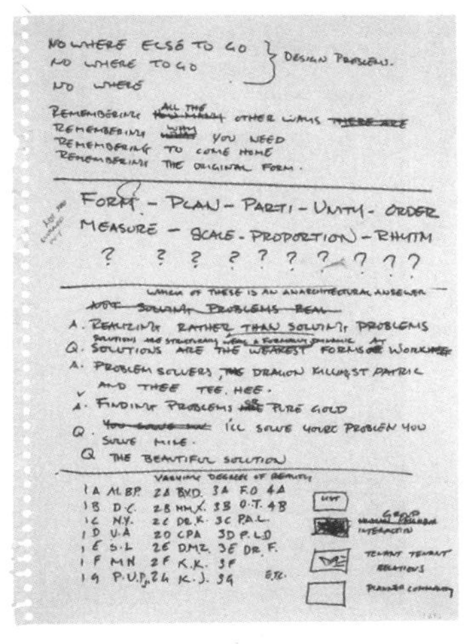

NO WHERE ELSE TO GO
NO WHERE TO GO
NO WHERE
} DESIGN PROBLEM.

REMEMBERING ALL THE OTHER WAYS
REMEMBERING YOU NEED
REMEMBERING TO COME HOME
REMEMBERING THE ORIGINAL FORM.

FORM - PLAN - PARTI - UNITY - ORDER
MEASURE - SCALE - PROPORTION - RHYTHM
? ? ? ? ? ? ? ? ? ?

WHICH OF THESE IS AN ANARCHITECTURAL ANSWER

A. REALIZING RATHER THAN SOLVING PROBLEMS
Q. SOLUTIONS ARE THE WEAKEST FORMS OF WORK
A. PROBLEM SOLVERS, THE DRAGON KILLIST PATRIC AND THEE TEE. HEE.
A. FINDING PROBLEMS PURE GOLD
Q. I'LL SOLVE YOUR PROBLEM YOU SOLVE MINE.
Q THE BEAUTIFUL SOLUTION

ANT ARCO TECTURE

ARC O TECTURE

*SOMEWHERE OUTSIDE THE LAW
II YOU ARE THE MEASURE
III A ROCKING CHAIR ESTATE.

Ant arco tecture, proposal for Anarchitecture, 1974

118 Gordon Matta-Clark 119

4

Mysterienspiel, 1934
Foto des vernichteten Gemäldes

102

103

Der Weg nach Golgatha, 1934
Foto des vernichteten Ölgemäldes

5

6

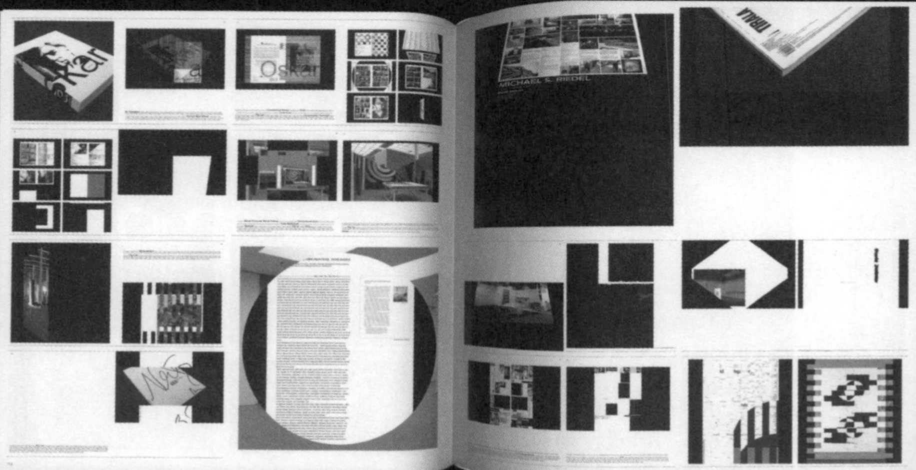

7

(INSERT - PAINTING OF CHILD IN A BOSTON HOME)

CHARLOTTE has had the painting brought back. She stares.

CHARLOTTE

If I could only get over my inhibitions for once.

(CLOSE SHOT OF RADIO PLAYING TCHAIKOVSKY'S FIFTH)

(PAN SHOT OF SKY - STARS BRIGHT)

8

1 Thomas Klefisch – 60 Monate, 60 Bilder
Bruno Kehrein (ed.)

2 10+1 Talents Messe Frankfurt
Hansjerg Maier-Aichen (ed.)

3 Vivace
Hanne van der Woude

4 Laurie Anderson Tisha Brown Gordon Matta-Clark, Pioneers of the Downtown Scene New York
Barbican Art Gallery (ed.)

5 Der Maler Peter Weiss. Bilder Zeichnungen Collagen Filme
Verlag Frölich & Kaufmann (ed.)

6 Pink Wave Hunter Part 1
Andro Wekua

7 Kunste zur Text, Michael Riedel
Matthias Ulrich, Max Hollein (ed.)

8 The Städel Paintings, John Baldessari
Martin Engler (ed.)

It is not easy to make universal statements about *the* magazine design, because it depends very much on what a magazine wants to communicate and what media role it should play: football magazine or fashion magazine, lifestyle magazine or underground paper, news magazine, or yellow press. However, most magazines have a lot in common: They appear periodically, have to assert themselves on the shelves of kiosks/bookstores, and as a rule they meet the reading expectations that correspond to "informative reading".

The grid in magazines A–5

"Informative reading" initially has an impact on the editorial structure of a magazine: Recurring editorial forms such as "cover story", "report", "advice column", "panorama", etc. are intended to offer the reader a structure that can be learned and facilitate orientation. For the same reason, the texts of the various editorial forms have similar lengths from issue to issue and the images are treated similarly in terms of size and placement. This is also a help for authors – they can "write on line" on the basis of the text lengths defined in the magazine grid, because they know how much space is given to them and how correspondingly short or detailed their text can be (one of the aspects in which the newspaper is similar to the magazine). For the design, "informative reading" means two things. On the one hand, there must be an unmistakable reading guidance. Headlines, sub-headlines, running and marginal texts as well as pictures and graphics are then arranged in such a way that, for example, a title story or a collection of useful tips or a report can be identified as such and easily grasped at the first glance 1. On the other hand, the design must be based on a grid consisting of small modules that offer possibilities for many different editorial forms. The recurring structure and esthetics are intended to achieve what is commonly referred to as "reader-paper-loyalty" in the industry. The cover page design must therefore be accordingly typical. In a nutshell: The readers expect the familiar with ever-new content. They expect, for example, "Spiegel" magazine to fulfill all visual and content-related expectations that arise when thinking of it. The same applies to "form", "11 Freunde" or "The Gentlewoman" magazines.

→ D1

Reading expectation
Informative reading

Double-page spread from "Spiegel" magazine, April 2017

„Wir atmen alle auf“

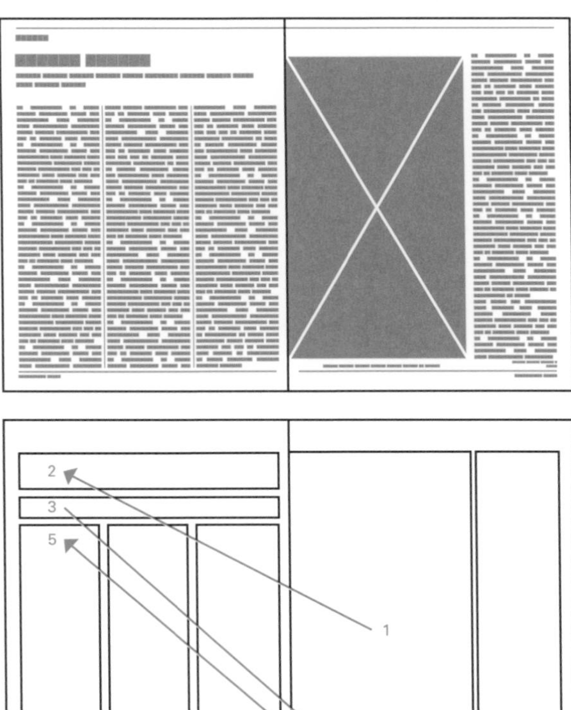

1 Someone who wants to read "informative" is only patient to a limited extent. We all know this: First we look at the picture while leafing through a magazine, then we read the headline (sometimes it's the other way round). Maybe we also read the caption – at the latest then we decide if we want to stay with the article or if we want to keep browsing. The layout must take this reception behavior into account.

A
A1
A2
A3
A4
A5
A6
A7
A8
B
B1
C
C1
C2
C3
D
D1
D2
D3
D4

What all magazines have in common is that they (must) cultivate their characteristics and the trust placed in them in order to retain their readers. The grid with its recurring structure and its creative interpretation (with regard to white spaces, reference edges, image positions, etc.) creates a distinctive basic pattern for each magazine, a "visual tone" by which readers can recognize a magazine, even if they are not aware of it. "Informative" reading, as is typical for the reception of a magazine, therefore has many facets. This is important to know, because it raises the question of the general validity of the previously described "rules" in dealing with text/image combinations.

The "grid laws" of "Spiegel" magazine apply only to it. Others apply to "Novum" magazine and yet others to "Homme" magazine or to publications with a lower circulation, such as fanzines. "Spiegel" magazine relies on creative calm and reliability[2]. Other magazines want to create creative restlessness by violating the harmony of text/image combinations. Pictures are no longer guided by text lines, are not placed in a comprehensible grid (sometimes they even have their own grid, different from the text grid, see Fig. 7) and have different sizes, which do not seem to originate from any comprehensible system. In short, they question order (in the sense of a creative harmony) – just as the special readership expects it to be. This style – to be found especially in contemporary fanzines and lifestyle magazines – serves a reading expectation in which the "unfamiliar" is perceived as particularly appealing (and which is then quite different from, say, "Spiegel" magazine): The reader's eyes look here and there for quick information or simply for entertainment (usually served by pictures, graphics, captions and headlines, always in a style that is intended to arouse curiosity) before they perhaps get caught up in longer passages of text[3].

A A1 A2 A3 A4 A5 A6 A7 A8 B B1 C C1 C2 C3 D D1 D2 D3 D4

Double-page spread from "Spiegel" magazine, no. 02, 2016

Es kommen härtere Tage

Ein Anschlag hätte den Stoff der nationalen Aufregung ebenso liefern können, ein Kindsmord, irgendeine andere Tat.

Double-page spread from "Spiegel" magazine, no. 18, 2017

Deutschland

Rechnungshof kritisiert Panzer-Deal

Double-page spread from "Spiegel" magazine, no. 18, 2017

Deutschland

Der Junge im blauen Kaftan

2 The "visual sound" of "Spiegel" magazine is unmistakable. Many graphic decisions (paper, format, font and gray value, grid, picture language, the ratio of printed to unprinted surfaces, the use of lines) ensure this. It goes without saying that this style is not found in "The Gentlewoman" or "Kicker". After all, every magazine wants to be unique.

Unnamed Fanzines Workshop, Mainz University of Applied Sciences

Geboren im Aufzug

xtrem

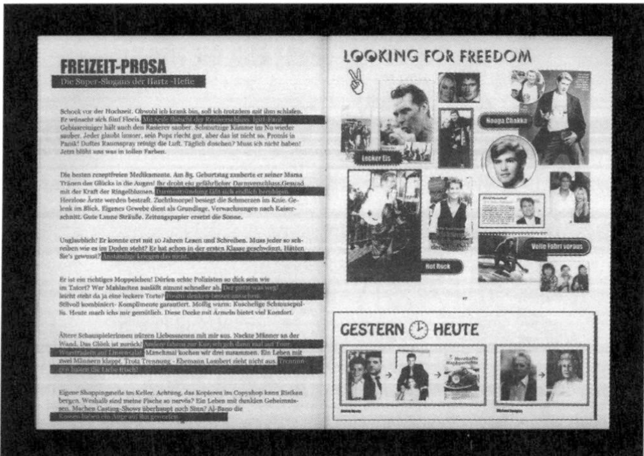
FREIZEIT-PROSA

LOOKING FOR FREEDOM

GESTERN HEUTE

3 Magazines have different charisma. They all maintain an individual visual climate that will repeat itself from issue to issue. Those who like the look will become sporadic or even permanent readers – provided that the design statement matches the content.

But even if it is less wild (and the "harmony laws" described in the non-fiction book chapter are observed in the text/image combinations), there are enough possibilities in magazine design to create different reading speeds and a corresponding creative "entertainment" [4]. Texts then do not always begin at the top of a type area, but are sometimes "lowered", i.e. several centimeters further down – or the text column ends much earlier than it should. Or there is a lot of white space on one side. Or a huge text in headline size dominates a whole page. Or texts protrude into images. Or pictures (and sometimes even texts) collide. Is there no grid underlying such pages? Yes, practically always. If these variances appear in a publication or a connected page section, they should be

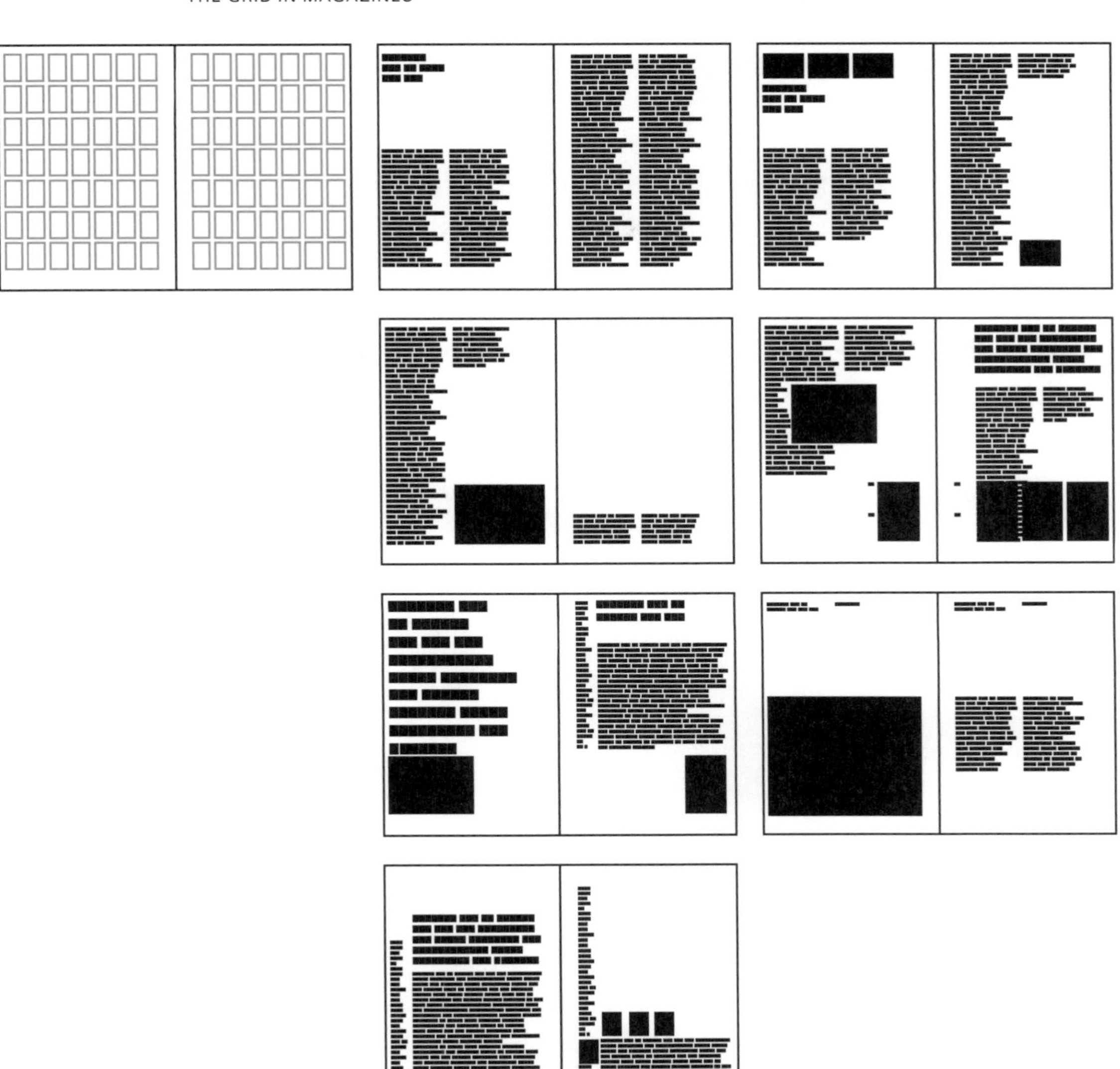

4 Grids are basic patterns that can be interpreted creatively. They can be filled depending on the desired appearance. The interpretive repertoire includes: lowered texts, shortened text columns, the definition of printed and unprinted areas, the decision to let texts flow into pictures, the size of headline texts, the drawing of "clotheslines", and the construction of "stages" and so on.

seen as planned interpretations of an existing basic framework. The fixed basic order of a magazine makes sense for another reason: It simply doesn't pay off (time, effort) to reinvent a weekly magazine from issue to issue.
The designers of such magazines gratefully revert to those principle layouts and grids that have been developed once (or are redeveloped for an occasional relaunch).

So you have to look at the grid in magazines as a "principle of possibilities": This is where all the basic conditions are defined within which macro-typography can unfold. The already mentioned "clotheslines" can then be set up or "stages" built. Or "disorder" can compete with "order". Especially the latter deserves a closer look: Even a supposedly coincidental "disorder" can arise from a grid idea. If, for example, two independent grids – one for the text, another for the images – are used. The illustrations on this double-page spread show how this works 5–7.

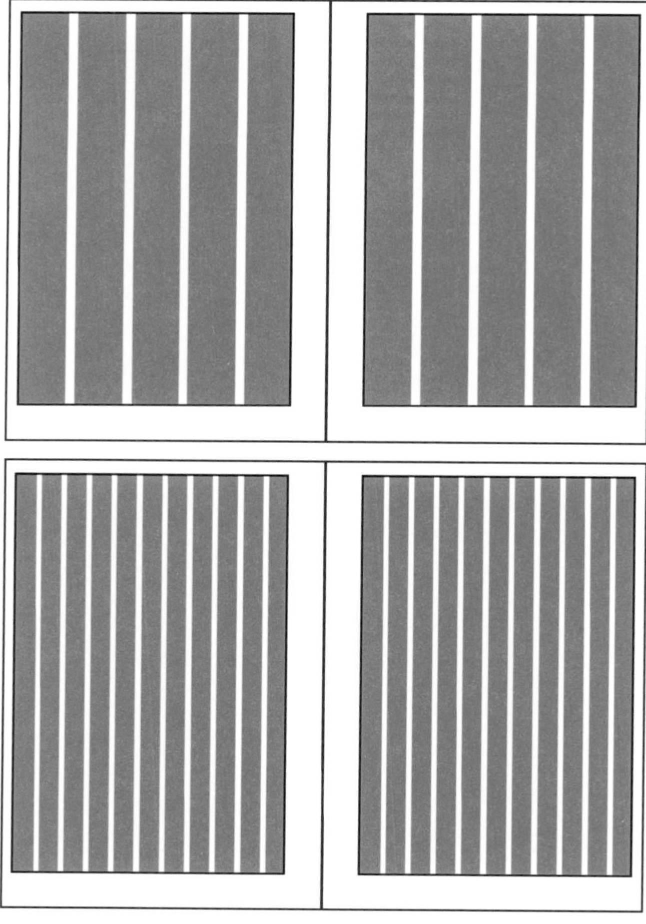

5 In this example we have created a 5-column grid for the texts. In order to be able to handle the images more flexibly later, we have created an 11-column image grid, which deliberately cannot be developed from the 5-column grid.

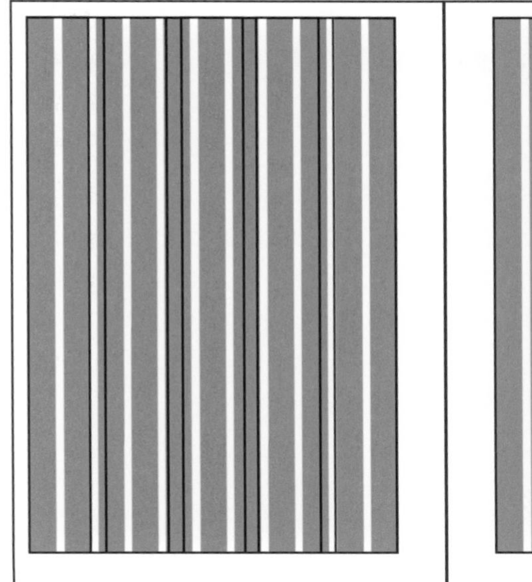
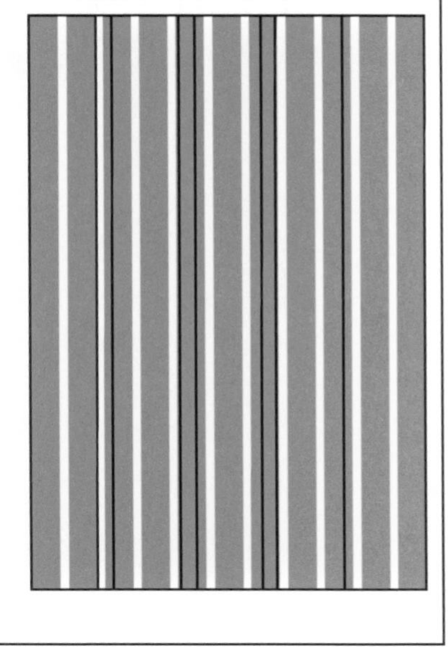

A
A1
A2
A3
A4
A5
A6
A7
A8

6 This illustration shows the text grid and the image grid.

B
B1

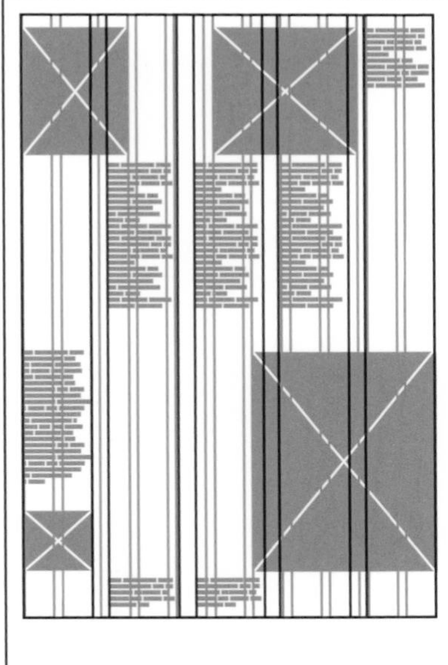
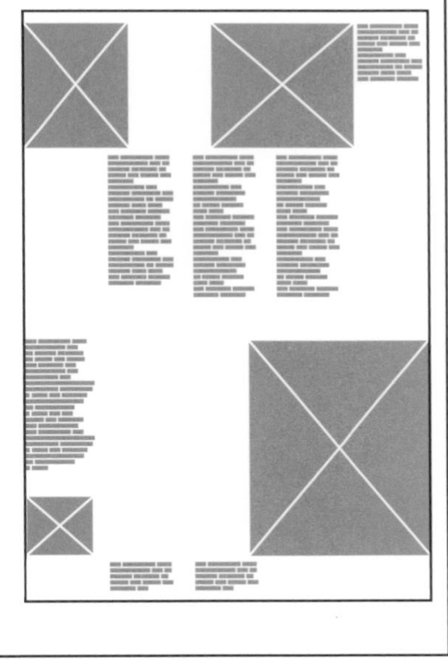

C
C1
C2
C3
D
D1
D2
D3
D4

7 A layout based on different grids for text and images could look like this. This design guarantees a certain creative restlessness – and yet "the wheel doesn't have to be reinvented" on every double-page spread, thanks to the reliable grid parameters.

Magazines are a dime a dozen. In recent years, their number has steadily increased (contrary to expectations) – this is especially true for limited print-run "special interest magazines", which are very popular with their fans. The big mainstream magazines, on the other hand, are struggling for advertising customers and with the digital upheaval in the media world. The battle for readers and their attention is one of the most important impulses to present a special and individual layout. The types of design described are therefore only a small part of the many ways in which magazines can present themselves.

Interview
Horacio Silva

Portrait
Annemarieke
van Drimmelen

Modern Mobility

Honey Dijon is all over the place, in a good way. One minute she's rocking a black-tie party in New York for the CFDA, and the next she's at Berghain in Berlin, jazzing up the famous techno club with her trademark sound that mixes old-school house from Chicago – her hometown – with anything from disco to funk to soul. Not for Honey the jeans-and-T-shirt uniform of her fellow DJs. By night, she's more likely to be in Alaïa or Givenchy. Maybe it's her combination of androgynous allure, musicality and old-fashioned politesse, but for Honey, it seems that all doors are always open.

Horacio Silva: Honey, I don't know anyone who moves in as many circles as you. One minute you'll be DJing at some too-cool-for-school night in New York, the next you're off to Cartagena for a *beaumonde* party.

Honey Dijon: I do move through quite a few. But I've always been interested in different lifestyles, sexual orientations and gender expressions. I relish that. The surprising thing for me is that I've managed all I have by playing underground house and techno.

HS: I can never remember who said it, but talking of social agility and mobility brings to mind that quote "The essence of style is someone who can be comfortable in any room."

HD: I'm a contributor to Style.com, so I've been thinking about exactly what style is a lot lately. I like to think of myself as a stylish person. Not because of the clothes that I wear – which for day normally consist of a perfect jean, a cashmere sweater and a blazer, incidentally – but because of the way that I live my life. Above all, I'm curious about people's experiences, so it doesn't matter to me how much money or what social standing they have.

HS: I think curiosity has a lot to do with it. From what I know of you, you're an autodidact who's devoured magazines for years and acquired so many that you have a special storage place for them.

HD: No, it recently got destroyed! There was a fire two units down from mine at Manhattan Mini Storage. The fire department doused all the rooms around it, and half my magazine collection got ruined. I had *The Face*, *Blitz*, Italian *Vogue* from when Steven Meisel first started photographing for it, French *Vogue*, *Details*, *Per Lui*, *Jill*...everything. I'm devastated.

HS: That's awful. How influential were they for you?

HD: Very! I grew up in a middle-class household on the South Side of Chicago, and I've been a huge magazine junkie since I was 12. They were my education in art, fashion, culture, living. I actually got into them because my uncle was a tailor. I used to go into his shop with my father to have his clothing fitted, and there were always *GQ*s around, dating back to the 1960s. The first time I saw them, which would have been about 1988, I was hooked. The ones from the late '70s with all the Charivari and Matsuda ads and the ones from the early '80s when Bruce Weber and Denis Piel were shooting for them – I couldn't believe there was this whole world that I'd never seen before.

HS: Which title best represented your generation, would you say?

HD: When I discovered *Details*, and particularly *Interview*, that completely changed the game. I mean, in the '80s and '90s, *Interview* was unbelievable – you'd have an artist interviewing a nightlife person, a bartender interviewing a designer. People from different social places all talking to each other. I guess that shaped the way I see the world.

HS: Do you think growing up in Chicago had an effect?

HD: Oh, it did. I grew up around

96

Honey Dijon

Coming to a music festival near you this summer, Honey Dijon likes her daywear simple and expensive. Here, she is wearing a white cotton shirt and white cotton trousers, both by EDUN. The gold jewellery is Honey's own.

97

1

Gerade bei Design ist manchmal die Entrückung der Weg, um eine Aufmerksamkeit gegenüber den Dingen herzustellen, durch die man sie dann wieder anders verstehen und sehen kann.

● When it comes to design, dissociation is sometimes the way to create attention for things, so that one can then understand and see them in a different way.

2

„Von unseren Freunden haben wir die besten Hochzeitsgeschenke bekommen. So wie die rosa Phallus-Vase oder den Chair One von Konstantins Assistenten."

E

Ein typisches Pariser Eckhaus am Boulevard des Batignolles im 17. Arrondissement: fünf Stockwerke hoch, Haussmann-Fassade und triangulär wie ein dickes Stück Camembert. Hier wohnt Pauline Deltour, zusammen mit ihrem Mann Nicolas und ihrer drei Monate alten Tochter. Über die mit Teppich ausgelegte Holztreppe steigen wir hoch in den zweiten Stock, wo Pauline gerade ihre Tagesmutter vor der Tür verabschiedet. Vor drei Wochen hat sie wieder angefangen, Vollzeit zu arbeiten, wie in Frankreich üblich. Nur mittwochnachmittags, also heute, kümmert sie sich selbst um ihre Tochter. Die sei aber *ganz* unkompliziert und schlafe normalerweise gut, meint sie gelassen. Für Gespräch und Fotos sollten wir genug Zeit haben. Während die kleine Anouk also friedlich nebenan im Kinderzimmer schlummert, bittet Pauline uns in den Salon.

Auf dem Weg dorthin stolpern wir über einen Zwillingskinderwagen mit zwei Babyschalen. Was, schon wieder schwanger? Nein, nein, lacht sie. Den habe sie nur für die *garde partagée* gekauft. So nennt man in Frankreich ein äußerst praktisches Betreuungssystem, bei dem man sich mit einer Partnerfamilie eine *Nounou*, also eine Tagesmutter teilt. Denn Kindergartenplätze sind auch in Frankreich schwer zu haben.

Pauline ist die natürlich schöne Französin, wie sie im Buche steht. Sie empfängt uns barfuß, ihr schwarzes, kinnlanges Haar trägt sie offen und ein bisschen wild, ist kaum geschminkt und gertenschlank, *bien sûr.* Dass sie vor nur drei Monaten entbunden hat, ist ihr bei bestem Willen nicht anzusehen. „Gut kaschiert", meint sie bescheiden, aber in Wahrheit gehört sie wahrscheinlich einfach zu dieser Gattung Pariserinnen, die nie ein Gramm zu viel drauf hat. Ohne Sport und Diät zu machen, versteht sich.

Wenigstens ist die Wohnung unaufgeräumt – bei dem Gedanken ertappe ich mich. Zwar schöne Designklassiker, der Slow Chair von Bouroullec oder die Lampe May Day von Flos, dafür aber Kartons und Tüten in der Ecke und eine Reihe von Bildern auf dem Boden, die darauf warten, an der Wand angebracht zu werden. Sehr sympathisch. Ich muss mich für *mein* Chaos zu Hause also doch nicht schämen. Doch die Freude währt nicht lange: „Wir sind erst vor Kurzem hier eingezogen", entschuldigt sie sich. Hätte man sich ja denken können.

In der vorherigen Wohnung habe es kein Zimmer für Anouk gegeben, erzählt sie. Seit dem Umzug vor ein paar Wochen leben sie nun im Kinderwagenland, in *poussetteland*, wie Pauline ihr Viertel nennt. Damit meint sie wohl, dass es weniger Bars und Kneipen gibt. Eine klassische Wohngegend. Besonders ruhig ist es deswegen trotzdem nicht. Von der angesagten Ausgehmeile Pigalle trennt sie nur der Boulevard de Clichy mit seinen blinkenden Sexshops, und von unten brummt der Straßenlärm des stark befahrenen Boulevard de Batignolles nach oben.

Ein gewisser Geräuschpegel gehört in Paris nun einmal dazu. Pauline gefällt das. Deswegen sei sie sogar von München wieder zurück nach Paris gegangen. Nach ihrem Studium an der Schule für angewandte Künste (ENSAAMA) zog die gebürtige Bretonin, die später in Angers aufwuchs, nach Bayern. Vier Jahre verbrachte sie dort, drei davon arbeitete sie mit Industriedesigner Konstantin Grcic zusammen.

Das Interview auf Deutsch zu führen würde ihr trotzdem schwerfallen, sagt sie. Auch ein Grund, warum sie irgendwann wieder zurück nach Frankreich wollte. Endlich wieder ihre eigene Sprache sprechen. Vor allem aber ging ihr die Münchner Sauberkeit auf den Keks. „Alles ist dort so perfekt. Man sieht weder farbige Menschen noch Obdachlose. Man hat fast das Gefühl, in einer Stadt aus Pappmaschee zu leben. Der Schmutz von Paris hat mir irgendwann gefehlt, der Lärm, die Dynamik."

Paris ist dagegen wie ein Ameisenhaufen. Eine ständige Inspiration. „Das Wimmeln ist ansteckend", findet sie. Pauline, die emsige Ameise. Ein Bild, das zu ihr passt. Mit ihren Anfang dreißig hat sie die gesamte Bandbreite des Designs schon fast rundum abgedeckt. Dass die Leute sie trotzdem oft als Produktdesignerin bezeichnen, geht ihr auf die Nerven. „Man hat mich

21

3

2

3

4

am Ende: »I hope my little preface which I intend to write at a time when I am not overburdened as during these weeks will not disappoint you too much.«[27]

Am 12. Dezember erhielt ich einen Brief von Matthias Becker mit Horkheimers versprochenem Vorwort. »During his serious illness of the past weeks«, schrieb Becker, »he was greatly concerned to make the deadline he had promised. We are a bit late, but I think that you will be very satisfied with his introductory words.«[28] Natürlich war ich nicht nur dankbar, sondern auch tief bewegt von dieser Geste. Ich übersetzte den Text und schickte ihn nach Montagnola, damit Horkheimer ihn, falls er es wünschte, korrigieren konnte. Das Vorwort erschien mit kleinen Änderungen, als das Buch im Frühjahr 1973 schließlich veröffentlicht wurde. Die wohl wichtigste Veränderung betraf seine Zweifel an dem ergreifenden Satz, dem der Titel dieses Vortrags entnommen ist: »Die Hoffnung, irdisches Grauen möge nicht das letzte Wort haben, ist zweifellos ein metaphysischer Wunsch.« In meiner Übersetzung änderte Horkheimer »metaphysical« in »non-scientific«, ließ aber die Formulierung »the hope that earthly horror does not possess the last word« stehen.[29]

Das waren aber nicht die letzten Worte Horkheimers an mich. Neben der Auseinandersetzung über den Titel reagierte er großzügig auf einen Aufsatz, den ich 1972 unter dem Titel *The Frankfurt School in Exile* veröffentlicht hatte, und er schrieb, wie ungeduldig er auf die Veröffentlichung des Buches warte, die, wie er hoffe, mit der bevorstehenden englischen Übersetzung der *Dialektik der Aufklärung* zusammenfallen würde. Am 10. März 1973 informierte er mich endlich, dass zwei Exemplare des Buches angekommen seien; sie seien »beautiful and [he was] happy with them.« Die letzten Worte dieses letzten Briefes, nachdem er darum gebeten hatte, ihm die Besprechungen zu schicken, waren schlicht Worte der Freundschaft: »How are you? Are you well in Berkeley; will you be coming any time soon back to Europe?«[30]

Vier Monate später, am 7. Juli 1973, starb Horkheimer im Alter von 78 Jahren in einem Nürnberger Krankenhaus und wurde auf dem jüdischen Friedhof in Bern beerdigt. Kurz nach seinem Tod bekam ich den Abzug eines Fotos, eines der letzten, die von ihm gemacht wurden, auf dem er, wie immer untadelig im Dreiteiler, *The Dialectical Imagination* liest. Es gibt wohl kaum ein bewegenderes Bild für einen Historiker als das, das den Helden der eigenen Erzählung zeigt, wie er sich dem Ende seines Lebens nähert und offensichtlich einen gewissen Trost in der Bemühung findet, ihn und sein Leben zu verstehen. In der Zeit, in der ich Max Horkheimer kannte, verlor er seine engsten Freunde, Adorno und Pollock, und seine geliebte Ehefrau Maidon, die im Oktober 1969 starb. In vieler Hinsicht war er eine geschwächte Gestalt, von Krankheiten geplagt und voller Misstrauen gegen die Lesarten seines Erbes auf beiden Seiten des politischen Spektrums.

28 Matthias Becker an den Autor, Lilienthal, Schweiz, 12. Dezember 1971; Sammlung des Autors.
29 Max Horkheimer an den Autor, Montagnola, 5. März 1972; Sammlung des Autors. In Jay (1976 [1973]: 10) heißt der Satz schließlich entsprechend: »Die Hoffnung, irdisches Grauen möge nicht das letzte Wort haben, ist zweifellos ein nichtwissenschaftlicher Wunsch.«
30 Max Horkheimer an den Autor, 10. März 1972; Sammlung des Autors.

Ich hatte ungeheures Glück, als Erster eine allgemeine Geschichte dieses Erbes vorlegen zu dürfen, und noch größeres Glück, mir dabei Horkheimers Vertrauen zu erwerben. Auch wenn ihm unübersehbar wichtig war, dass meine Erzählung ihm zur Ehre gereichte, fühlte ich mich nie gedrängt, das Material in rosigerem Licht erscheinen zu lassen, als die Dokumente hergaben. Ich kann seine – und Felix Weils – Ängste, ihr Denken könnte auf einen nicht näher definierten jüdischen Geist oder auf die Erfahrung der Weimarer Juden reduziert werden, völlig nachvollziehen, auch wenn ich nach wie vor glaube, dass sich eine nicht reduktionistische Analyse dieser Dimension ihrer Geschichte als fruchtbar erweisen könnte. Der Ausgang des Streits über meinen Titelvorschlag war für alle Seiten zufriedenstellend. Die Alternative legte den Schwerpunkt auf ihr Denken statt auf ihr Leben, wo er hingehört, und ich konnte *Permanent Exiles* schließlich für eine Sammlung über eine Gruppe von Emigranten nutzen, die weniger einheitlich war und keine gemeinsame intellektuelle Position vertrat.

Was mich vielleicht am meisten bewegt, ist die Tatsache, dass vier Jahrzehnte nach Horkheimer Tod und nach dem Erscheinen von *The Dialectical Imagination* die Flaschenpost, die die Frankfurter Schule ins Meer geworfen hatte, auch weiterhin an unerwarteten Küsten auftaucht und von neuen Lesergenerationen geöffnet wird, die darin die Inspiration zur Entwicklung einer kritischen Theorie des 21. Jahrhunderts finden. Ob »metaphysisch« oder »nichtwissenschaftlich«, der Wunsch, mit Hilfe einer solchen Theorie die Greuel einer Welt zu mindern, die von dem Utopia, das die Frankfurter Schule ersehnte, noch weit entfernt ist, ist auch heute noch sehr lebendig.

Aus dem Amerikanischen übersetzt von Irmgard Hölscher

Literatur

— Adorno, Theodor W. 1964: Zur Bekämpfung des Antisemitismus heute, in: Das Argument 29. 6, 88–104.
— Adorno, Theodor W. 1986 [1962]: Zur Bekämpfung des Antisemitismus heute, in: Gesammelte Schriften 20. 1: Vermischte Schriften I. Frankfurt a M.: Suhrkamp, 360–383.
— Adorno, Theodor W. und Herbert Marcuse 1999: Correspondence on the German Student Movement, in: New Left Review 1. 233, 123–126.
— Adorno, Theodor W. und Max Horkheimer 2006: Briefwechsel 1927–1969. Hg. von Christoph Gödde und Henri Lonitz. Band 4: 1950–1969. Frankfurt a. M.: Suhrkamp.
— Bloom, Allan 1987: The Closing of the American Mind. How Higher Education Has Failed Democracy and Impoverished the Souls of Today's Students. New York: Simon & Schuster Paperbacks.
— Boll, Monika und Raphael Gross (Hg.) 2009: Die Frankfurter Schule und Frankfurt. Eine Rückkehr nach Deutschland. Göttingen: Wallstein.
— Brown, Norman O. 1959: Life Against Death. The Psychoanalytic Meaning of History. Middletown: Wesleyan University Press.
— Feuer, Lewis 1980: The Frankfurt Marxists and the Columbia Liberals, in: Survey 25. 3, 156–176.
— Feuer, Lewis 1982: The Social Role of the Frankfurt Marxists, in: Survey 26. 2, 150–170.
— Gay, Peter 1968: Weimar Culture. The Outsider as Insider. New York und Evanston: Harper and Row.
— Horkheimer, Max 1968: Kritische Theorie. Eine Dokumentation. Hg. von Alfred Schmidt. Frankfurt a. M.: S. Fischer.
— Jacobs, Jack 2015: The Frankfurt School, Jewish Lives, and Anti-Semitism. Cambridge: Cambridge University Press.

5

travel while you can

6

WHEN YOU
COME TO
THE FIGHT
AFTER
ROUND
FOUR
Black in Dark in
AND
THE HALLS
DON'T BLOCK
GO HOME
FOR Y'ALL MAY
THE DOOR
DON'T BLOCK
Bureau Mirko Borsche
Black in Dark
P. 129
Projects
P. 28

7

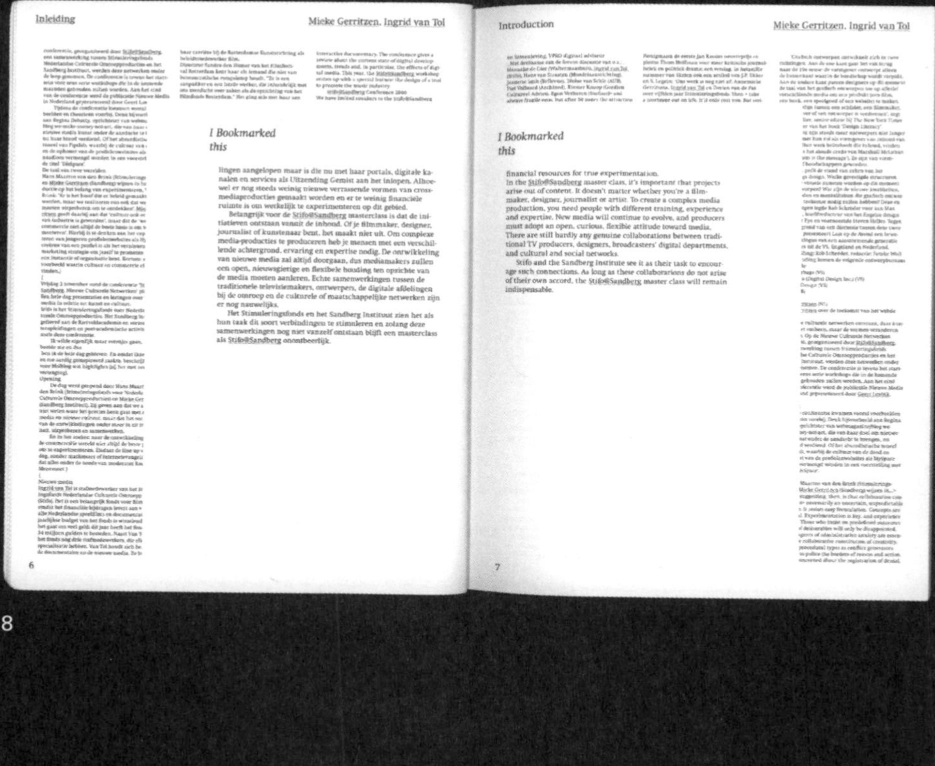

Inleiding
Mieke Gerritzen, Ingrid van Tol
I Bookmarked
this
6
Introduction
Mieke Gerritzen, Ingrid van Tol
I Bookmarked
this
7

8

9

44

Irma Boom, book designer

entretien par Peter Biľak

traduit de l'anglais par Jean-François Allain

Irma Boom, book designer

10

No clear-eyed assessment of the ominous system can help but see that the tide of political change over the past twenty years has been moving swiftly and relentlessly against us. Our defeats and setbacks have imposed constraints on the nature of resistance everywhere. We have all had to fight against not just the ascendency of the neoliberal bloc and the reactionary right, but we have also had to push back our own pessimism, a pessimism that capitalist hegemony is all too happy to nurture and feed.

It doesn't help that, with the defeat of the socialist experiments of the 20th century, two generations of organizers and activists have now come of age politically with few visible and viable alternatives to imperialism and neoliberalism. The fight against the enemy, as trying as it has been, has been no more difficult than our internal struggle with the troubling idea that noble, doomed resistance may be all that is left to us. I've spent too many sleepless hours haunted by the fear that vistory may be nothing more than an unattainable dream.

The danger in this insidious notion is profound. Without a clear conviction that another world is indeed possible, we resign ourselves all too easily to the idea that simply "putting up a good fight" is enough. We absolve ourselves of the responsibility of finding ways forward. We forgive our own shoddy, sloppy practice, just as we forgive our comrades'. We quickly lose all incentive for rigorous reflection on and evaluation of our work. We stop striving for improvement and excellence. The doubt takes control'

We are at a critical point in history. With the dire condition of people and of the planet, the stakes are high and rising. Opportunities for socialist liberation are emerging as are opportunities for reactionary barbarism. Harnecker insists that the quality of our organizing and movement-building work matters. The opposition is constantly revamping and refining, improving and innovating. Our success demands excellence. It is not enough for us to simply try, as Mao once warned, we have to dare to win.

—Adapted from Steve Williams' review of Marta Harnecker's *Ideas for the Struggle*

It is perfectly clear that political parties across the spectrum today are unquestioningly committed to maintaining the capitalist growth economy, seemingly oblivious to the catastrophe that this out-dated development agenda holds in store for people and planet – a catastrophe that, in some respects, has already arrived. In short, a universal 'growth fetish' defines representative democracies today, essentially enforced by a crude liberalism that presumes interference in the so-called free market is illegitimate. Regulatory tinkering, at most, is permitted. Empire marches on.

A worrying aspect of this political blindness and paralysis is that it may be built into the very structure of representative democracies. Unable or unwilling to look beyond the short-term horizon of the next election, politicians are essentially prohibited from taking a geological view of things, which is necessary for the preservation of our biosphere. To avoid making hard decisions, environmental costs are pushed into the future, all glossed over by a techno-optimism that promises ecological salvation through technology, innovation, design, and market mechanisms. From this perspective, there is no need to question affluent lifestyles or conventional modes of development. One consequence of this non-confronting myth is that the voices of future generations fall on deaf political ears – rendering our democracy decidedly 'unrepresentative' in this glaring way.

In this context, democracy as we know it today seems to be a deeply flawed – or, at least, grossly incomplete – mode of political organization and practice, unable to deal with the defining challenges of our times. For those people who are uncomfortably aware that limitless growth is a recipe for ecological (and thus humanitarian) disaster, the idea of trusting our growth-orientated 'representatives' to lead the way to a just and sustainable economy seems a delusion too large to swallow. Like Kafka, we will be waiting a long time.

Furthermore, one only needs to watch a single session of 'question time' in parliament to become convinced beyond doubt that democratic debate today has degenerated into shallow, often juvenile, power-hungry bickering, expressed in simplistic sound bites – a televised manifestation of 'fiddling while Rome burns'. It tempts one to despair. Certainly, one has to turn away.

Accordingly, wild democracy begins with the premise that the 'normal' party politics of representative democracy lies, for the foreseeable future, at least, beyond hope and redemption. Voting cannot possibly complete our civic duty, because our range of representatives is depressingly limited – Shorten or Turnbull? Clinton or Trump? – a political 'Sophie's choice'. Whether we look to the parliamentary Left or the parliamentary Right – both poles are shaped by the growth paradigm – we are guaranteed to lose.

We must, therefore, reinvent democracy for our moment in history. We must explore the democratic 'wild' beyond the ballot box.

— Sam Alexander

11

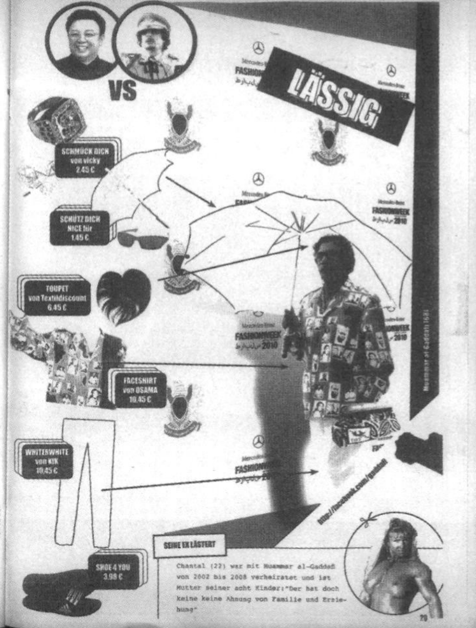

12

THE GRID IN MAGAZINES

1 The Gentlewoman

2 form

3 The Weekender

4 Freimodekultur. POPGender, Mode, Fotografie und Texte

5 West–End: Neue Zeitung für Sozialforschung

6 Lodown Magazine

7 Slanted

8 _Nieuwe Culturele Netwerken/ _New Cultural Networks

9 11 Freunde

10 Back Cover

11 Adbusters

12 Fanzine

A

A1

A2

A3

A4

A5

A6

A7

A8

B

B1

C

C1

C2

C3

D

D1

D2

D3

D4

Newspapers resemble magazines in many respects. Here, too, there are fixed columns and article lengths, but also strictly defined image sizes and placements. On the one hand, this must be the case so that the newspaper can be produced daily with the least possible effort. Journalists, for example, are guided by the text volumes available in the layout. On the other hand, the aim is to create trust through design recognition.

The grid in newspapers A—6

The keyword is called (as with the magazine) "reader-paper-loyalty". Readers "get used" to text lengths, picture spaces and the whole style of a newspaper [1] and have trained themselves unconsciously to a very specific rhythm of information absorption. I always notice this when the "Süddeutsche Zeitung" (SZ) – my favorite daily newspaper – is not available and I then have to resort to another German-language newspaper, for example the "Frankfurter Allgemeine" (FAZ). Both are comparably respectable quality newspapers [2]. And yet at the FAZ, visual circumstances of reading that I don't even notice anymore at the SZ catch my eye: How is the title page sorted? How much information is there and how long does it take to read the texts? Where are the comments and how long are they? Where are the announcements for the inner part or are there any at all? And I'm only concerned about all this because the FAZ is unfamiliar to me.

Reading a daily newspaper – this also applies to the online versions – should be quick and convenient. The tolerance for even the smallest disturbances or differences in information reception is correspondingly low. This is not even a matter of design quality. And it's not about the political coloring of the articles (even if the content perspective and the language style are important parts of the "reader-paper-loyalty").

It is simply our convenience, or better said, our rational calculation of when and where we want to invest how much time. And that's why we pay different attention to the daily newspaper – a medium that is already used in the afternoon to pack fish or ends up directly in waste paper – than, say, a reference book for design.

"Süddeutsche Zeitung",
Issues from May 3rd–5th, 2017

A
A1
A2
A3
A4
A5
A6
A7
A8
B
B1
C
C1
C2
C3
D
D1
D2
D3
D4

1 Every newspaper has its own rhythm in terms of content and design. On a daily level, the creative scope is extremely limited: The parameters developed (text lengths, text and image sizes, type of pagination, etc.) are almost irrevocable and must be filled directly by the author with the current events of the day.

Trumps Welt: Was war wirklich los in Schweden? › Die Seite Drei

Süddeutsche Zeitung

NEUESTE NACHRICHTEN AUS POLITIK, KULTUR, WIRTSCHAFT UND SPORT

Das Streiflicht

Pferde auf Eis

Schulz rückt ab von Agenda 2010

Der SPD-Kanzlerkandidat räumt „Fehler" seiner Partei in der Sozialpolitik ein. Diese will er nun korrigieren – und eine Mindestrente einführen sowie die Befristung von Arbeitsverträgen erschweren

Kein Platz für Helden

Deutschland hängt an traditionellem Familienbild

Laut OECD-Studie tragen die deutschen Frauen im europäischen Vergleich am wenigsten zum häuslichen Einkommen bei

Pence sichert EU Partnerschaft zu

US-Vizepräsident betont Trumps Wunsch nach Zusammenarbeit

Riad will Spezialeinheiten nach Syrien schicken

Neues Firmenregister soll wahre Eigentümer zeigen

Weitere Ermittlungen im Fall Beckenbauer

München hat die meisten Staus

DAS WETTER

13°/3°

Frankfurter Allgemeine

ZEITUNG FÜR DEUTSCHLAND

Dienstag, 21. Februar 2017 · Nr. 44/8 R0

HERAUSGEGEBEN VON WERNER D'INKA, JÜRGEN KAUBE, BERTHOLD KOHLER, HOLGER STELTZNER

F.A.Z. im Internet: faz.net

Pence: Unsere Geduld mit der Nato ist endlich

Nicht ohne mein Smartphone

Schulz' Vorteile

Von Jasper von Altenbockum

Wer den Krieg nährt

Von Reinhard Veser

Heute

Der Irrsinn in Pakistan

Frankreichs Ratlose

Ja zum Nô

Noch schneller

Das Überraschungsei

Beton gegen Terror

SPD-Kanzlerkandidat Schulz will Agenda 2010 korrigieren

Mehr Geld für Arbeitslose und Rentner, mehr Mitbestimmung für Arbeitnehmer

In der Ostukraine ist kein Frieden in Sicht. Schuld daran ist Moskau. Kiew muss gestärkt werden.

Kabul verlegt Truppen an die Grenze zu Pakistan

Protest gegen Raketenbeschuss aus Pakistan nach Terroranschlag / Flüchtlinge im Visier

Hans D. Barbier gestorben

Merkels Reise nach Algerien abgesagt

Südsudan erklärt Hungernotstand

Im „Exorzismus-Prozess" Haft für Hauptangeklagte

2 Two beautiful picture puzzles for designers: Which of the two newspapers is more informative for you? Which one looks more serious and which one appeals most to you? And what is the reason for that, in terms of the creative means?

Designers are rarely required to participate in the design of a daily newspaper. Nevertheless, the newspaper as a medium has a number of interesting aspects that can be useful in everyday design. Essentially, the question is how to place text and images on large areas. The following four illustrations show the most common layout options: staircase style 3, block style 4, shovel style 5, chimney style 6.

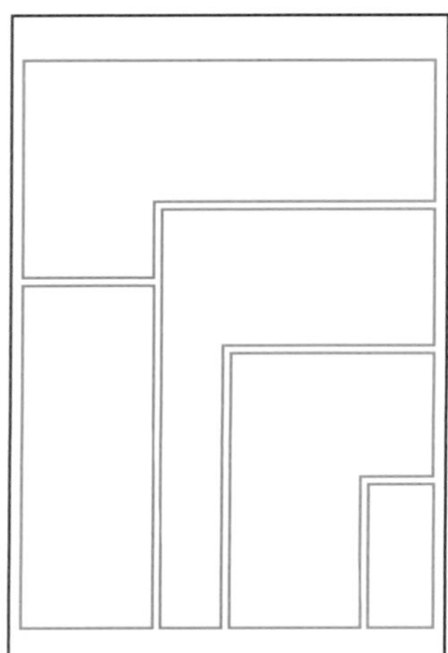

3 Staircase style: The article ends and article beginnings are offset towards each other so that "stairs" are created horizontally.

4 Block style: Articles are wrapped in blocks to form small units.

→ D1

Readability
Legibility

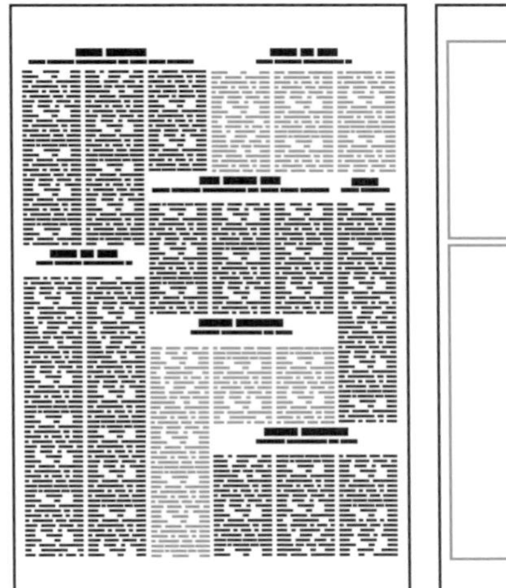

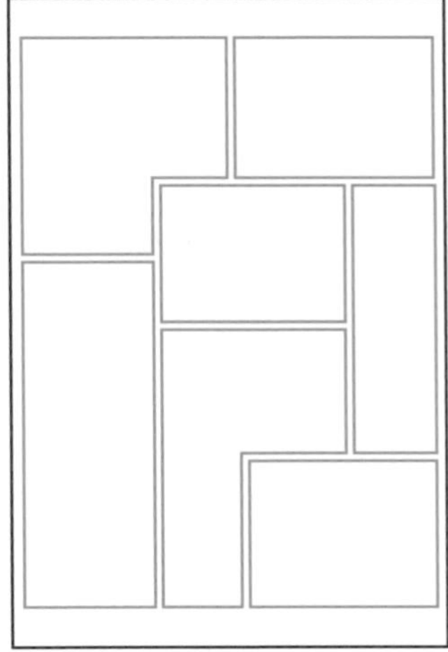

5 Shovel style: The articles are placed in both staircase and block style.

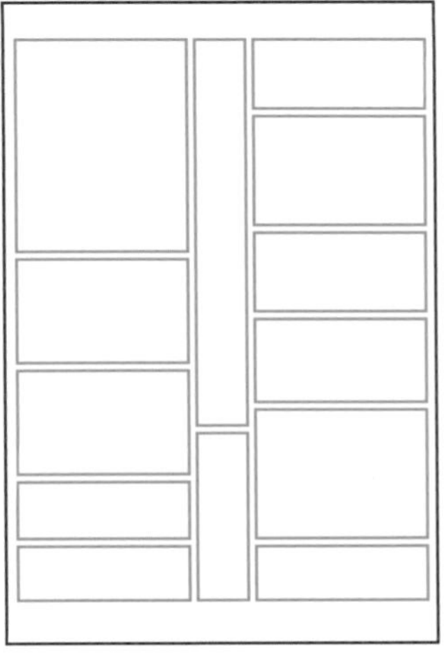

6 Chimney style: The articles form long columns or, in the case of short articles, are grouped together in one column.

In addition to the various methods for wrapping texts and placing images, daily newspapers offer good micro-typographic illustrative material (font sizes, line spacing, gray values, etc.). This is because they take great care with regard to readability and legibility – provided they are quality newspapers. But the rough typography of tabloids also has its justification. It is supposed to deliver on trash promises – if possible, from a distance.

Even if the medium “newspaper” in its printed form seems to have become outdated somewhat, the daily newspapers appearing worldwide are an immense factor of visual communication. They also serve as sources of inspiration. Not to mention the detailed reporting, which in view of the sometimes overwhelming flood of information on the Internet still offers important orientation and assessments.

Bye-bye Britain

»Als wirksames Instrument zur Kriminalisierung der Deutschen (…) wird immer noch der Völkermord am europäischen Judentum herangezogen«

South Korea vote raises hopes of detente

Left-leaning candidate sweeps to presidency

Moon Jae-in favours new engagement with North

Profile

Liberal on same page as US

Judge in Jakarta jails 'blaspheming' Christian governor for two years

Trump team delays decision on quitting Paris climate accord

Environment protection boss favours withdrawal

President's daughter and husband want US to stay

Current immigration policy would have kept Chaplin out of US, says De Niro

All of us in film owe a debt to Charlie Chaplin, who wouldn't pass today's extreme vetting

Irish police drop Fry prosecution

Türkische Journalisten klagen über Folter

Abgeordnete der Oppositionspartei CHP berichten über Misshandlungen Inhaftierter

„Ein Maßstab für die Demokratie"

PEN-Vize Feuchert über den Zustand der Meinungs- und Pressefreiheit weltweit und die Wege zu mehr Medienkompetenz

ZUR PERSON

Le Pen hat ein Euro-Problem

Die Kandidatin des rechten Front National will von einem schnellen Ausstieg aus der Währung nun nichts mehr wissen

Attempt to revolutionize education

Migranti, vertice a tre a Parigi «Un codice comune per le Ong»

Approccio condiviso con Germania e Francia. Ma l'Eliseo non ammorbidisce la sua linea dura

Ministri

Africa ed Europa

Il modello Madrid Quel muro eretto nel Mediterraneo con diplomazia (e soldi al Marocco)

di Andrea Nicastro

La parola

CEUTA

L'attacco

Molotov all'hotel che ospita rifugiati a Brescia

Il retroscena

di Fiorenza Sarzanini

In cifre

A Bruxelles

L'Italia chiede la ripresa della distribuzione dei profughi che si trovano nel nostro Paese

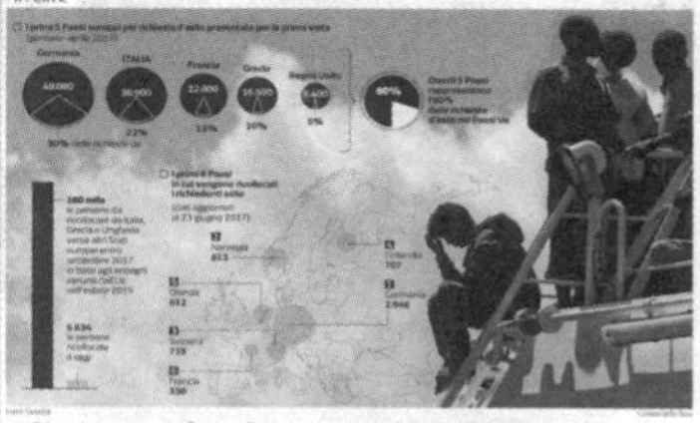

Gli aiuti e i fondi Così Minniti ha ottenuto garanzie dai due alleati

Appello ai sindaci: ognuno faccia la sua parte

200

Profughi e Ong

Il videomessaggio

Di Maio: Macron bravo (con le frontiere altrui)

Strutture e Residence

Nel centro dei profughi contro i profughi: «Basta nuovi arrivi»

Kaba, leader della protesta nel campo di Cona: non c'è più posto. Il prefetto: ne spostiamo dieci al giorno

Andrea Pasqualetto

Macron triomphe et doit réconcilier un pays divisé

Sa large victoire face à Marine Le Pen laisse les coudées franches au nouveau président pour des élections législatives décisives

Emmanuel et Brigitte Macron, devant la Pyramide du Louvre, dimanche 7 mai.

MACRON ENTEND S'APPUYER SUR UN PREMIER MINISTRE LOYAL ET SANS AMBITION PRÉSIDENTIELLE POUR 2022. PAS QUESTION D'INSTALLER À MATIGNON UN FUTUR ADVERSAIRE

Résultats du second tour

66,06 %

33,94 %

25,38 %

11,49 %

« LA RÉPUBLIQUE EN MARCHE »

« UN VOTE UTILE »

« La tâche qui nous attend est immense »

CHRONIQUE

PAR FRANÇOISE FRESSOZ

L'illusion de Giscard d'Estaing

15 בני אדם חולצו חיים מהריסות רעידת האדמה באיטליה; מניין ההרוגים עלה ל-250

קולומביה חתמה על הסכם שלום עם ארגון המורדים FARC

הדמוקרטיה באפריקה מתערערת עוד לפני שהתבססה

Ten eerste

Székesfehérvár, Hongarije: 'Laat Soros niet het laatst lachen'. Foto AFP

Antisemitisch luchtje rond Hongaarse campagne tegen Soros

Jonna Jan Hoitland

Premier Viktor Orbán heeft vaker de vijandkaart gespeeld

Bouwtoezicht blijft onder de hoede van gemeenten

Joost de Vries, Den Haag

Ik las opeens in een ochtendblad dat er nu kennelijk een andere visie is ontwikkeld

Ronald Plasterk, minister van Wonen

School geeft leerling-koks iets te voorbarig hun einddiploma

Ten eerste

Ontbossing in Brazilië. Veel diersoorten moeten tot 80 procent van hun leefgebied missen. Foto Andre Penner / AP

De uitsterfgolf, we zitten er al middenin

Een vermaarde bioloog trekt aan de alarmbel over iets dat we eigenlijk allemaal al wisten: dieren sterven in rampzalig tempo uit. Belangrijkste oorzaak is de menselijke overbevolking.

Maarten Keulemans, Amsterdam

Het is heel simpel: we staan aan de rand van de afgrond; het gaat allemaal nog veel erger worden

Jelle Reumer

WIE IS PAUL EHRLICH?

HOE GAAT HET MET DE DIEREN?

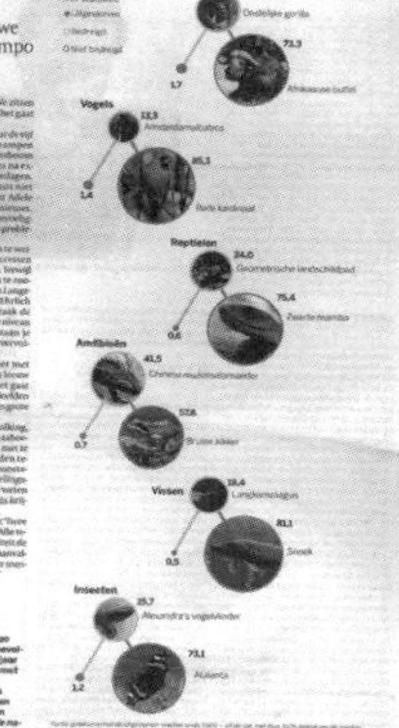

1 Die Zeit

2 The Guardian

3 Frankfurter Rundschau

4 The New York Times

5 Corrierre della sera

6 Le Monde

7 Haaretz

8 De Volkskrant

Web design approaches are to a large extent determined by the technical conditions on which this medium is based. These – similar to our user behavior – are subject to constant change, which is very rapid, as can be seen by the growth of digital possibilities and the accompanying changes in our reading habits.

The grid in web design A–7

An example of this might be that it wasn't so long ago that web design only had to deal with the display options required for monitors whose size differed only slightly. The websites were inflexible: When the visible section became smaller, you had to scroll horizontally to make hidden content visible at the edge 1.

This uncomfortable state was soon addressed: In order to allow a grid-related adaptation to the different sizes, the layouts became "liquid". This means that as the screen width became narrower, the columns of the layout also became narrower (up to a tolerable size) 2.
In the meantime, however, the number of devices on which websites could be accessed due to built-in browsers has increased. These should displayed without loss of information and comfort: on smartphones (portrait and landscape), on tablets (portrait and landscape), on laptops, on fixed monitors, and so on. With these requirements in mind, layouts had to be more than just "liquid". They have also become "adaptive": If the width of the layout changes, there are so-called "breakpoints" (i.e. display widths stored in the source code). If these breakpoints are exceeded or undercut, either by the end device itself or by narrowing the window, they trigger a change in the display defined in the source code 3. They therefore ensure that the layout changes by leaps and bounds after a phase of "liquid" narrowing – for example, when a three-column layout becomes two-column and then one-column after a certain width. This structural flexibility, consisting of "liquid" and "adaptive" control mechanisms, is called "responsive web design".

→ D1

Breakpoints
Source code

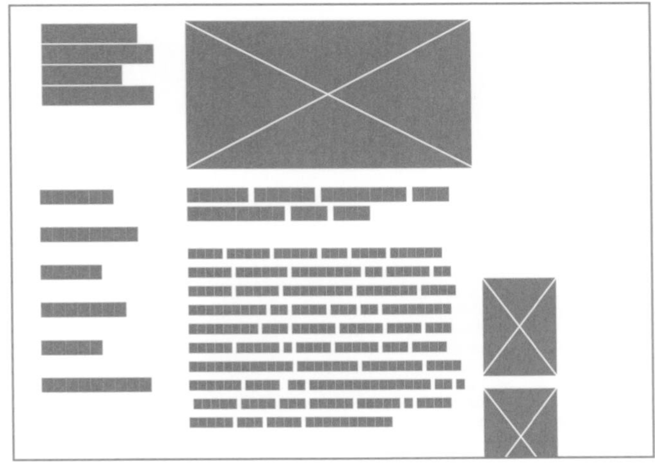

1 Inflexible web design: The classic website of the 90s was "hard coded", i.e. optimized for a (then) common display size. If the format or the resolution of the output device changed, parts of the website "disappeared", the user had to scroll horizontally to see everything.

A
A1
A2
A3
A4
A5
A6
A7
A8
B
B1
C
C1
C2
C3
D
D1
D2
D3
D4

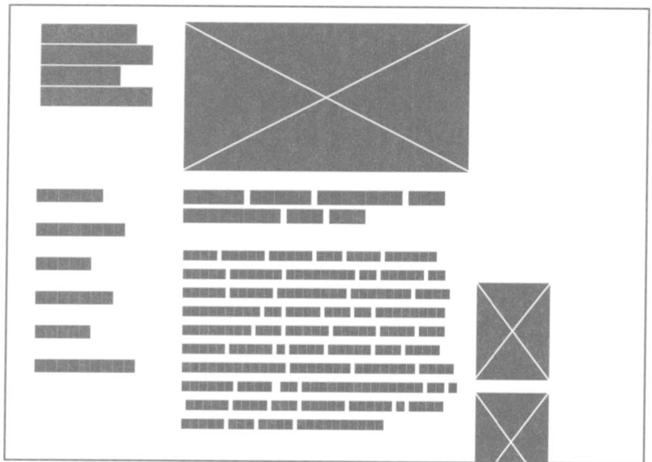

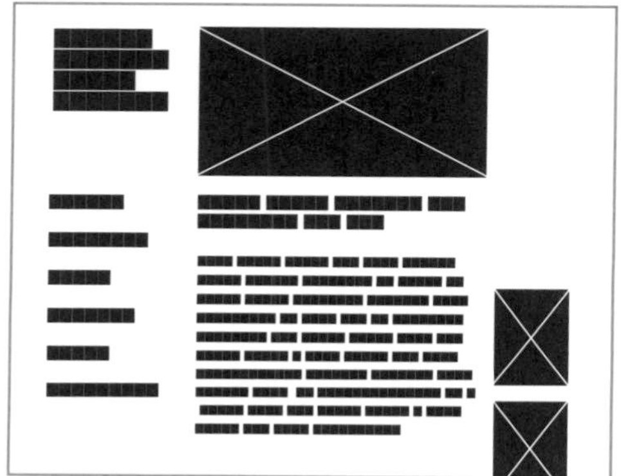

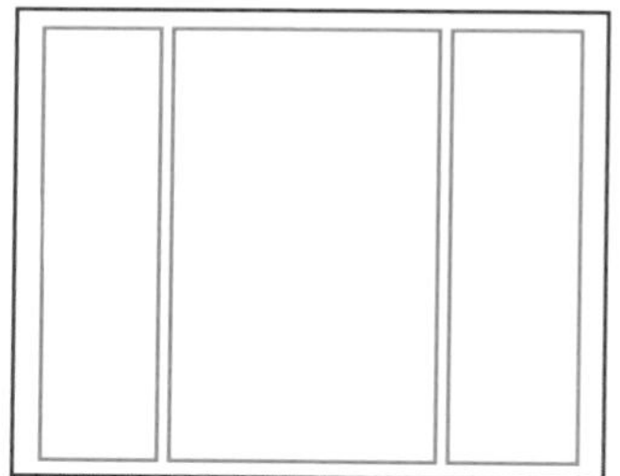

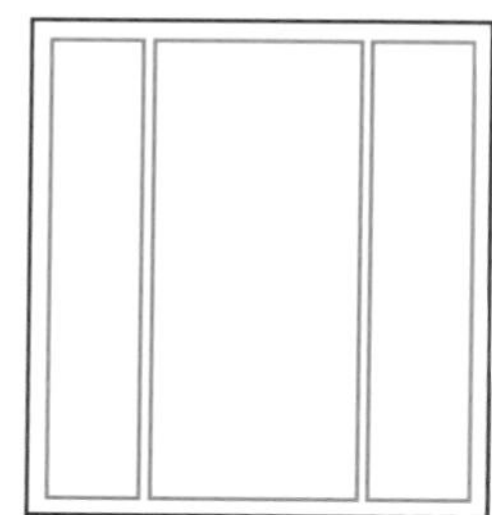

2 "Liquid" web design: The layout adapts horizontally to different screen widths. The vertical distances remain the same.

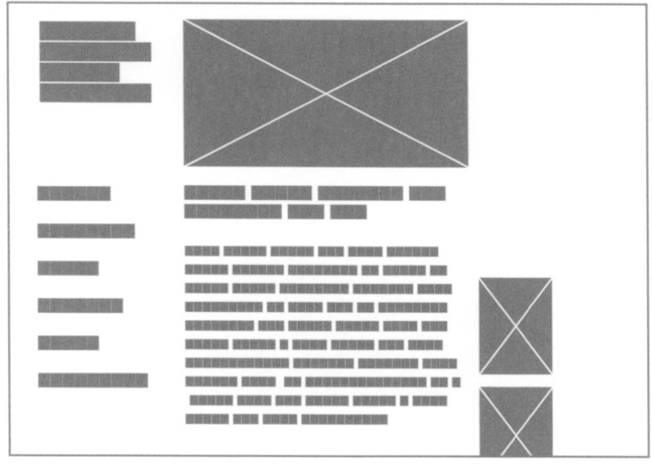

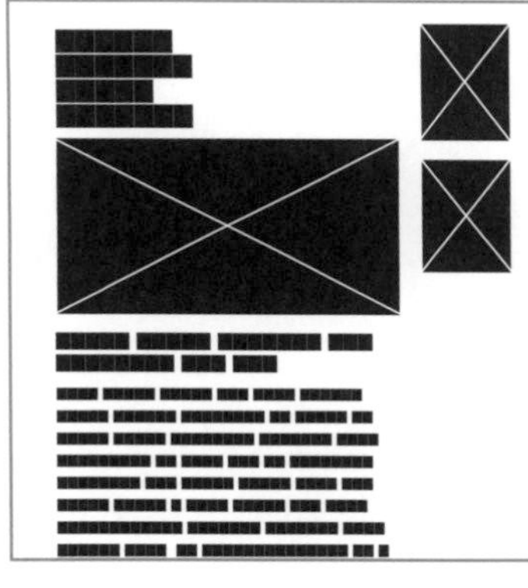

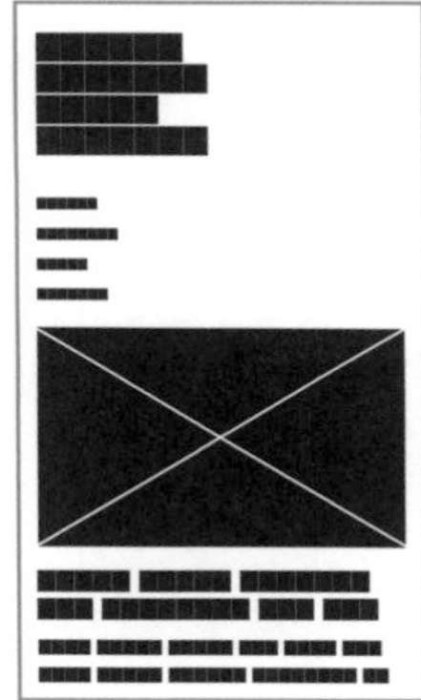

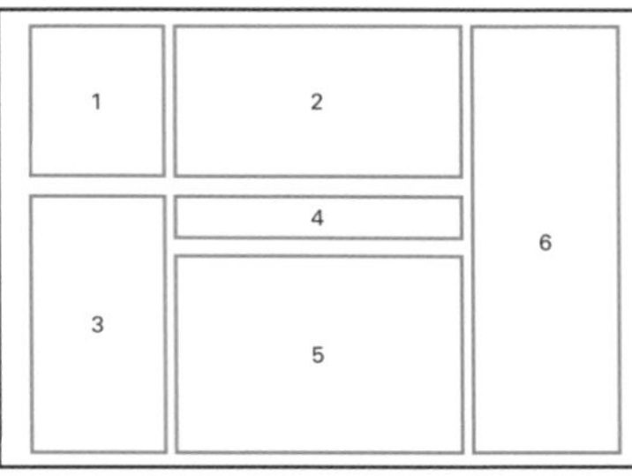

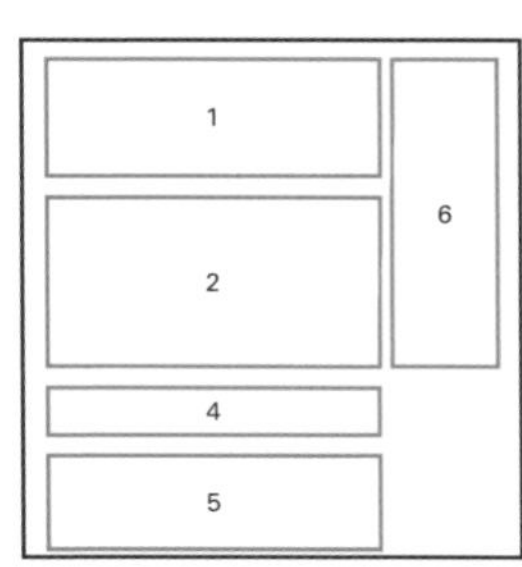

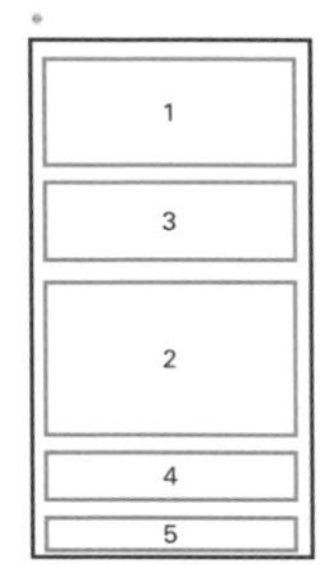

3 The "liquid" is now joined by the "adaptive" web design: The illustrations show the sudden change in the information structure, the number of columns changes. This occurs when the "breakpoints" take effect.

A
A1
A2
A3
A4
A5
A6
A7
A8
B
B1
C
C1
C2
C3
D
D1
D2
D3
D4

"Responsive web design" is, currently, the ultimate state of affairs, because it enables content to be optimally presented for the respective device [4]. In terms of design, this is something new: The layout is losing significance and with it the grid in the sense of a single ordering principle (because many different grids are now in demand).

This sounds logical: If there is no fixed format, the grid loses its status as an invisible structural generator that provides information about the medium and origin of content. The design of websites is usually a design of templates (i.e. templates or "page types"). If all conceivable reading devices are to be taken into account, there must be an enormous number of templates. When the website is loaded, it is decided which of these templates will be used. To put it simply, the code "asks" the browser for the reader and gets an answer; if the data is not yet known, for example if you are currently dragging the window smaller, an algorithm decides which width is the best solution.

In order to take all the different formats into account, content must be divided into many small "information figures". These are text groups and headings, images or image groups, colored areas, and possibly illustrations and graphics. These "modular information figures" can be related flexibly to each other. Depending on the reader, they can be positioned next to each other or repeatedly next to each other, but also above or below each other, depending on what is necessary and how it is defined by the programmer. This is a design from "inside out" – in contrast to a design from "outside in", which starts with the definition of format, type area and grid. The advantage of this method, which relies on "information figures" instead of defined layouts, is obvious: It cannot get more flexible with regard to the various reading devices. The recognition, the "branding" of a website, is based on the handling and the character of the font, the image perception, the colors, and so on.

→ D1

CMS
XML
XSLT
XSLFO

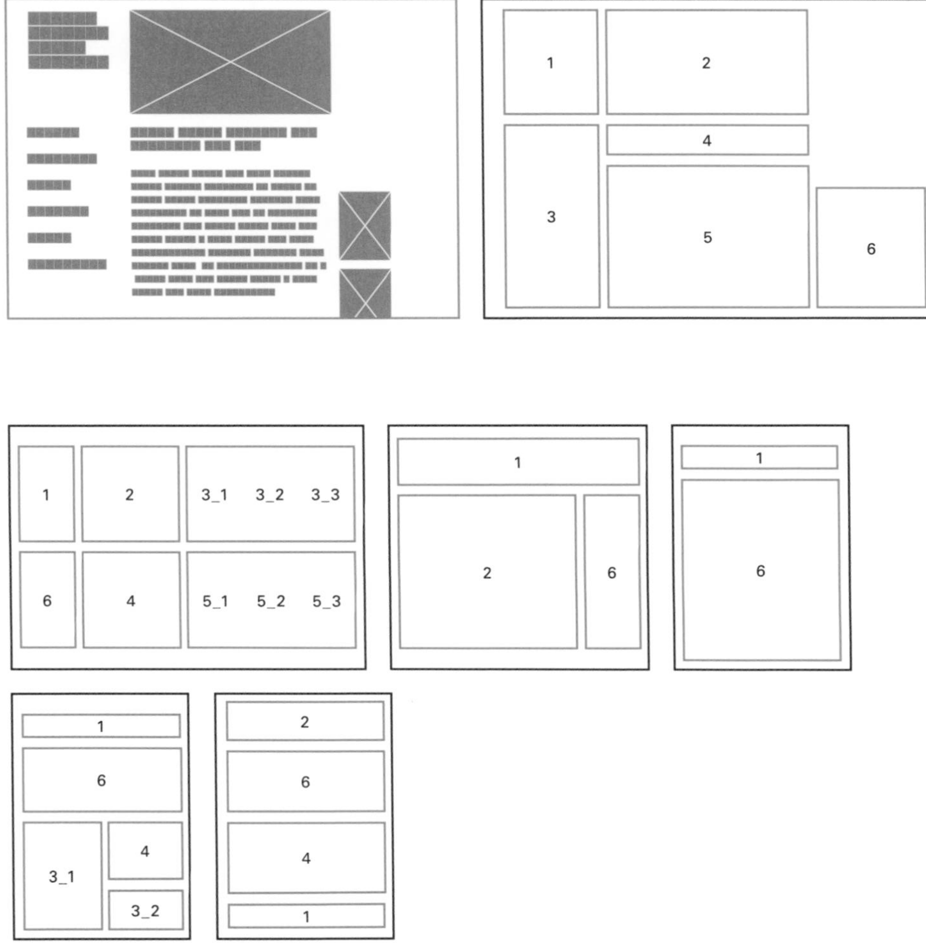

4 There are no patent solutions for using grids in the different formats. Depending on the layout and the desired result, there are different ways. "Responsive web design" is the most flexible system when it comes to using as many different options as possible:
Information figures (images, graphics, texts) can always be regrouped in the optimal size for the respective end device – depending on the space available.

This development from layout grids to flexible positive information figures is not only a response to the different display formats, but also ensures that applications in different operating systems, as web applications implemented in the browser, as desktop apps or even as print products are possible.
A good example of this is the T3N web magazine, which generates its print layout from a Content Management System (CMS). Typo3 is used to produce the magazine. "With the help of Typo3 and a web-based publication infrastructure based on XML, XSLT and XSLFO, T3N is typeset completely dynamically and generated at the push of a button", according to the makers.

A
A1
A2
A3
A4
A5
A6
A7
A8
B
B1
C
C1
C2
C3
D
D1
D2
D3
D4

The technical framework of web design has produced new ways of working and new insights that have changed the methodology of design. The physical format is becoming less important, and the format of the monitor is not necessarily relevant. Web designers have no control over a final layout because it no longer exists. Instead, design must offer a variety of possibilities (for example in the form of numerous "page types"). The working process in web design is interdisciplinary and not linear – from design to prototyping to programming and back again, tests and their results lead back to the design phase and so on. Designers and programmers are jointly responsible for what the possibilities of a website must look like. The emphasis is on flexibility, with numerous forms ready to accommodate a wide variety of content. Technical questions, such as which programming language should be used, make the differences to design in print particularly clear. In addition, the direct evaluation of communication between sender and addressee is also new. The terms "user experience", "interaction style", "usability", "engagement time" or "personas" signify the changes in the relationship between sender and addressee: User behavior influences the design more directly than ever – and vice versa 5.

This chapter should be considered an introduction even more than the previous ones. Specific tips and the description of technical procedures would make little sense and go beyond the scope of this book due to the variety of possibilities. In addition, the above-mentioned speed with which the web continues to evolve is simply too high. When this book is published, new findings, new technical possibilities, new requirements and new user behavior will already have been evolved. In order to stay up to date, you should regularly check the websites of experts (smashing magazine, T3N, 960.gs, ia.net, praegnanz.de, and others).

→ D1

User experience
Interaction style
Engagement time
Personas
Native display

arte media library, desktop browser view

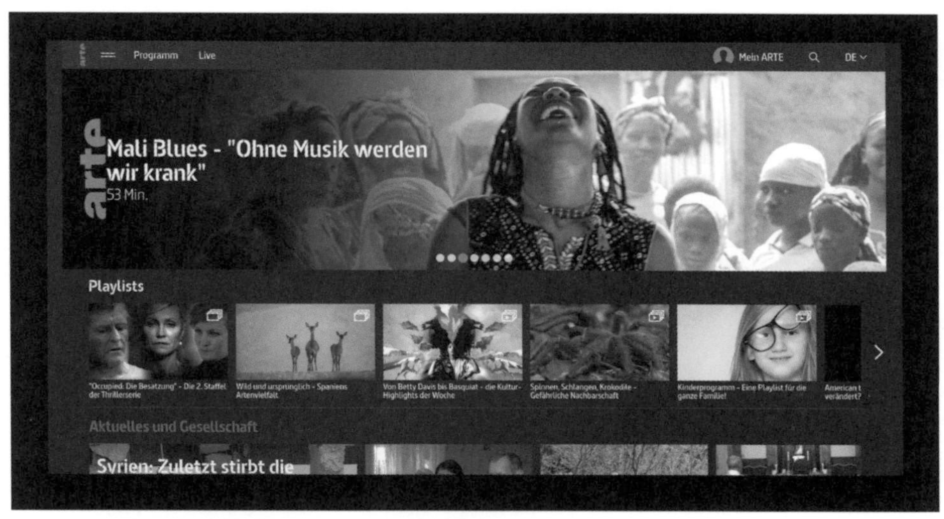

A
A1
A2
A3
A4
A5
A6
A7
A8

arte media library, tablet view

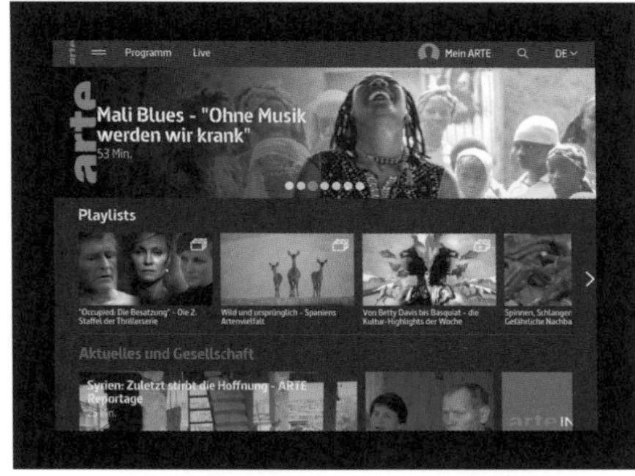

B
B1

C
C1
C2
C3

Left: mobile browser view

Right: native app view

D
D1
D2
D3
D4

5 The arte media library shows what it should be like: The contents are divided into information groups. If the monitor size (desktop) changes, the grid reacts in a "liquid" fashion. If the width falls below a breakpoint (in this case the portrait format smartphone browser display), the grid reacts "adaptively". With the mobile app, the content design is explicitly designed for smartphones. In this case one speaks of a "native display".

From the infinite variety of possible examples, I have selected some websites: They show how their appearance changes from display size to display size. This unrepresentative selection is intended to sensitize you to the current state of web design. In addition: browse the web yourself and follow the development.

www.faz.net/aktuell/
Frankfurter Allgemeine
Sonntag, 11. Juni 2017
POLITIK WIRTSCHAFT FINANZEN FEUILLETON SPORT GESELLSCHAFT STIL TECHNIK & MOTOR WISSEN REISE BERUF & CHANCE RHEIN-MAIN
Parlamentswahl in Frankreich
Auf dem Weg zur ganzen Macht
Die wichtigsten Fragen
Frankreich entscheidet, ob Macron auch regieren kann

1_1

Frankfurter Allgemeine
Die wichtigsten Fragen
Frankreich entscheidet, ob Macron auch regieren kann
F.A.S. Exklusiv
Nächster Ausgang Zollunion?

1_2

Frankfurter Allgemeine
Parlamentswahl in Frankreich
Auf dem Weg zur ganzen Macht
Die wichtigsten Fragen
Frankreich entscheidet, ob Macron auch regieren kann
F.A.S. Exklusiv
Nächster Ausgang Zollunion?

1_3

Hallo daar
BEZOEK STEDEL
DE COLLE
STEDELIJ
STEFAN TCHE
NIEUW FAMILIE R
JUMP INTO TI
“IK BEN EEN
Koop ticket
Nu te zien
Openingstijden en prijzen

2_3

Stedelijk Museum Amsterdam
https://www.stedelijk.nl/nl
Hoogtepunten uit de collectie
STEDELIJK BASE
BEZOEK STEDELIJK MUSEU
DE COLLECTIE
STEDELIJK BASE
STEFAN TCHEREPNIN —
NIEUW FAMILIE RONDLEIDIN
JUMP INTO THE FUTURE
“IK BEN EEN GEBOREN E

Dagje uit? Bekijk wat er te doen is voor
Families
Menu
EDELIJK MUSEUM AMSTERDAM →
DE COLLECTIE
STEDELIJK BASE
HOOGTEPUNTEN
STEDELIJK-ICONEN
1880-NU
AD MASTERS → TENTOONSTELLING, 27 JAN T/M 3 JUNI 2018
NIEUW FAMILIE RONDLEIDING →
JUMP INTO THE FUTURE — A

3_1

TM RSI SGM 1960-90
Research Archive
Cover Index
Chronological / Random
1960

3_3

TM RSI SGM 1960-90
Research Archive
Cover Index
Chronological / Random
1960

3_2

Naturally, Djurek's 2018 vintages will sport Gordian on their labels, a perfect marriage of content and form.

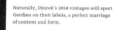

MMXVIII
GORDIAN
NIKOLA DJUREK † TPTQ

SPRING RAF SIMONS 2018
MANHATTAN BRIDGE, NEW YORK CITY

4_3

Gordian, an elegant sans-serif with very slightly modulated strokes, is rooted in classic Roman square capitals, figures designed to be engraved in stone. Besides wine making and font designing, Djurek has also practiced stone carving, which is reflected in the subtle chiseling of Gordian's flaring stroke endings. These traditional roots, however, combine with modern characteristics (wider B, E, F, P and S characters, plus a complete set of lowercase letters) to create a distinctly 21st century typeface, and there is also a generous selection of alternative glyphs which can serve to give the text either a more classical or more modern feel.

Gordian has four weights designed for intermediate text sizes, each with true italics and small caps. It also includes 12 stunning display styles in two versions, Kapitalen (four weights of plain single capitals) and Knot (eight sets of entangled double capitals), the latter featuring smart OpenType functions that create various interactive patterns. See the PDF presentation.

Naturally, Djurek's 2018 vintages will sport Gordian on their labels, a perfect marriage of content and form.

MMXVIII
GORDIAN

Factory Sample
23—Joy Division

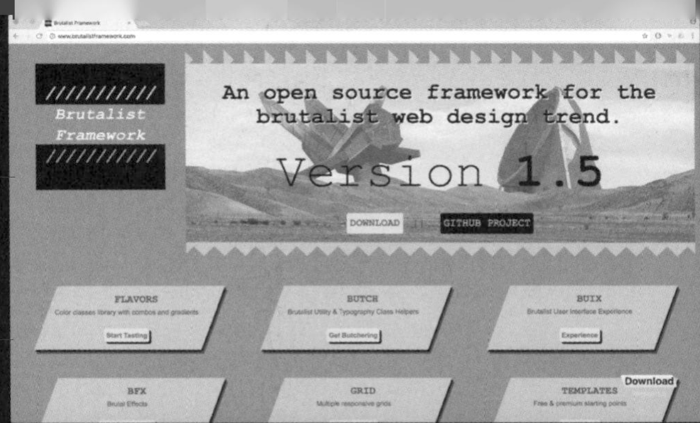

5_1

5_2

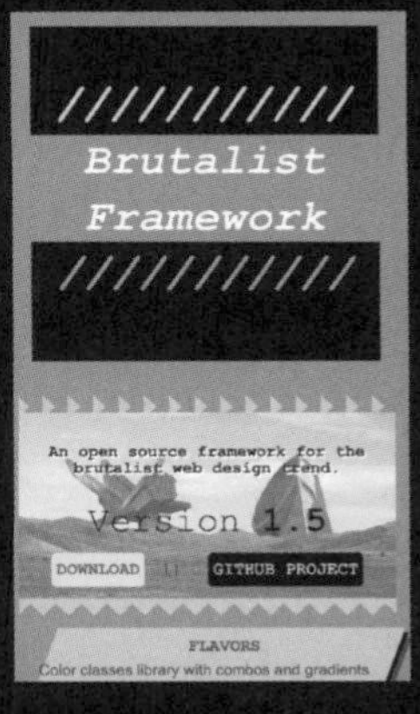

5_3

OPEN SOURCE
PROJECTS
GILLETT SQUARE
ABOUT

6_1

OPEN SOURCE
PROJECTS
GILLETT SQUARE
ABOUT

OPEN SOURCE
PROJECTS
GILLETT SQUARE
ABOUT

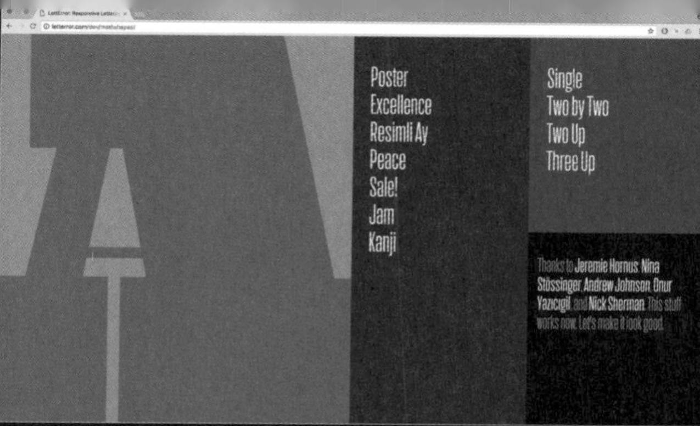
Poster
Excellence
Resimli Ay
Peace
Sale!
Jam
Kanji
Single
Two by Two
Two Up
Three Up
Thanks to Jeremie Hornus, Nina Stössinger, Andrew Johnson, Onur Yazıcıgil, and Nick Sherman. This stuff works now. Let's make it look good.

7_1

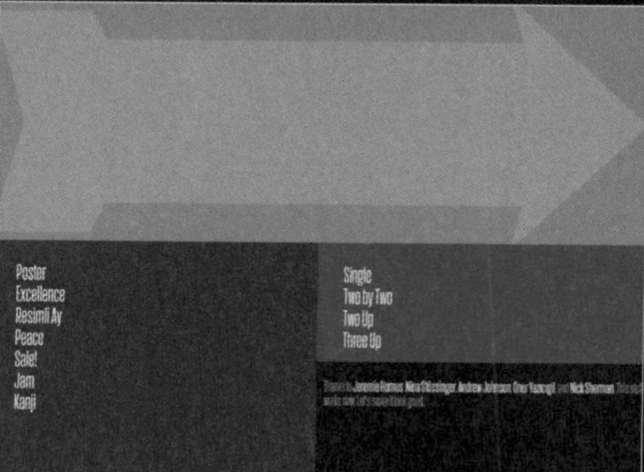
Poster
Excellence
Resimli Ay
Peace
Sale!
Jam
Kanji
Single
Two by Two
Two Up
Three Up

7_2

1
1.000 Words
Manifesto
Allan Chochinov
A
Manifesto
Now!
Experimental Jetset
Manifesto
Debate
About
Exhibition
Book

8_3

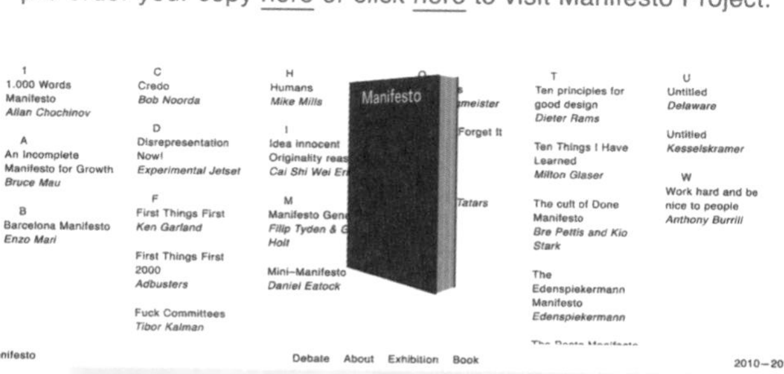
We will print a new limited edition of Manifesto, the book. Please pre-order your copy here or click here to visit Manifesto Project.
1
1.000 Words
Manifesto
Allan Chochinov
A
An Incomplete
Manifesto for Growth
Bruce Mau
B
Barcelona Manifesto
Enzo Mari
C
Credo
Bob Noorda
D
Disrepresentation
Now!
Experimental Jetset
F
First Things First
Ken Garland
First Things First
2000
Adbusters
Fuck Committees
Tibor Kalman
H
Humans
Mike Mills
I
Idea innocent
Originality reas
Cai Shi Wei Er
M
Manifesto Gene
Filip Tydén & G
Holt
Mini–Manifesto
Daniel Eatock
Manifesto
T
Ten principles for
good design
Dieter Rams
Ten Things I Have
Learned
Milton Glaser
The cult of Done
Manifesto
Bre Pettis and Kio
Stark
The
Edenspiekermann
Manifesto
Edenspiekermann
U
Untitled
Delaware
Untitled
Kesselskramer
W
Work hard and be
nice to people
Anthony Burrill
Manifesto
Debate
About
Exhibition
Book
2010–2014

Museum für Zeitgenössische Kunst
/Musée d'Art Contemporain
/Museum of Contemporary Art

Ausstellungen & Veranstaltungen & Vermittlung & Sammlung & Infos de/fr/en

01.08.–14.10.2018:

PRAGMATISMUS UND SELBST-ORGANISATION

&
01.08–14.10.2018

9_1

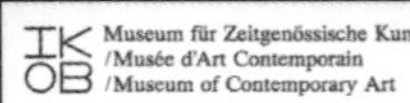

Museum für Zeitgenössische Kunst
/Musée d'Art Contemporain
/Museum of Contemporary Art

Ausstellungen & Veranstaltungen & Vermittlung & Sammlung & Infos
de/fr/en

01.08.–14.10.2018:

PRAG-MATIS-MUS UND SELBST-ORGANISATION

&
01.08–14.10.2018
STAR WORK № 29 DE KRUISIGING
Philippe Vandenberg
&
Adrien

9_3

Museum für Zeitgenössische Kunst
/Musée d'Art Contemporain
/Museum of Contemporary Art

Ausstellungen & Veranstaltungen & Vermittlung & Sammlung & Infos de/fr/en

01.08.–14.10.2018:

PRAGMATISMUS UND SELBST-ORGANISATION

&
01.08–14.10.2018
STAR WORK № 29 DE KRUISIGING
Philippe Vandenberg
&

Adrien Tirtiaux ELFTE ARBEIT FÜR DAS IKOB (HOMOGENISIERUNG DER SAMMLUNG)

05.09.–12.09.2018:
DAS IKOB ZEIGT SICH IN BRÜSSEL -

9_2

89+——→About

89plus is a long-term, international, multi-platform research project co-founded by Simon Castets and Hans Ulrich Obrist, investigating the generation of innovators born in or after 1989. Without forecasting artistic trends or predicting future creation, 89plus manifests itself through panels, books, periodicals, exhibitions and residencies, bringing together individuals from a generation whose voices are only starting to be heard, yet which accounts for more than half of the world's population.

Marked by several paradigm-shifting events, the year 1989 saw the collapse of the Berlin Wall and the start of the post- Cold War period, and the introduction of the World Wide Web and the beginning of the universal availability of the Internet. Positing a relationship between these world-changing events and creative production at large, 89plus introduces the work of some of this generation's most inspiring protagonists.

Since an introductory panel held in January 2013 at the DLD – Digital, Life, Design conference in Munich, 89plus has conducted research internationally, in Hong Kong and Miami with Art Basel's Salon series, in Singapore as part of Singapore International Festival of

which culminated in the project 'Vessel Verse' by Sarah Abu Abdallah and Abdullah Al Mutairi at Art Dubai 2016.

89plus has developed a series of residencies with various partners internationally including the Park Avenue Armory in New York, the agnès b. / Tara Oceans Polar Circle Expedition, and the Google Cultural Institute in Paris, which culminated in a one night exhibition at Fondation Cartier, Paris. Also in Paris, 89plus presented a video screening on the Filter Bubble as part of Prospectif Cinéma program at Centre Pompidou. 89plus also collaborated with Musée d'Art Moderne de la Ville de Paris (MAM), organising series of solo and duo shows as interventions in MAM's exhibition, 'Co-workers'.

In late 2013, 89plus partnered with Fondazione Sandretto Re Rebaudengo and the Serpentine Galleries for a new annual award for emerging talent, the 'Re Rebaudengo Serpentine Grants'. The 89plus Marathon was held at London's Serpentine Sackler Gallery in late 2013, followed shortly after by the 89plus Americas Marathon: Autoconstrucción at Museo Jumex, Mexico City.

10_2

89+——→About

89plus is a long-term, international, multi-platform research project co-founded by Simon Castets and Hans Ulrich Obrist, investigating the generation of innovators born in or after 1989. Without forecasting artistic trends or predicting future creation, 89plus manifests itself through panels, books, periodicals, exhibitions and residencies, bringing together individuals from a generation whose voices are only starting to be heard, yet which accounts for more than half of the world's population.

Marked by several paradigm-shifting events, the year 1989 saw the collapse of the Berlin Wall and the start of the post- Cold War period, and the introduction of the World Wide Web and the beginning of the universal availability of the Internet. Positing a relationship between these world-changing events and creative production at large, 89plus introduces the work of some of this generation's most inspiring protagonists.

Since an introductory panel held in January 2013 at the DLD – Digital, Life, Design conference in Munich, 89plus has conducted research internationally, in Hong Kong and Miami with Art Basel's Salon series, in Singapore as part of Singapore International Festival of the Arts, in Cape Town with Design Indaba, in Madrid with ARCOmadrid, in New York and Rio de Janeiro as part of the MoMA PS1 exhibition 'Expo 1', and in Dubai with Art Dubai, which culminated in the project 'Vessel Verse' by Sarah Abu Abdallah and Abdullah Al Mutairi at Art Dubai 2016.

89plus has developed a series of residencies with various partners internationally including the Park Avenue Armory in New York, the agnès b. / Tara Oceans Polar Circle Expedition, and the Google Cultural Institute in Paris, which culminated in a one night exhibition at Fondation Cartier, Paris. Also in Paris, 89plus presented a video screening on the Filter Bubble as part of Prospectif Cinéma program at Centre Pompidou. 89plus also collaborated with Musée d'Art Moderne de la Ville de Paris (MAM), organising series of solo and duo shows as interventions in MAM's exhibition, 'Co-workers'.

In late 2013, 89plus partnered with Fondazione Sandretto Re Rebaudengo and the Serpentine Galleries for a new annual award for emerging talent, the 'Re Rebaudengo Serpentine Grants'. The 89plus Marathon was held at London's Serpentine Sackler Gallery in late 2013, followed shortly after by the 89plus Americas Marathon: Autoconstrucción at Museo Jumex, Mexico City.

In early 2014 The LUMA Foundation hosted the inaugural exhibition, '89plus / Poetry will be made by all!', in Zürich, driven by a residency series and an ongoing project which is publishing 1000 books by 1000 poets. A second iteration of 'Poetry will be made by all!' was presented as part of the exhibition, 'After Babel' at Moderna Museet in Stockholm throughout summer 2015. 89plus continued its collaboration with The LUMA Foundation in 2015-16 with the group exhibition, 'Filter Bubble', which included over 40 international artists, and again in 2017 with the group exhibition, 'Americans 2017'.

In August 2015 89plus undertook a research trip to Ghana, South Africa and Ethiopia, in partnership with the Google Cultural Institute and Another Africa, to meet and conduct workshops with 89plus practitioners at Nubuke Foundation, Accra; Keleketla! Library, Johannesburg; and Addis Ababa University. In August and September 2016, selected workshop participants from each city worked with these local partners to develop project proposals for the Google Cultural Institute Residency in Paris in late 2016. There are more details about this project on the Google Arts & Culture website.

2016 projects included 'Bunny Rogers: Wringer', a solo exhibition at Foundation de 11 Lijnen, Oudenburg, and 'Qidian', a group exhibition at Zendai Zhujiajiao Art Museum as part of the Shanghai Project.

89plus is grateful for the support of The LUMA Foundation
89plus.com is kindly supported by DLD – Digital, Life, Design

10_1

89+——→About

89plus is a long-term, international, multi-platform research project co-founded by Simon Castets and Hans Ulrich Obrist, investigating the generation of innovators born in or after 1989. Without forecasting artistic trends or predicting future creation, 89plus manifests itself through panels, books, periodicals, exhibitions and residencies, bringing together individuals from a generation whose voices are only starting to be heard, yet which accounts for more than half of the world's population.

Marked by several paradigm-shifting events, the year 1989 saw the collapse of the Berlin Wall and the start of the post- Cold War period, and the introduction of the World Wide Web and the beginning of the universal availability of the Internet. Positing a relationship between these world-changing events and creative production at large, 89plus introduces the work of some of this generation's most inspiring protagonists.

Since an introductory panel held in January 2013 at the DLD – Digital, Life, Design conference in Munich, 89plus has conducted research internationally, in Hong Kong and Miami with Art Basel's Salon series, in Singapore as part of Singapore International Festival of the Arts, in Cape Town with Design Indaba, in Madrid with ARCOmadrid, in New York and Rio de Janeiro as part of the MoMA PS1 exhibition 'Expo 1', and in Dubai with Art Dubai, which culminated in the project 'Vessel Verse' by Sarah Abu Abdallah and Abdul-

10_3

Wikipedia Random Article Collection is a growing archive inspired by content generated from Wikipedia's random article search function. By clicking once, participants use Wikipedia's random article search function to generate endless content. Each printed article is inspired by and created from images and text found in the online original- as well as any wikipedia worm-hole discovered. The collection supports a web-to-print-based artistic practice which utilizes search engines and other algorithmic operations as content generators. As such, the entire Wikipedia Random Article Collection and/or individual zines are available as PoD. Wikipedia Random Article Collection is featured in The Library of the Printed Web which was included in The Book Affair at the opening of the 55th Venice Biennale and NY Book Fair 2013, 2014, 2015. A small sampling of articles are also owned and available for check-out at the Chattanooga Public Library. To contribute work, or for any other inquiries, please contact Lauren Thorson.

1974 Academy Awards
Lauren Wade

11_1

Wikipedia Random Article Collection is a growing archive inspired by content generated from Wikipedia's random article search function. By clicking once, participants use Wikipedia's random article search function to generate endless content. Each printed article is inspired by and created from images and text found in the online original- as well as any wikipedia worm-hole discovered. The collection supports a web-to-print-based artistic practice which utilizes search engines and other algorithmic operations as content generators. As such, the entire Wikipedia Random Article Collection and/or individual zines are available as PoD. Wikipedia Random Article Collection is featured in The Library of the Printed Web which was included in The Book Affair at the opening of the 55th Venice Biennale and NY Book Fair 2013, 2014, 2015. A small sampling of articles are also owned and available for check-out at the Chattanooga Public Library. To contribute work, or for any other inquiries, please contact Lauren Thorson.

1974 Academy Awards
Lauren Wade

11_2

Wikipedia Random Article Collection is a growing archive inspired by content generated from Wikipedia's random article search function. By clicking once, participants use Wikipedia's random article search function to generate endless content. Each printed article is inspired by and created from images and text found in the online original- as well as any wikipedia worm-hole discovered. The collection supports a web-to-print-based artistic practice which utilizes search engines and other algorithmic operations as content generators. As such, the entire Wikipedia Random Article Collection and/or individual zines are available as PoD. Wikipedia Random Article Collection is featured in The Library of the Printed Web which was included in The Book Affair at the opening of the 55th Venice Biennale and NY Book Fair 2013, 2014, 2015. A small sampling of articles are also owned and available for check-out at the Chattanooga Public Library. To contribute work, or for any other

11_3

BALENCIAGA
SUCHE
LOGIN
DAMEN
ALLES
HERREN

12_1

BALENCIAGA
SUCHE
DAMEN
ALLES

BALENCIAGA
SUCHE
LOGIN
DAMEN
ALLES

1 faz.net

2 stedelijk.nl

3 tm-research-archive.ch

4 typotheque.com

5 brutalistframework.com

6 opensource.london

7 letteror.com

8 manifestoproject.it

9 ikob.be

10 89plus.com

11 random-wikipedia.com

12 balenciaga.com

A

A1

A2

A3

A4

A5

A6

A7

A8

B

B1

C

C1

C2

C3

D

D1

D2

D3

D4

This chapter deals with other applications of grids in bundled form. It deals with their use in signage, the design of business stationery and posters. Why are these (so variously complex) areas not presented in separate chapters? Because the design possibilities in the three applications are too great to give general practical tips on how to use grids. The following texts are therefore intended as basic introductions.

Further applications
A—8

Signage

Signs (also known as orientation systems) are designed to help people find their way around. The locations for such orientation aids can be airports or sports stadiums, clinics or museums, industrial parks or office towers, residential complexes, or swimming pools. In all cases, information should ensure that visitors (i.e. strangers) understand how they have to behave in order to find certain places. Orientation systems can convey simple facts, but also complicated ones. It is easy to imagine, for example, that an airport signage system is a rather complex matter. A signage of this kind not only has the task of satisfying the information needs of individuals, it is also intended to guide them – for example by directing streams of visitors to information hubs and leading them from there to (optionally different) destinations.

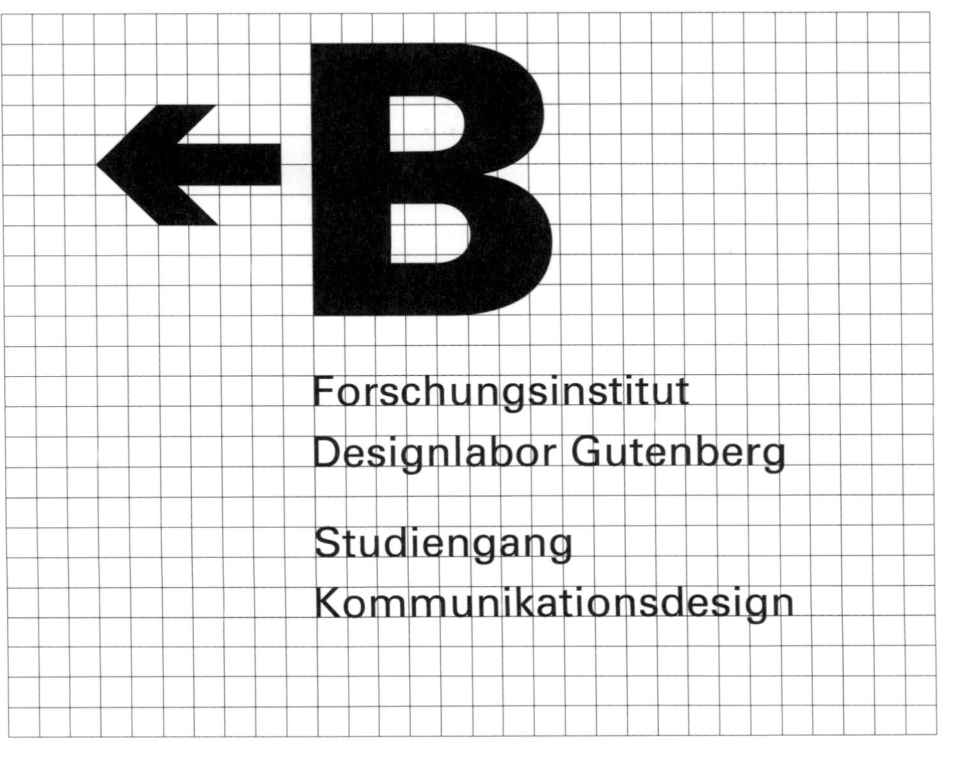

1 The (normally invisible) grid of a grid system in this principle representation deals with an essential aspect of signage:
It is about the representation of information hierarchies on the basis of conceivably clear graphic structures. The grid regulates the placement of the elements and thus considerably aids communication. In addition, it ensures recognition when different sign and column sizes are used, for example.

An important criterion in the design of a signage system is the rapid communication of its contents. In the ideal case one does not consciously deal with the signage, because it functions without problems – one looks, understands and then steers towards the desired goal 1.
There are a number of design criteria that enable such problem-free orientation – always provided that the concept of the signage is optimally adapted to the respective architectural conditions. First of all, the signage system must be recognizable as such. From a design point of view, this means that there is a range of mutually coordinated sign sizes (e.g. signs hanging from the ceiling, wall signs and steles in recurring formats, etc.). A coordinated color concept and a specific typography also ensure recognition.

Fonts, pictograms and directive symbols must, on the one hand, be in harmony with the formats and, on the other hand, take into account the defined reading distances while ensuring the greatest possible orientation comfort. We know such signage from many places (hospitals, public authorities, railway stations, stadiums, and airports) and quickly "learn" to identify and search for their individual components and to orient ourselves along them. Here, the grid is particularly responsible for standardization and structural order.

In addition, designers are constantly developing new forms of orientation – be it typography painted on the ceiling, light and typography projections, sounds, or floor coverings (and many more ideas). How conventional or unconventional a signage system is depends on the purpose, the architecture, the audience it is intended for and the courage of the designers, clients and architects.

Business stationery

The grid and stationery? Sounds a bit strange, but even an ordinary business letter needs a structure. At least if you want to save costs and time and have to send many letters (still practiced by offices, law firms or universities even today, in digital times). For such cases there are the rules laid down in DIN 5008 for writing and design in the office and administration sector. It's very helpful to take a look. And it's absolutely essential if you're dealing with the above-mentioned customers.
DIN 5008 [2] not only regulates how, for example, abbreviations are to be handled or how something is to be emphasized in the text, but also establishes design rules. They refer to the letter paper format DIN A4. On the right you can see a German standard business letter with all the information about where to place which information and where to fold it.

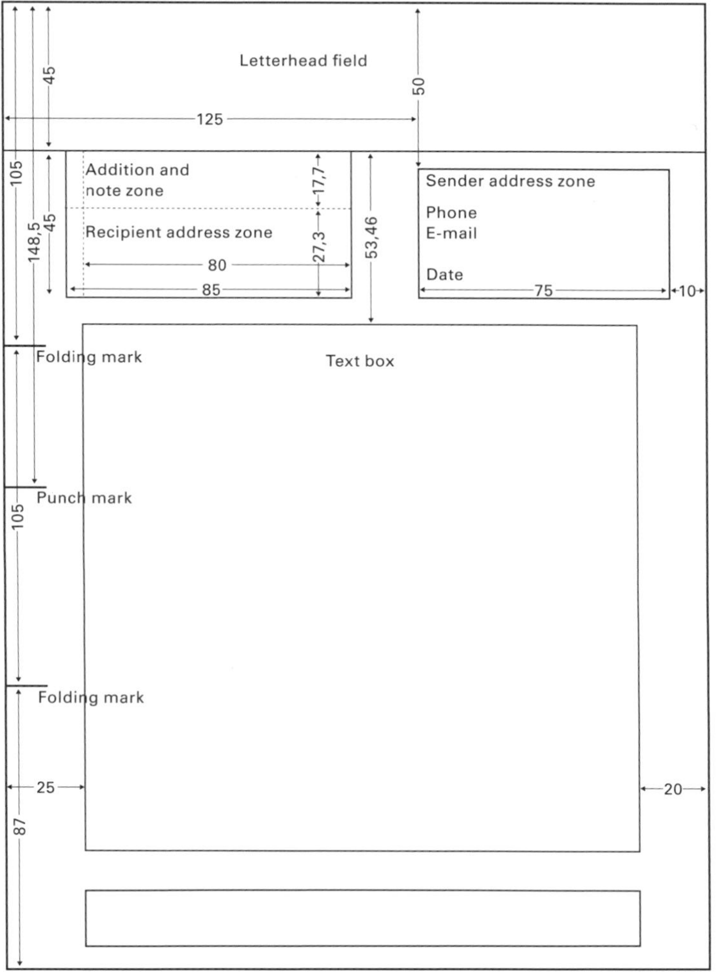

2 The DIN 5008 standard business letter specifies where text should be written on the letter and where the sender's information should be located (logo, address, etc.). Together with the folding information, it is matched to a DIN long envelope (DIN C4), in whose window the sender line and address are visible.

The design of a standard business letter can therefore be very specifically regulated. If one is, however, in charge (whether as designer, artist, or private person) or has a customer, to whom the functional advantages of the standard business letter appear secondary – then actually everything is possible. The only limits here are set by the post office, which has linked its handling conditions to a list of postage charges. The conditions apply to the envelope form and total weight. In addition, the address on the envelope must be legible.

A
A1
A2
A3
A4
A5
A6
A7
A8
B
B1
C
C1
C2
C3
D
D1
D2
D3
D4

That the standard business letter is valid in Germany, but not automatically worldwide, sounds plausible. Other sheet formats (e.g. the letter format in the USA), other envelopes (e.g. in the Netherlands) generate their own rules and change the appearance of the letters.

Printed business stationery does not just consist of business letters and envelopes. There may also be invoice forms, greeting cards or text messages, stickers, pre-printed large-scale envelopes, postage stamping machines, and so on. However, the business card is still the most frequently used. It is even used among the so-called "digital natives", in part because it gives a small first visual impression in a very analog, fast way. Here, too, everything is possible in terms of content and design. The only restriction is if you want to make things easier for the recipients of a business card is to make it easy to transport. Ideally, it should be made of stiff yet somewhat flexible cardboard and have the format of a check card (it is usually inserted into the appropriate compartment of the wallet). Even if the digital world knows many new – and perhaps better, because faster – forms of visual communication, printed business stationery is still part of almost every corporate design.

→ D1

DIN 5008
DIN A4 (DIN 476)
DIN C4
Letter format
Corporate design

Poster

What do grids have to do with the medium poster? After all, everything is allowed here and you don't have to follow any structural rules. Well, if the quote (by Uwe Loesch) is correct that the "poster is an area that catches the eye", then a poster works especially well if the content message can be captured particularly quickly. That doesn't have to apply to every poster – there are program posters, hard-to-decipher but hip in-scene posters, and many more. If, however, fast communication is desired, then reading guidance becomes particularly important.

Poster “a labour of love”,
U. Voelker

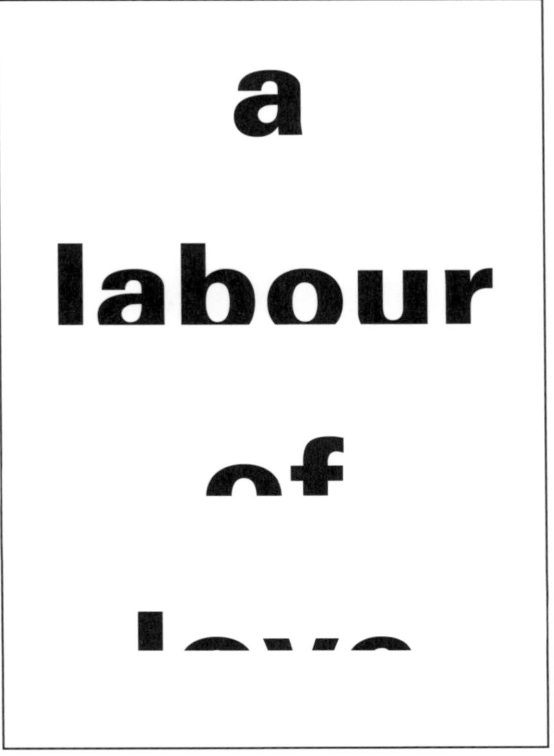

A
A1
A2
A3
A4
A5
A6
A7
A8
B
B1
C
C1
C2
C3
D
D1
D2
D3
D4

3 As a medium that communicates quickly, the poster has its own unique possibilities, because it offers the content and its creative staging as complete information – served “at a glance”.

With posters, designers can be quite manipulative. What is seen first followed by what, what should be retained and what should cause viewers to think about afterwards? This is a question of how information is distributed on the surface. And wherever information is distributed some form of grid is already inherent. The medium poster – as a large surface on which all content gathers – has its very own laws. It’s not a place to leaf through like a publication, but where everything is perceived at once, at a glance, so to speak. The design of a poster can take place in such a variety of ways that patent recipes for applying grids are out of place. It’s even hard to say anything about font sizes. Sure, a large font is easy to read from a distance 3. But a very small font could also attract the viewer to come closer to the poster and in this way achieve the best effect in terms of content. The best advice at this point is therefore: The more posters you have seen, the bigger your repertoire will be.

Chapter A ends with signs, stationery and posters. At this point I will refrain from showing examples. Orientation systems and business stationery usually consist of many parts and are available in infinite variations. There are simple examples and complex ones, some are not limited to printed matter, but also have digital characteristics. This variety contains many different laws. Showing them goes beyond the scope of this book. You should continue to study the application possibilities in relevant specialist publications.

The situation of posters is similar. They can fulfill many different purposes (for example as advertising posters, as cultural posters or as artistic posters). They can be small, there are City Light posters and huge 18/1 billboards. Each purpose and each format has different design requirements. It is impossible to show examples here without highlighting a particular style. Here, too, the following applies: Continue your studies in the appropriate specialist media.

PRIMATE
K-LUX JS STA
FR.14.09.07

B Design Process – First Steps

Design actually means "visual communication" — Always the same: sender, content, addressee — What distinguishes the visual from the verbal — Drawing as a first step — About attributes and analogies — Design is visual rhetoric — I think aloud and draw small

In the previous chapter A of the book I explained what you should pay attention to when using graphic grids in practice. In this chapter I would like to focus on the design process itself. But before I let you participate in my considerations and initial sketches, I have to say a few words about the conceptual framework.

Idea and sketch
B — 1

Let's start with the term "communication". It describes the process of exchanging or transmitting information.
The term has many levels of meaning. I focus on the one that describes the interaction between people. There is verbal, gestural and mimic communication, which we learn from an early age and which we master without consciously grasping every process. As a rule, we only think about communication when we perceive disturbances or when we have intentions whose implementation requires the development of communicative strategies. Normally, however, we communicate spontaneously and cheerfully throughout the day.

We designers are not that relaxed. We are less concerned with the exchange of information than with the graphic transmission of information – the technical term is "visual communication". Here the following scheme, which actually applies to every form of communication, acquires a methodical meaning: There is a sender, content and an addressee.
Methodical, because visual communication is always planned in contrast to everyday verbal, gestural and mimic interaction 1. The spontaneity is missing.* One of the reasons for this is that the visual method must make use of various media carriers that have their own visual laws.

*
for more information, see the chapter
"Stimulus, response and other phenomena",
C2

Every reader knows examples of planned visual communication: The logo of a company should communicate its characteristics, it was constructed accordingly and tested on the target group. A newspaper layout should "communicate" the specific journalistic level, accordingly graphic elements (e.g. font, layout, pictures) were determined, which are associated with journalistic levels of this kind by the target group. A website should have a very specific effect, interaction principles and functions were specifically selected and graphic elements combined in such a way that they trigger the desired reflexes in the target group. In all cases, the respective design of content should make it possible for the addressee to understand the sender visually.

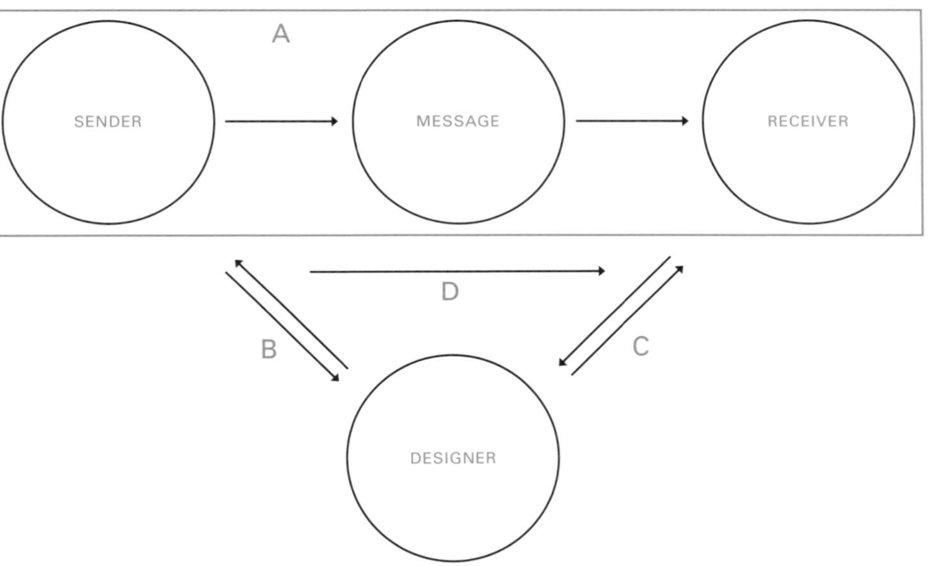

1 A desired visual communication process (A) is first moderated by the designer: He/she must fathom the intentions of the sender and understand his/her message (B). He/she must analyze the reception behavior of the receiver (C). The designer advises the sender on the intention as well as on the evaluation of the receiver's analysis and subsequently on the choice of medium (B).

Once the intentions, the message and the receiver behavior have been analyzed, the designer designs the message (D).

We designers proceed accordingly step by step: We must first understand what the sender wants to say*. In consultation with the sender, we determine what charisma his/her content should have. Then we take a closer look at the addressees and analyze them and their socio-cultural environment – for example, what visual environment characterizes them, what values they live by, what taste they have. As a result of this preliminary work we know which communicative intentions the sender has and we know which visual signals and stimuli are necessary to trigger the desired reaction in the addressees. And now we designers commence to generate the visual analogies necessary for this communication process. “Creating visual analogies” means nothing other than finding adequate graphic forms for described intentions and agreed terms. Terms such as “serious” or “informative” or “loud” or “attractive” are typical attributions from a multitude of combinable attributes that can serve as definitions for a desired impression of the design. Which graphic means these concepts use depends on those to whom the message is directed. “Serious” is implied by different means to 23-year-old female law students than to 27-year-old plumbers, 35-year-old dropouts or 54-year-old managers (not to mention all the different national and cultural interpretations of “serious”). The better one knows the target group, the more accurate the design can be. There are many ways to start designing.

Visual analogies are rhetorical means of communication: They should achieve an effect that is intended. This is essentially the description of visual communication. And one thing is clear: The more we know, the more we have already seen of the world and its communication, the more different people we met with their needs, habits and values, the greater is our communicative ability – in terms of our visual vocabulary, our creative empathy and in terms of our consultant quality.

→ D1

Visual analogy, see Visual rhetoric

* Of course, we designers occasionally also act as authors. In this case we are sender and designer at the same time. This does not change the structure of communication.

On the following pages, I will explain what considerations go through my mind when developing an exemplary layout idea. For clarity reasons, I deliberately leave out a detailed sender and receiver analysis and concentrate on what happens when a visual analogy is to take shape. The task I am tackling here is to create an entertaining and informative magazine layout. The following sketches show how I translate the terms “entertaining” and “informative” into graphics (as a target group, I’ll target you, the reader of this book).

Most of you immediately sit at the computer. This can work, but it has its pitfalls: In order to start playing around with layout programs, for example, you have to define some parameters that should better remain open at this point (format, fonts, etc.). So I’ll start by drawing around a bit. The advantage: Ideas can be quickly discarded and changed or concretized. Moreover, design is not only rational analysis, but also based on intuitive ideas that can be fixed while drawing.

So let’s go ...

A
A1
A2
A3
A4
A5
A6
A7
A8
B
B1
C
C1
C2
C3
D
D1
D2
D3
D4

... I start thinking about an informative and at the same time entertaining magazine and record my thoughts as sketches.

Step 1
I can best think in drawing terms when the sketch is so small that I can't even *try* to be precise. The original size of my small sketches: each 12 x 23 mm.

Regardless of the size of the sketches (everyone has their own preferences), it is advisable to sketch several double-page spreads at once. Reason: "Entertaining" can also be the surprising change of the layout from one double-page spread to the next. The attribute "informative" can be visualized by continuing elements over several pages. After all, the reader will later browse through the magazine and not just stare at one page.

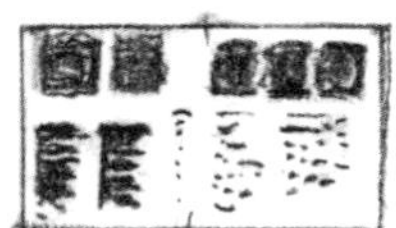

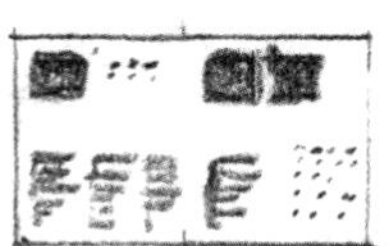
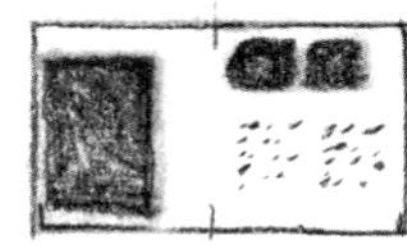
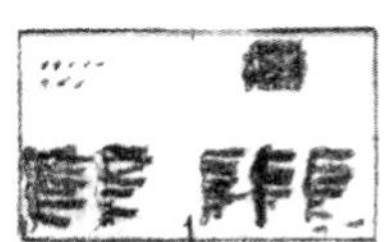

Step 2
I liked the little sketches. They contain restlessness, but also order.

That's important despite all entertainment aspects, because anyone who wants information needs a certain amount of peace for reading. I want to cultivate the interplay of restlessness and order, so I make the sketches a little bigger. They look as if I could handle a three-column grid.

Step 3

I draw a three-column grid. My sketches so far suggest that I should choose narrow margins. This is not bad, because working with narrow margins corresponds to the current fashion. This signals a topical time reference that you might like.

But I can see that the layout is too static. In my head, characteristics for “entertaining” emerge – the design has to be surprising and lively, in other words: more dynamic. The scribble tells me what I don’t want: a three-column grid that seems stiff and inflexible. I can hardly shift anything in the course of the double-page spreads.

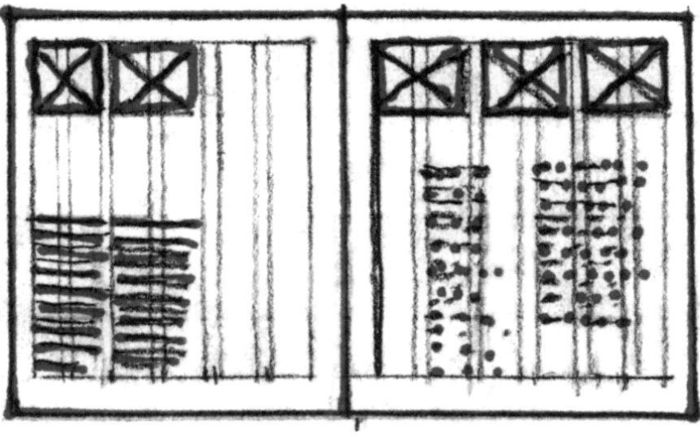

Step 4

Now the grid has become six-columned. I am dissatisfied.

What promised to become restless in my first scribble (“restless” is also a characteristic that I assign to the goal “entertaining”) is now too neat. What to do?

A
A1
A2
A3
A4
A5
A6
A7
A8
B
B1
C
C1
C2
C3
D
D1
D2
D3
D4

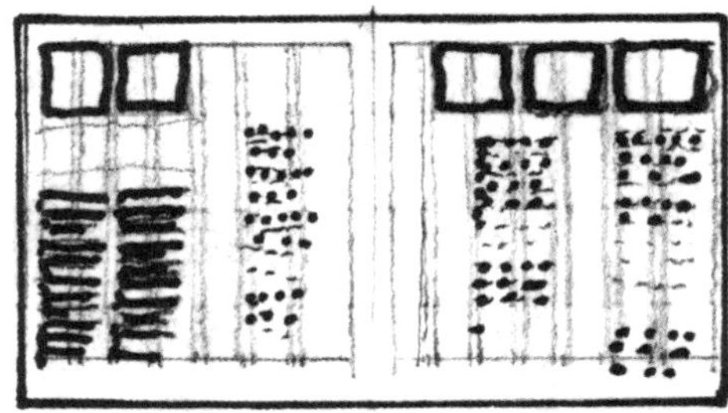

Step 5

I think I know what to do: The format is wrong! It should be a bit wider (like in my first small sketches). In addition, I need more possibilities to offset edges against each other – for example, there shouldn't always be a left-justified setting under the left edge of an image.

So I choose a seven-column grid, which gives me this flexibility (maybe I'll have to make it even smaller later, let's see). And also the font has to be livelier. I like my sketches quite well: a running text that looks pretty bold, otherwise many small dots distributed on the double-page spread. This could be a monospace font (its special design as a former typewriter font always results in a faulty and "perforated" type face).
I establish "clotheslines", which run through the format horizontally and on which I can recurrently hang pictures and texts on the pages.
By the way, now I am quite happy to sketch and not to work in a layout program, because the spontaneous format expansion went fast and I was not forced to enter millimeters into the document settings (which always require a concrete idea). After all, this is only a vague idea.

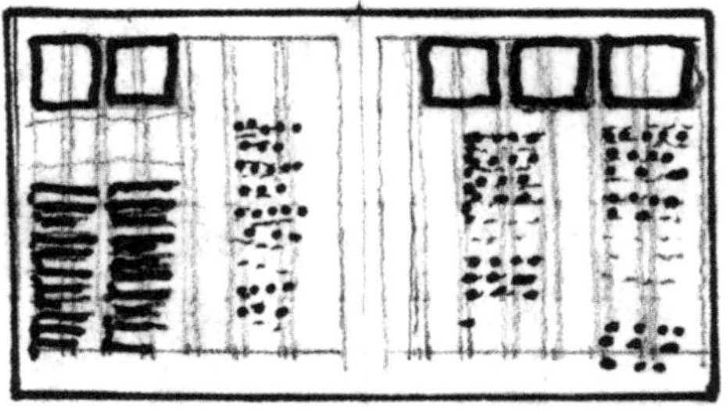

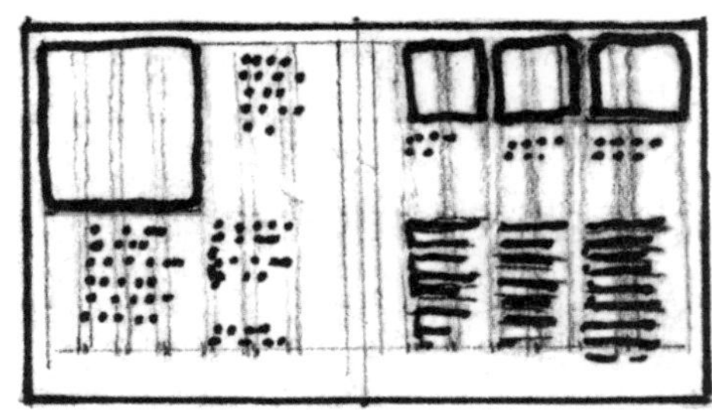

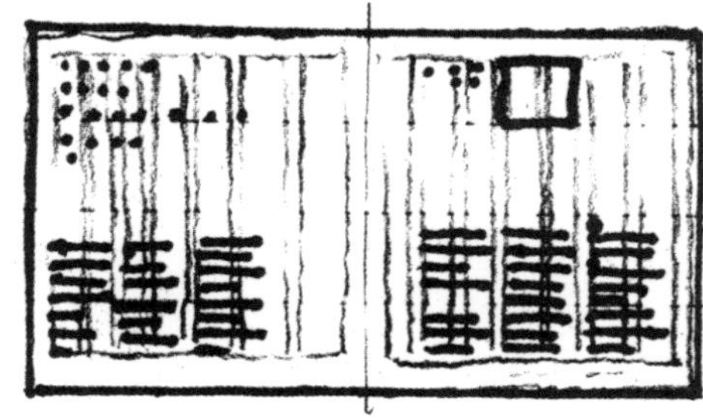

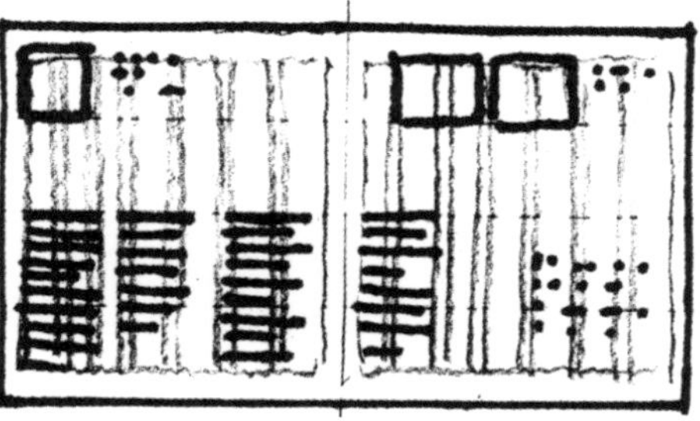

Step 6
I take the decisions made in steps 1 – 5 (narrow margins, seven-column grid, font tonality) as a basis and draw another four double-page spreads based on the initial mini layout sketches. I am satisfied. For in the course of drawing and thinking, my thoughts have become ordered. I know roughly what I want – or at least enough to now sit at the computer and get started.

Perhaps in the course of the further design everything will be completely different, but perhaps I have already laid an important foundation with the sketches, who knows. But as an introduction the sketches were helpful.

A
A1
A2
A3
A4
A5
A6
A7
A8
B
B1
C
C1
C2
C3
D
D1
D2
D3
D4

The core message of this chapter is that thinking while visualizing can bring clarity to your concept. Ideas are created while doing.

The expectations regarding the results of such an approach are therefore less directed at the quality of the sketched designs, but rather at the ideas and considerations that arise during sketching. In other words, the sketches can be lopsided and crooked (like the sketches I've presented here). What matters are the thoughtful aha-effects.

Herewith I would like to conclude the discussion of practical and lead over to chapter C. In it I will discuss some theoretical information that forms the basis of creative action.

A

A1

A2

A3

A4

A5

A6

A7

A8

B

B1

C

C1

C2

C3

D

D1

D2

D3

D4

獨家獅頭鵝現江湖
獅頭鵝 $58/斤
獅頭鵝全食
陳年滷水獅頭鵝
特首也『潮』撐
鵝頭頸
30元条
2009/06/03
滷猪手

C Background Information

Organization is half the battle — From overall impression to detail — About design, power and responsibility — Stimulus and response — The four sides of a message — Nothing goes without grammar — Intuition and method — Order and adventure — Learning from art — The new emerges from contradiction

A
A1
A2
A3
A4
A5
A6
A7
A8
B
B1
C
C1
C2
C3
D
D1
D2
D3
D4

In chapters A and B of the book, I have described the role that grids play in design practice. But this tendency to organize is not a fad of petty designers. They only do what is necessary. Let's be honest: Life is hardly imaginable without the support of various systems of organization (including the graphic grid). This also applies to the most unconventional and wildest among us. We all need identifiable patterns, structures and meanings to guide us. And guidance is necessary in view of the vast amount of impulses, news, stimuli and signals that we are exposed to every day and that we have to evaluate.

Humans need order
C — 1

We want to be able to tell from the first few pieces of information whether we should react to a signal or ignore it. Our environment should be predictable, because reliable structures mean having it easier in everyday life. To this end, our world consists of a myriad of order systems and conventions that we share with others. We do not even notice them but take them for granted. We only become fully aware that such conventions exist when we come across other conventions in other cultures that we do not know – do they shake hands or not, how do they say goodbye, which side of the street do they drive on, from which end do they read books, is it enough to shake hands to seal a deal, how do they express politeness, and so on. We are familiar with such situations when we visit foreign countries or have foreigners as guests.

But with a sharpened eye, our own systems of order and conventions can easily be identified – whether they are infrastructural, material, cultural or intellectual. Have a look around 1: Socks and the shirts are kept separately; for storage, cupboards are used that are located in rooms of an apartment, which in turn is divided into several functional rooms; the apartments are components of houses that carry numbers for a better overview; they are located on streets that have names so that they can be distinguished; houses and streets form towns and villages that are connected to others by streets; these lead through fields, forests or meadows, which in turn are used for a specific purpose. Transport and communication systems provide networks connecting towns and cities; they are based on plans drawn up by professionals who have been provided with the necessary knowledge through training systems.

http://bit.ly/2vWvGwY

A

A1

A2

A3

A4

A5

A6

A7

A8

http://bit.ly/2E1kyRD

B

B1

C

C1

C2

C3

http://bit.ly/2nLhClz

D

D1

D2

D3

D4

1 We are usually not aware of the systems of order in our everyday lives. Nevertheless, they are a great help: sorted clothes, clearly arranged books on the shelf and also the actually unpopular road traffic regulations ensure that we can focus on the things that are really important to us.

Based on information collected, structured and didactically prepared in databases and books, the training systems are part of a political structure the conditions of which were created by a defined social system... and so on and so forth.

Human being's drive to recognize orders, to learn them or to create them may be considered archaic 2. Adrian Frutiger undertook a small model experiment to illustrate this original drive: Imagine a drawn square that is "empty", i.e. that shows an inner white surface. Sixteen points should now be drawn into it in a random manner (i.e. following no ordering principle). Frutiger writes in his book "Signs and symbols"*: "How difficult it is to set these sixteen elements in such a way that they stand as if by chance, unrelated to each other, without evoking a certain structure, an image, a geometric or figurative idea, becomes clear here. In contrast to this scattering process, it is very easy to design and conceive a multitude of figures or arrangements with the sixteen elements. A paradoxical conclusion can be drawn from this realization: that the creation of an order is easier than the creation of a disorder, a disform."

This example by Frutiger refers to "creating", in another example he deals with "seeing". He changed the positions of the dots on an ordinary die (the "1", for example, no longer sits in the middle but in a corner of the surface) and wrote about the irritations caused by these changes. It is the image of the visible die surface (the arrangement of the points in the surface) that informs us first and not the value (the number of points) alone. A small deviation from the convention already creates uncertainty, although the content of the information (the die value) itself has not changed 3.
The perception of the human being therefore proceeds from the overall impression to the detail, the "image" of information provides important first impressions regarding its nature and credibility.

*
Signs and symbols, Adrian Frutiger
→ Further reading p. 162

https://go.nasa.gov/2BRfBsH

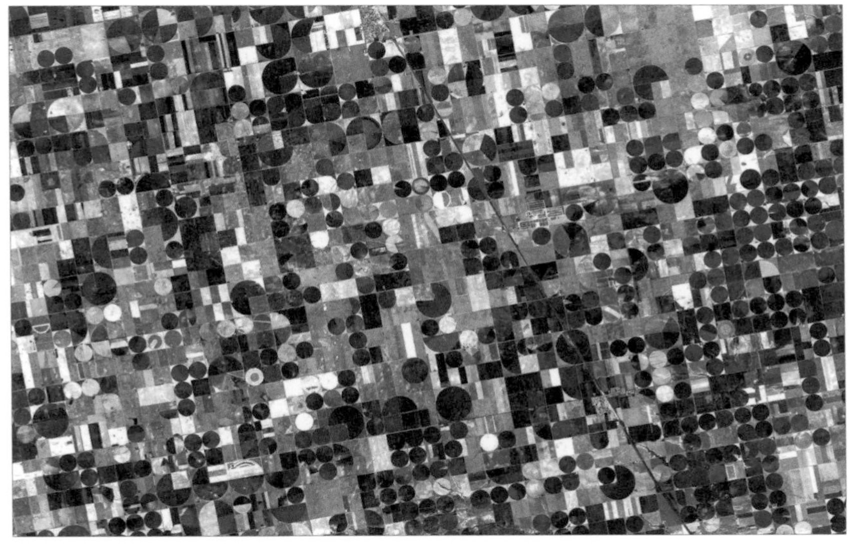

A
A1
A2
A3
A4
A5
A6
A7
A8

2 The greater the distance with which one looks at the world, the more fascinating the images of our well-organized life are. What this photograph of irrigation systems does not show are contracts, building permits, annual balance sheets, family structures and ownership. There is no "just like that" on earth.

B
B1

http://bit.ly/2nE8FKx

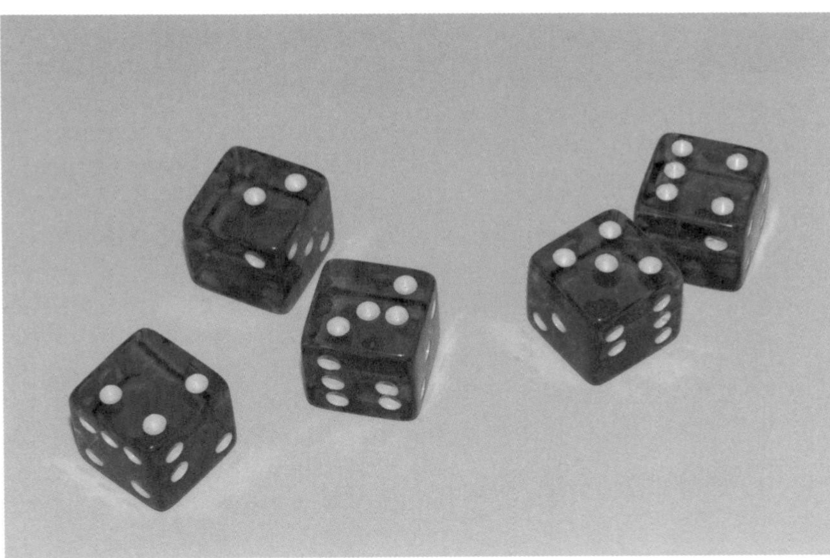

C
C1
C2
C3
D
D1
D2
D3
D4

3 The dice look interesting. But you probably wouldn't play for money with these dice if someone invited you – would you?

Examples: A novel should look like a novel from a distance, just like a newspaper or instruction manual. Even before you start dealing with the content, the layout says something about its specific character. The design manifested in the grid ensures this.

Before designers can begin with the design, they must interpret the content to be visualized. Only then can they start to take care of the design. They pour, so to speak, content into an adequate form that is already equipped with rough media layout parameters, so that books or magazines, for example, can be immediately recognized as such. Some contents can even have a particularly demanding effect on the design. This becomes clear when you want to design a poem, for example. If the alignment determined by the author is disregarded here, the literary intention is no longer comprehensible to the reader. The same applies if the poem is not placed on the surface in the arrangement typical of poetry[4].

The structuring and medial allocation of visual information not only meet the human need for orientation but are also absolutely necessary – both with regard to "doing" or better, "sending" (from the designer's point of view) and "seeing" or more correctly, "receiving" (from the addressee's point of view). The grid as a macro-typographic organ of order is thus an indispensable component of communication – in terms of its simplification and uniqueness.
The terms "sending" and "receiving" are elementary components of human communication. Looking back at the history of humanity, the "sending" and "receiving" of visual information represents the beginning of human civilization. Even the Sumerians tried cuneiform script that reveal an attempt to structure content[5]. In the history of all writing systems worldwide, the organization of visual content – whether symbols, drawings or writing – played a decisive role. After all, the essence of language fixation (and writing is nothing else) consists of its linearity and its unambiguous nature suitable for repetition. In prehistory, if an image of hunting an animal could be transformed into a pictogram, it could be repeated as a symbol. At such a moment a form of written communication emerged, as symbols could be learned, passed on and used.

→ D1

Macro-typography
Pictogram

"Das Ringelnatz Lesebuch"
Joachim Ringelnatz

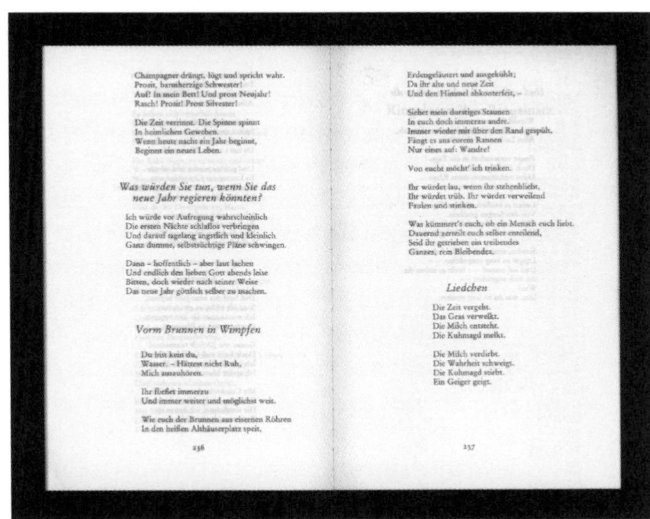

Champagner drängt, lügt und spricht wahr.
Prosit, barmherzige Schwester!
Auf! In mein Bett! Und prost Neujahr!
Rasch! Prosit! Prost Silvester!

Die Zeit verrinnt. Die Spinne spinnt
In heimlichen Geweben.
Wenn heute nacht ein Jahr beginnt,
Beginnt ein neues Leben.

Was würden Sie tun, wenn Sie das neue Jahr regieren könnten?

Ich würde vor Aufregung wahrscheinlich
Die ersten Nächte schlaflos verbringen
Und darauf tagelang ängstlich und kleinlich
Ganz dumme, selbstsüchtige Pläne schwingen.

Dann – hoffentlich – aber laut lachen
Und endlich den lieben Gott abends leise
Bitten, doch wieder nach seiner Weise
Das neue Jahr göttlich selber zu machen.

Vorm Brunnen in Wimpfen

Du bist kein du,
Wasser. – Hättest nicht Ruh,
Mich auszuhören.

Ihr fließet immerzu
Und immer weiter und möglichst weit.

Wie euch der Brunnen aus eisernen Röhren
In den heißen Althäuserplatz speit,

236

Erdengeläutert und ausgekühlt;
Da ihr alte und neue Zeit
Und den Himmel abkonterfeit, –

Siehet mein durstiges Staunen
In euch doch immerzu andre.
Immer wieder mit über den Rand gespült,
Fängt es aus eurem Rannen
Nur eines auf: Wandre!

Von eucht möcht' ich trinken.

Ihr würdet lau, wenn ihr stehenbliebt,
Ihr würdet trüb. Ihr würdet verweilend
Faulen und stinken.

Was kümmert's euch, ob ein Mensch euch liebt.
Dauernd zerteilt euch selber enteilend,
Seid ihr getrieben ein treibendes
Ganzes, rein Bleibendes.

Liedchen

Die Zeit vergeht.
Das Gras verwelkt.
Die Milch entsteht.
Die Kuhmagd melkt.

Die Milch verdirbt.
Die Wahrheit schweigt.
Die Kuhmagd stirbt.
Ein Geiger geigt.

237

4 The picture of the poem shows how it should be read. Any typographical intervention regarding the alignment is prohibited.

http://bit.ly/2GKLTZQ

5 The Sumerians worked the fields, bred animals, traded and had means of payment, in short: They already lived in a structured community. But this was not possible without (visual) communication.

A
A1
A2
A3
A4
A5
A6
A7
A8
B
B1
C
C1
C2
C3
D
D1
D2
D3
D4

When using letters, which we are used to in visual communication today, the same thing happens in principle. By learning and applying the abstract letter code, we automatically adopt the principles of order inherent in it – starting with the necessary distance between the letters that we observe, the distance that separates the lines, or the direction in which we write. We do this intuitively, just as we always compare signs or arrangements of signs (from pictograms to writings to layouts) with our visual memory. Frutiger, in his above-mentioned book, presented morphological boards showing how much people look for familiar shapes and patterns in graphic signs 6.

Such interpretation attempts, however, do not only affect signs, but also surfaces and accordingly layouts. For example, the fact that a sign (text or image) at the top of an otherwise white sheet appears unstable, yet the same character placed at the bottom seems stable, indicates that we are visually conditioned in many ways. In this example, we are guided by our experience of gravity, according to which everything floating is unsupported, whereas what is below is on "solid ground". All interpretations are influenced by the respective cultural conventions, some interpretations more so than others. Thus it can be assumed that those people who read and write from left to right also feel "dynamics" when moving from left to right. An example from micro-typography shows us how finely balanced (and how unconsciously) such a feeling is: The Humanist Serif is regarded as "dynamic" because of its still rudimentary handwritten style (curves and tapering connections, soft curving of the serifs, inclination to the right), the Rational Serif is regarded as "static" because of its stronger emphasis on the vertical 7.*

But graphic elements that we do not consciously see also have an influence on our perception. This refers to white spaces – whether between or around blocks of text, between lines, between words, or within letters.

→ D1

Morphology
Micro-typography
Humanist Serif
Rational Serif

*
The anatomy of type,
Stephen Coles, Erik Spiekermann
→ Further reading p. 163

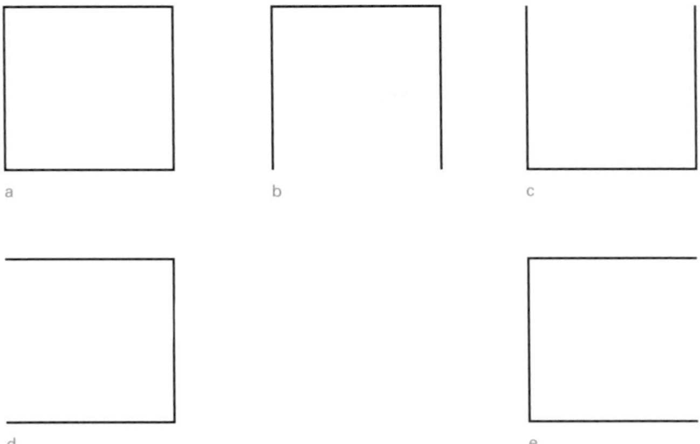

A
A1
A2
A3
A4
A5
A6
A7

6 Anyone who has grown up in the European cultural area will probably agree on the same interpretation: a) a closed space, b) a protective shelter, c) a vessel, d) an opening that feels like an entrance, e) an opening that feels like an exit. A8
These interpretations are based on learned patterns, according to which there is a top and bottom and a left-to-right dynamic. The basis for the latter sensation is the direction in which we read and write.

B
B1

C

GARAMOND

C1

Suddenly I was on the sea at night (the sea was stormy), the next ship C2
clock in my field of vision pointed to three. A host called for a dog – C3
the first tentative morning light lit up the sky, but I couldn't sleep because there was a splinter in my heart. I remember thinking that I had to brush my teeth urgently, but I couldn't find any tooth powder. Then the ship reached New York.

D

BODONI

D1

Suddenly I was on the sea at night (the sea was stormy), the next ship clock D2
in my field of vision pointed to three. A host called for a dog – the first ten- D3
tative morning light lit up the sky, but I couldn't sleep because there was a
splinter in my heart. I remember thinking I had to brush my teeth urgently, D4
but couldn't find any tooth powder. Then the ship reached New York.

7 The Garamond is regarded as a "dynamic" old-style serif typeface, because it has a flowing character due to its humanistic writing style (corresponding to the reading direction). Due to its classical origin, Bodoni emphasizes the vertical more strongly and is therefore regarded as "static".

The Chinese philosopher Lao-Tse is claimed to have said that a wheel is made of sixteen rods, but that it is not only the rods that make up the wheel, but their clever arrangement[8]. This statement points to a basic principle of creative activity, which consists in keeping and omitting, in the interplay of black and white, in the interplay of matter and space. If, against this background, one once again recalls design results that are perceived as particularly appealing, then the unprinted surface could unfold a surprising significance in these examples. A closer look reveals that the proportions between the printed and unprinted surface are anything but arbitrary. And it becomes clear here at a later stage that a grid that ensures the precise division of the surface is also an esthetic aid. The "invisible" part of the graphic owes its effect to its accuracy and commitment.

To sum up, it can be said: Order is an elementary component of life – whether you rebel against it, need it or want to ignore it. It is so elementary because we are dependent on orientation in the (perceived) chaos of a confusing world.

We designers know about the effect of visual codes and how to create visual order. When we use grids to help visualize information, we make orientation easier for people. Because with their typical media characteristics, grids allow unambiguous classifications. We designers are therefore not only responsible for the visible elements of the design, but also for the invisible ones – namely for the structure. It is thus in our power whether and how the designed overall impression communicates the content. The designer's knowledge, the resulting power and the associated responsibility form the basis of our profession.

A
A1
A2
A3
A4
A5
A6
A7
A8

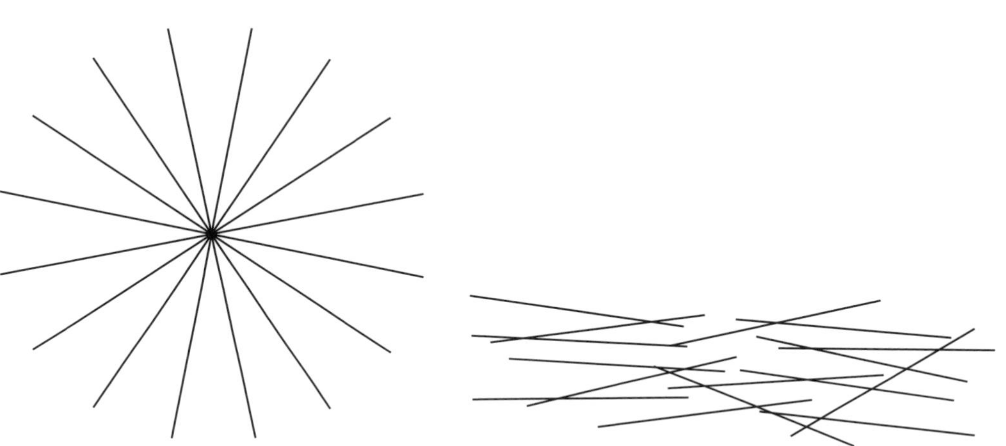

B
B1

8 The example of the "clever arrangement of rods", on which the static of a wheel is based, can be transferred to many areas: whether it is a matter of design (grids, fonts, layouts), or material or immaterial constructions of all kinds. In all cases, aspects that are not visible always play a role.

C
C1
C2
C3
D
D1
D2
D3
D4

Visual communication is essentially based on a "sender-receiver" model. This is what the previous chapters have already shown in one way or another. It comes to mind to ask whether or not findings from general communication psychology are suitable for being transferred to the visual realm, because even there, in verbal communication, the "sender-receiver" situation plays a decisive role.

What does this have to do with grids? We communicate in everyday life in describable behavior patterns without being aware of it. What seems random to us follows invisible interpersonal rules – same as in design, where an invisible order directs our senses. The visualization of communication on a psychological level therefore supports the attempt to make visual constructions comprehensible and projectable.
Since an interaction between "sender" and "receiver" is rarely possible in visual communication (in the sense of a direct response, which in turn generates an answer, etc.), the "sender-receiver" situation is dealt with here primarily from the sender's point of view.

Stimulus, response and other phenomena C—2

The psychological principles, which I would like to address in more detail, initially relate to verbal communication and form a small section of a complex subject area. It is about the "stimulus – response" principle and the associated duality of "expression" and "effect". In addition, I shall introduce the principle of the "four sides of a message" and describe what the terms "message level" and "meta level" mean. Finally, I would like to introduce a famous axiom by Paul Watzlawick. I have chosen these aspects because their parallelism to visual communication can be used to describe important creative functionalities. If one looks around in everyday life, one comes across a first, proven communication psychology pattern: "Creating associations", a method that constitutes the essential part of advertising (together with "exemplary" and "benefit promising").
"Whether or not I move towards something or turn away from it depends strongly on the feelings the object triggers in me. The nature of the feelings in turn depends on the experiences I have made with them (...)" says the psychologist Schulz von Thun.* As an example, he cites a child who received a shot from a doctor, a process that was painfully remembered by the child. A week later at the hairdresser's,

the child begins to cry. The reason is that the white coat of
the hairdresser reminds the child of the painful visit to the
doctor (also a white coat). In communication psychology,
according to Schulz von Thun, one speaks here of a "classical A
conditioning": Certain feelings are triggered on the basis
of earlier experiences of association. This is well known in A1
advertising: It uses stimuli with positive connotations A2
(natural landscape, good-looking and mostly young humans,
beautiful weather, prosperity, health etc.) to create an asso- A3
ciation with products, which do not have necessarily some- A4
thing to do with the positive stimuli mentioned. If this A5
"stimulus – response" model is transferred to design, it be- A6
comes clear that designers have much to gain if they can
empathize with the associating experiences of the receivers A7
of a visual message: Which cultural conventions generate A8
which expectations? How serious, for example, must a book
appear so that it can be recognized as such by a certain circle
of readers and at the same time be distinguished from other
literary genres? When and how does a website functionally
and innovatively affect a defined target group? In all cases,
it is a matter of generating a predicted response from certain B
addressees with a targeted stimulus. B1

Conditioning according to the "stimulus – response" pattern
is based on the principle of "expression" and "effect". In verbal communication, self-expression serves to communicate C
something to someone and to trigger a reaction from the
other person. According to Schulz von Thun, "expression" C1
and "effect" can be in balance with each other. As an example C2
he cites a child who has injured itself and therefore screams
("expression"). The parents rush to help ("effect"). In this C3
example, both components are in a harmonious relationship,
because the expression of real pain has the desired appeal
effect. But if the same child cries now, in memory of the D
achieved effect, with (conscious or unconscious) calculation
also without serious cause, then it uses the tested "expres- D1
sion" to achieve an actually not appropriate "effect" – namely D2
that the parents rush to it worriedly too. There is then no D3
balance between "expression" and "effect" – the expression
is corrupted for the sake of effect. D4

The example sounds almost banal in its obviousness, and yet the behavior to achieve an "effect" (whether appropriate or not, whether conscious or not) determines our daily lives. This is especially true for designers, because achieving

*
Six tools for clear communication,
Friedemann Schulz von Thun
→ Further reading p. 164

"effect" with an "expression" is part of their core business. Therefore, it is worth asking: Where does the corruption of the "expression" of design begin in order to achieve "effect"? How can harmony be created between "expression" and "effect" in design?
And: Doesn't the diversity of people demand ever new forms of "expression" in order to create an individual "effect"?

If the latter were true, designers would have to have a large repertoire of creative expression. A consistent creative "style" could only be justified if one were to communicate comparable content to the same target group in the same continuous manner – this is true sometimes, but everyday graphic design usually is more diverse. "Differentiation" instead of "run of the mill" must therefore be the solution for design. Another basic principle of verbal communication suggests this conclusion. It is called (according to Friedemann Schulz von Thun): the "four sides of a message" 1.

There are four aspects that make up verbal communication – all take place at the same time:
1) the factual aspect (the communication of a fact),
2) the relationship aspect
(the treatment of the fellow human being through the way of communication),
3) the self-revealing aspect
(what does the way of communication say about yourself),
4) the appeal aspect
(what do you want to achieve with communication).

Actually, all four aspects can be transferred to the design process – with the unbeatable advantage of being able to use them with a foresighted sense of proportion (in contrast to the complex simultaneity of all aspects of the spoken word). That means, however, that in every visual communication the questions of what is to be communicated, the relationship to the addressee, the own formative contribution and the effect to be obtained must be answered again. Although designers cannot avoid providing general answers to these questions (they do not communicate with individuals, but with target groups), such an analysis of the communication situation must precede every design assignment. What then follows can be called the graphic "coding" of a message: A whole series of visual and also haptic messages should be helpful to enable the receiver to understand the message correctly.
In communication psychology, every message is seen as a web of verbal and nonverbal messages. The sender therefore communicates on two levels. It does not only depend on what

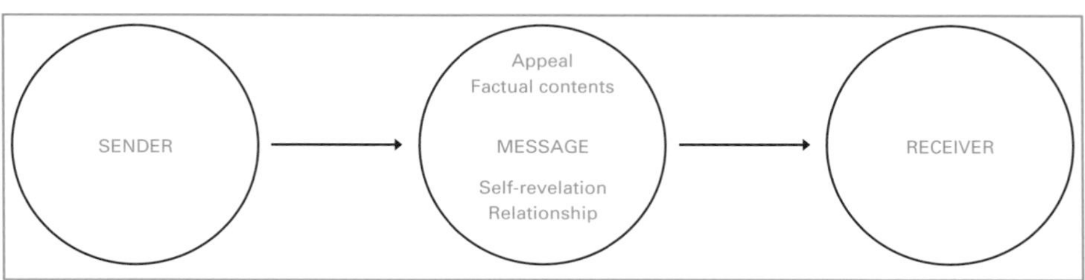

1 The model of interpersonal communication (according to Schulz von Thun) is based on the fact that each message contains four aspects. It does not only depend on what you say, but also on how and to whom.

the sender says (on the verbal message level in the described "four-sided" way), but also on how it is commented nonverbally (on the meta level). The gestures, the facial expressions, but also the context or the tone are regarded as nonverbal. The messages of both levels support each other regarding how the message is to be understood, they "qualify" each other. If, for example, the sentence "I think this poster is great" is accompanied by positive facial expressions, then one speaks of a "congruent" message – both levels point in the same direction. If the same sentence is accompanied by a pejorative grimace, the nonverbal contradicts the verbal level. One then speaks of an "incongruent" message: The grimace would give the verbal statement a new meaning. Such "incongruent messages" make up a large part of interpersonal communication (just think of ironic remarks and the like).
It follows that the verbal level is inconceivable without the nonverbal level. Each level communicates even if one would try to "switch it off" – for example by sitting silently in the corner. Watzlawick has formulated a meta-communicative axiom* for this: "You cannot not communicate". All behavior has a communicative character – whether one speaks or remains silent, acts or does not act.

Of course, this principle also applies to visual communication: Every graphic utterance says something and thus enters into an evaluative relationship with the content. This can happen in a "congruent" way – if the design supports the intention of the content or "incongruent" if the design contradicts the content. However, in visual communication it cannot play a role of commenting on and controlling interpretation, which the meta-level plays in a verbal statement.The reason for this is that in verbal communication the signals of both levels reach the receiver simultaneously – but not in visual communication. Here the design (through the layout) sends signals to the receivers before they can devote themselves to the content (e.g. by reading the texts). This "non-simultaneity" makes it dangerous to send a message "incongruently". If the design promises something other than what the content says, then the receiver will perceive the communication as ambivalent – if he or she gets involved with it at all. This means: A variability of the creative expression can only take place within "congruent" boundaries. "Incongruence" makes visual communication complicated.

In many respects, visual communication follows the rules that apply to verbal communication. Two major differences should be emphasized here once again:
First, visual communication is based on sending messages and information. The individual receiver usually remains unknown, and his or her reaction to what is sent cannot reach the sender in the sense of interaction. Because this is the case, design must speculate about its effect. Secondly: Visual communication can be planned. This became clearest with the principle of the "four sides of a message". In verbal communication, a word or sentence already contains all "sides of a message". This is the simultaneous "firing" of a conglomerate of conscious and subconscious messages, accompanied and commented on by nonverbal signals. The interplay between the message level and the meta level (whether "congruent" or "incongruent") makes verbal communication complex and spontaneous. This simultaneity is missing in visual communication. In return, one can work with time, calculation, empathy and knowledge. It is possible to try and discard different approaches before the visual message is finished and sent. It is then received by the receiver, with whom it first communicates at the creative level, before the content can have an effect.
Since receiving of a visual message proceeds from the overall impression to the detail, the design must not contradict the content. Against this background, it follows that it makes sense to use all visual instruments available to us with particular conscientiousness and cleverness.

*

Pragmatics of human communication,
Paul Watzlawick
→ Further reading p. 164

As has already been mentioned several times in this book, perception can be controlled. If, for example, you have studied the visual conventions of a target group, you can begin to speak their "language". This does not mean confirming the target group's viewing habits in advance, so to speak copying them. There may well be a reason legitimized by the content for the design to violate conventions. However, the receivers must be able to recognize the violations as such. They must be able to decode the visual "language" addressed to them.

Each visual "language" has its own visual grammar that is derived from the respective communication situation.
In its basic structure, such a grammar has four building blocks: the medium, the grid, the font and the image.

A
A1
A2
A3
A4
A5
A6
A7
A8
B
B1
C
C1
C2
C3
D
D1
D2
D3
D4

So far the treatment of the topic "order in design" has focused on many aspects of craftsmanship. What received little attention is the question:
How large is the share of the intuitive in the design process?
Is it possible to design (and "construct") solely by planning, or are there irrational components without which good design is not possible?
Is the focus on methods or is it rather intuition that makes the difference? I would like to illuminate the tension between these two poles here.
It has a long tradition and began when people began to consider the two disciplines "science" and "art" as opposites.

Intuition and method in design C—3

While science and art were still close relatives* in the Renaissance and up to the time of the Enlightenment, a new point of view emerged around the middle of the 19th century: Science had the goal of maximum "objectivity", while artists were expected to adopt a decidedly "subjective" point of view. This postulated dichotomy basically continues to this day. And yet the opposites have repeatedly converged in some areas.

The reasons for this – in the late 19th and early 20th centuries – were based on the progressing industrialization and political upheavals. A new form of communication emerged – "applied arts", of which graphic design is one component. Whether it was advertising for products, advertising for political positions or communication in public space in general: Increasingly, typesetters and printers (there were no designers in today's sense at the time) became designers and implementers in equal measure. In collaboration with them, many protagonists of the then artistic avant-garde discovered the power of visual communication. And it was precisely these artists who made it possible again to close the gap between art and knowledge.

→ D1

Method
Science
Art
Applied arts

* Artists such as Michelangelo, Leonardo da Vinci or Albrecht Dürer dealt with art, anatomy and technical inventions.
In the Renaissance, humanism began to change the understanding of art.
A "new" image of man came into being that was oriented towards the value of the individual life and the world of things – in contrast to the theocentric view of the Middle Ages.

This can be seen, for example, in the attitude of the Bauhaus protagonists, the art school* that set out to unite science, technology and art. Their goal was to develop ethical and
esthetic standards for the benefit of society. A

The collaboration of technology and art was a typical feature A1
of the early 20th century. Only with planning could the A2
mass production of goods be promoted, which should now
be available to everyone. Only with planning could these A3
goods be advertised, in the sense of a calculated effect on the A4
target groups. Only with planning could one advertise A5
political positions in the form of enlightenment and propa- A6
ganda. The emerging job profile of graphic design as a hybrid
of calculated action and artificial design was the result of A7
these requirements. A8

However, the rational dynamics floating above all this could not hide the fact that the "objectification" of design aimed at by science was ambivalently assessed.**
Wassily Kandinsky (the later Bauhaus teacher) already
expressed this in 1912 in "Über die Formfrage": B
"(...) In short: the true form (...) arises from the combination
of feeling and science", while Paul Klee (also a Bauhaus B1
teacher) stated in 1928 in "Exakte Versuche in der Kunst"
with regard to the limits of scientific approaches:
"(...) One proves, justifies, supports, constructs, one orga- C
nizes; good things. But one does not arrive at totality (...)". C1

According to Kandinsky and Klee, the role of the "intuitive" C2
moment, which is fed by the subjective perception of
the artist or the designer, is an elementary component of the C3
design process. If one wanted to test this comprehensible
thesis, one would only have to conceive a small experiment
and invite several designers to design – on the basis of iden- D
tical information regarding the sender, the content, the target
group and the desired effect. The results would be – what D1
a surprise – quite different. In principle, this experiment is D2
part of everyday design when, for example, a customer
requests several agencies to "pitch" on the basis of one and D3
the same briefing, i.e. to compete for the most convincing D4
creative solutions.

* The Bauhaus is used here as a representative of many currents of that time that dealt with the role of art and design in the social context. Examples are Art Nouveau, Futurism, DADA, Constructivism, de Stijl.

** Experimente zu einer Theorie der Praxis. Historische Etappen der Designforschung in der Nachfolge des Bauhauses. Claudia Mareis, kunsttexte.de

There is therefore an unpredictable part to the design process, namely the personality of the designer. This, in turn, is shaped by all sorts of factors – such as experience, socialization, mentality and the general cultural conditioning. In other words, the personality of the designer consists of subjective sensations and intuitive elements of action.
On the other hand, design is also not a "product of chance". The methodical approach to a task in visual communication is necessary and common if the effect is to be calculable.
In the previous chapter the psychology of communication has already been discussed. As described there, it is based on patterns that make a methodical approach possible.

The most important finding when looking at these patterns is that they are predictable factors that influence creative decisions.
The personality of a designer is expressed in his/her attitude towards society. And so it is not surprising that the Bauhaus teaching consisted of a mixture of artistic, analytical and methodical contents, precisely with the aim of training responsible personalities. This view was continued in post-war Germany in the 1950s and 1960s. The Hochschule für Gestaltung Ulm* promoted the continuation of holistic teaching. In addition to the core subjects of visual communication, the subjects of visual rhetoric, semiotics and sociology were also taught. Teachers such as Otl Aicher, Tomás Maldonado or Horst Rittel, however, changed the idea of design as it had prevailed in Bauhaus times with their theses on the projectable effect. Thus, after Bauhaus-oriented beginnings (influenced by the first director of the HfG Ulm, Max Bill), the aim was to combine "science and design" – but if possible without art with its unpredictability.

This period saw the founding of the Design Methods Movement* in the USA. An essential thesis of this movement was that there were design processes whose structures could be transferred to a wide variety of disciplines – such as architecture, economics or technology. Design is projectable and thus a rational process – free of individual and intuitive influences. This idea soon began to collide with

→ D1
Semiotics
Hipster

*
The Hochschule für Gestaltung Ulm (Ulm School of Design) existed from 1953–1968. Its goal was to establish practical application more firmly in product design and visual communication education and in this way intensify the connection between theory and practice.
With this objective, the HfG Ulm turned away from the model of the Bauhaus and stood for a design without borrowing from art.

the thought of pop culture, which also began in the 1960s
and lasted beyond the 1970s. Postmodernism with its mantra
of "Anything goes" then finally replaced the positions of
Modernism in the 1980s. The belief in "certainties" and A
"necessities" in design waned. In the 90s, the design process
was almost reversed: The individuality (and thus the intuitive A1
part) of the designer and his/her subjective view became A2
more important, while the importance of semiotic knowledge
and strategic planning diminished. The so-called "hipster" A3
design can also be seen in this tradition, which – beginning A4
in the 2000s – shaped design worldwide (at least in all west- A5
ern/capitalist-oriented countries). In recent years, on the A6
other hand, opulent design has slowly disappeared in favor of
a more sober design aimed at authenticity. In this way, it A7
corresponds with the social zeitgeist, which has made con- A8
cepts such as "sustainability" and "credibility" its idioms.

The methodical and the intuitive/artistic approach thus
played very different roles over the course of time. Whatever
the ups and downs of the relationship, the specific designer
approach to solving communicative problems did not go B
unnoticed outside the design sector. What was first sketched
in the short time of the Design Method Movement in the B1
1960s and was first conceived by the HfG Ulm – namely a
methodically structured approach to solving problems in
visual communication** – has been adopted by some eco- C
nomic sectors. Over the years, an approach has established
itself that operates under the technical term "Design C1
Thinking" and claims to have deciphered the "DNA" of C2
design processes.
This is based on the assumption that tasks and problems can C3
be solved better if people with different skills and disciplines
work together. This multidisciplinary approach should provide space for creative work. The aim is to produce a result D
that has undergone several quality assurance process steps.
An exemplary sequence is: D1
definition (order), research (background), finding ideas D2
(solutions), prototyping (elaboration), selection (justification),
implementation (delivery), learning (feedback). D3

D4

*
The Conference on Design Methods took place in the USA in 1962 and established the Design Methods Movement.
The aim of this design theory movement was to advance the systematization of design processes – without "disturbing" intuitive and thus uncontrollable influences.

**
Designing programmes, Karl Gerstner
→ Further reading p. 163
typographie, Otl Aicher
→ Further reading p. 162

In the book "Design Thinking"* it says: "While creativity in design is important, design is an activity that serves economic as well as creative goals. The design process helps ensure that a design satisfies all such considerations. The process seeks to generate a number of possible solutions and utilizes various techniques or mechanisms that encourage participants to think outside the box in the pursuit of creative or innovative solutions."

It is very possible that the synergies that are being sought actually lead to better solutions than unstructured ways of working. Such a methodical approach is also motivated by the idea that there can be a calculable and thus incorruptible basis for design processes. In the best case, designers then use well-defined processes that read like instructions for action. In the worst case, the method only generates efficiency and the question may arise as to whether it provides the desired creative scope to a sufficient extent with its defined steps. Sometimes they can't be big enough.

Because there is another task that design has to solve: the development of "something new". What does that mean? As a layperson (or client) one experiences all cultural manifestations, whether it is art, architecture, music or communication. These everyday experiences are contrasted with the expertise of designers. Their expertise lies in areas that are beyond the imagination of laypersons. Laypersons can only refer to the canon they know and which they usually perceive only subconsciously. It is difficult for them to imagine "something new".

*
Design Thinking, Gavin Ambrose, Paul Harris
→ Further reading p. 163

It is up to us designers to add new forms of communication and appearance to this canon. They are necessary because the development of the world confronts us with challenges that can often not be met by conventional means. Or they are simply necessary because you want to differentiate yourself from the existing. “New” arises when one includes intuition and chance in addition to rational analysis.

This is where experiments come in, whose welcome components which are often coincidences. There are many possibilities in design, for example generative design. For example, there are programs* that create layouts generated by “chance”. The creative development work makes it possible. Method (here: the computer program) and intuition (here: decisions based on the random principle) support and help each other, as you can see.

In this context, it is worth looking at art. It is teeming with works in which intuitive action is at the center of planned artistic processes. Here are three randomly chosen examples: The American artist Jackson Pollock painted so-called drippings. Picture “Number 32” is famous:

“Kunst+Zufall: Analyse und Bedeutung”, Christian Janecke

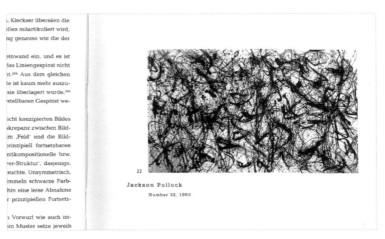

, Kleckser übersäen die
llen mitartikuliert wird,
ng genauso wie die der

einwand ein, und es ist
das Liniengespinst nicht
nt.[204] Aus dem gleichen
te ist kaum mehr auszu-
sie überlagert wurde,[205]
stellbaren Gespinst we-

icht konzipierten Bildes
skrepanz zwischen Bild-
m ‚Feld' und die Bild-
prinzipiell fortsetzbaren
ntikompositionelle bzw.
ver-Struktur', dasjenige,
suchte. Unsymmetrisch,
mmeln schwarze Farb-
hin eine leise Abnahme
r prinzipiellen Fortsetz-

n Vorwurf wie auch im-
ein Muster setze jeweils

22

Jackson Pollock

Number 32, 1950

1 “Number 32”, Jackson Pollock, 1950

* “Evolving Layout” is the name of such a plug-in. It was developed by Denis Klein and Raymond Vetter for Adobe InDesign. With the help of the plug-in, design elements on a page are grouped again and again and resized. These “random” layouts offer unexpected solutions and are a source of inspiration. http://www.evolvinglayout.com/

Black lines with drops form an abstract tangle, which is due to chance, because the paint dripping from a stick onto the canvas is only conditionally controllable 1.
The French artist Niki de Saint Phalle shot at canvases that had previously been prepared with paint and gypsum.
The paint running through and the destroyed plaster particles created a "random" picture 2.
The Dutch artist Herman de Vries produced a series of pictures that he called "random objectivations". The 1967 painting "collage V67-30 randomised distribution" shows ninety-two identically designed small white rectangles on a black surface. The positions of the white rectangles are random (in this case using a random number program) 3.

If you take a closer look at the examples I came across while reading the book "Kunst + Zufall"*, they show that order as a synonym for what can be planned – the seemingly "free space" of artistic creation – plays an unexpectedly important role here. For without the parameters on which the examples are based (prepared canvas, the choice of a stick as a color carrier, the choice of white rectangles of the same size, etc.), they would not have been possible in this way. "Setting up parameters" means nothing other than defining a linear or non-linear action, deciding on material, defining formats, in other words making many decisions that form the framework of an experimental arrangement consisting of intuitive actions.

In order to develop something new, different components are needed. They ensure creativity.

The psychologist Peter Kruse coined the term "indirect spaces of possibility" when he spoke of the conditions for creativity. We are not able to be creative on demand (the order "be creative!" is a paradox). Creativity can only develop within systemic framework conditions. One of these conditions is called "diversity". Kruse says that intelligent systems work with differences and thus create internal tensions, which in turn create unstable phases. These provoke changes in process patterns. He calls the possibility of transition into new patterns creativity. His conclusion: New things arise from contradiction, not from harmony.

*
Kunst + Zufall, Christian Janecke
→ Further reading p. 163

"Niki de Saint Phalle",
Pontus Hulten

A

A1

A2

A3

A4

A5

A6

A7

A8

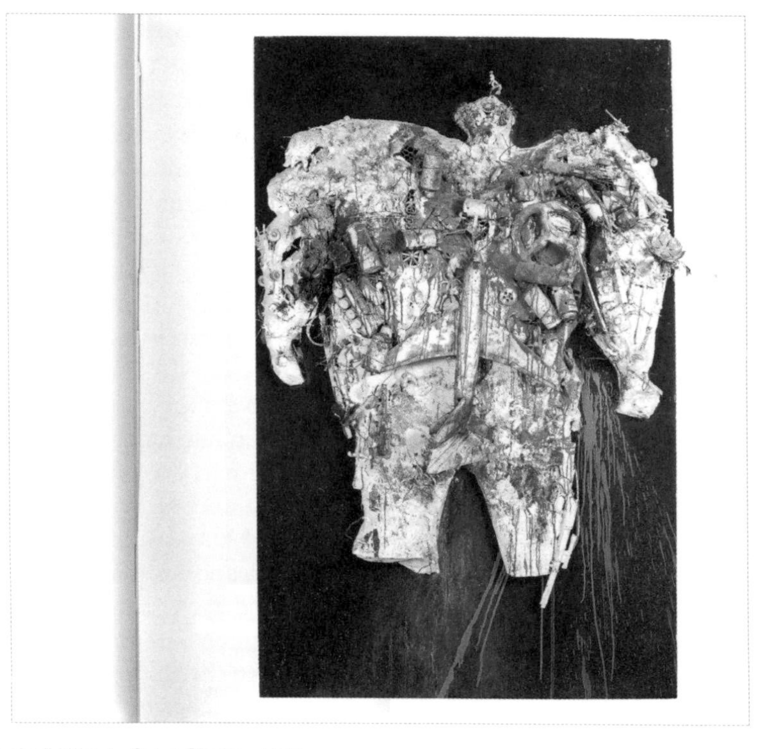

B

2 "La mort du patriarche", Niki de Saint Phalle, 1972 B1

"Kunst+Zufall",
Christian Janecke

C

C1

C2

C3

D

D1

D2

D3

D4

einen Zufall, der sich
tradiert wird. Irgend-
er schon ‚Geschichte',
np zwar initiierte, das
aß bloßer Zufall vielen
grundeliegen könnte,
iamp hegte die Hoff-
ann akzeptieren: „Mit
nen, als eine Möglich-
'elt auf Zufall begrün-
as, was passiert in der
kausaler Zusammen-

rg. Auch an den Stel-
rm von richtungswei-
kräftigen, zufälligen
n' lief nun ein *frischer*,
e Begegnung nicht ab
eines Werkes aus![167]

rtigte seit den frühen
ectivations" („Zufalls-
iegt die Verwendung
htung, Größe, Hellig-
Bildelementen festge-
dlichung', sondern die
entes im Sinne einer

nach dem Zufall vor-
ntstanden. Auf einem
undneunzig identisch
Streifen in zufälliger
lden. Die Anzahl der
erteilung und die Aus-
die Fläche durch ein
k ein zufälliges Koor-
ünstlers genügte wohl
fallszahlenprogramms
nig umständlicher das
ebenso eine Nummer

leistungsstarker Com-
prechendem Graphik-

114

13

Herman de Vries

collage V 67-30 randomised distribution, 1967

115

3 "collage V67-30 randomised distribution", Herman de Vries, 1967

In the further course of his argumentation, Kruse draws up three characters that are not very successful in themselves, but together are able to generate creativity. Kruse calls the first character "Creator" – that's the lunatic, the trouble-maker, who always comes up with new ideas. He calls the second character "Owner" – that is the knowledge owner who masters a subject in depth. He calls the third character "Broker" – that is the mediator, the networker, who knows people who know something. These three characters are symbolic of our brain.

Kruse in an interview from 2007*:
"(…) When I bring the Creator and the Owner together, I get ideas, an idea pool arises from knowledge and instability. This is the cortex. When I bring the Owner and the Broker together, I have two evaluators. Both must be able to evaluate what corresponds to the limbic system. When I bring the Broker and the Creator together, I have an ascending reticular activity that excites me again and again. And if you bring these three things together – excitement, resolution, and evaluation – then you have a brain. (…)"

In the same interview Kruse points to another module for creativity: "(…) Build networks. The moment you build networks, you create a situation in which the non-linear feedback effects repeatedly provide for the dissolution of stable states. This means that feedback mechanisms and diversity are extremely positive for creativity (…)".

If Kruse's argumentation is applied to the tension examined here, then creativity can only arise if method and intuition are parts of one and the same design process. This means, however, that both components must be equally valued – if one wants to fully exploit the creative possibilities.
"Soft" factors such as intuition are difficult to calculate and limit temporally, which is one reason why the method is often preferred. This should not prevent you, dear reader, from internalizing the bipolarity of creative work.

*
https://www.youtube.com/watch?v=oyo_oGUEH-I (in German)

So cultivate your methodical knowledge and develop intuitive self-confidence. It is helpful if you constantly question your patterns of behavior and reception; if you look for models of design that lie outside your cultural sphere; if you sometimes “go over the top” in your thoughts and designs. In other words, just do more often what you normally never do.

Search for adventure within order.

氫氣
鍺烷
硅烷
氯氣
三氯化硼
三氟化硼
氨氣
二氯氫硅
Phosphine in Hydrogen
Phosphine in Silane
磷烷混合硅烷
Arsine in Hydrogen
砷烷混合氫氣
TOXIC / POISON
FLAMMABLE
GASES
有毒 / 易燃氣體
NO SMOKING
不准吸煙
CAT.2D.G.STORE
第二類危險倉
MSDS
FIRE HOSE REEL
Nitrous Oxide
Carbon Hexafluoride
Trifluoromethane
Nitrogen
Liquid Nitrogen
Helium
Oxygen
Argon
Carbon Dioxide
Sulfur Hexafluoride
Carbon Tetrafluoride
氧化亞氮
六氟化碳
三氟甲烷
氮氣
液態氮
氦氣
氧氣
氬氣
二氧化碳
六氟化硫
四氟化碳
CAT.2D
有毒
TOXIC
NO SM
不准
第二類

D Appendix

This chapter explains various terms used in the text of this book. In addition, it is used to enable the search for terms in the texts. The glossary is your introduction to information research, which you should all do independently – depending on your needs and interests.

Glossary

D — 1

A

Algorithm
→ p. 90

Applied arts

Applied arts is the term used to describe the disciplines of art that deal with the design of everyday objects and everyday communication. In applied arts, the application and functional communication have first priority. Applied arts include architecture and interior design, graphic design, product design, arts and crafts and fashion design. → p. 140 → Art

Art

Here is the lexical definition of the term (excerpt): "Art, the creative and formative transformation of inner and outer contents of experience into a work that transcends them and is perceived by the viewer as an esthetic value (...) The source of art is imagination, inventiveness, fantasy, creativity, i.e. the creative power of the artist. (...)"
Source: German dtv Lexikon,
vol. 10 (own translation) → p. 140 → Science

Asymmetry

plays an important role in design as a counterpart to symmetry. Put simply, a symmetric layout stands for "harmony", while an asymmetric layout is capable of generating tension. Asymmetrical design was a characteristic feature of Modernism.
→ Symmetry

B

Baseline grid
→ p. 34

Binding
→ OFC – OBC (book covers)

Binding types

There are different ways to bind a book, magazine or booklet. The type of binding also influences the layout. If, for example, thread-stitching is used on a book, it can be opened particularly well and the pages can be pushed apart – this makes sense for thick books. The reason for this is the stable design of thread-stitching, because the pages are sewn together at the back. This robustness when pushing a double-page spread apart allows slightly narrower inside margins than with other types of binding. Thread-stitching is comparatively expensive. Adhesive binding and staple stitching are cheaper. Most people know the latter from booklets. Adhesive binding is stable, but not as robust as thread-stitching. The type area of a double-page spread quickly runs the risk of "disappearing" into the inside margin, as more caution is required when pushing a double-page spread apart – in the worst case, pages can come loose. There are a number of other types of binding: spiral binding, binding with book screws, etc. They all have different influences on the widths of the inside margins.
→ p. 14

Book formats

In the past, many designers have been concerned with defining the ideal proportionality of the aspect ratios of a book block. It is not possible to list here all the findings that have been presented in numerous specialist books. Here are a few examples of proven aspect ratios: 1:2 / 2:3 / 3:5 (ratios from the → Fibonacci sequence), and 5:9. The → golden ratio is 1:1.618. The DIN formats are not suitable for book formats. → p. 14

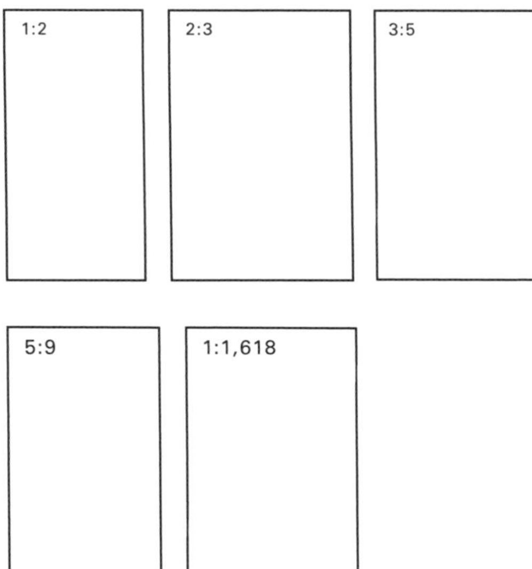

Breakpoints (web design)

When designing a website (in "responsive web design" mode), breakpoints play a decisive role. These are the points at which the design of a website changes noticeably, for example when the "containers" break.
For example, CSS (Cascading Style Sheets) can be used to change a four-column layout from a certain width to a layout with two columns. An important question is at which widths (or heights) a breakpoint should be set. There are different techniques, ways and means to determine the optimal breakpoints: setting breakpoints using the standard widths of the devices, setting breakpoints using a grid or aligning breakpoints according to content (content first). → p. 86

C

CMS

is the abbreviation for Content Management System. It is software that allows the management of content (text, image, sound, video, etc.) of a website (or intranet site). A website that is to be maintained regularly has a backend and a frontend. The frontend is what the visitor to the website sees. The backend, on the other hand, can usually be reached via a protected link. Here the contents are administered.
Content management systems normally do not require any programming knowledge. → p. 91

Columns

→ p. 10

Consultative reading

→ p. 24 → Reading expectation

Corporate design(CD)

The term describes the visual appearance of a company or institution. The CD is a sub-area of the corporate identity, which is composed of different sub-areas: for example in the rules on behavior (Corporate Behavior) or in the rules on the internal and external communication of the company (Corporate Communication). The detailed structure of a corporate identity can be found in relevant technical literature. → p. 106

D

Design Thinking

→ p. 144

Desktop app

→ p. 91

DIN 5008

DIN 5008 provides recommendations for business correspondence. This concerns both the design and the syntax. The recommendations deal with the typographically correct use of punctuation and characters, words, formulas, numbers and numerical structures. DIN 5008 also describes how texts can be structured or how tables are composed.
→ p. 104

A
A1
A2
A3
A4
A5
A6
A7
A8
B
B1
C
C1
C2
C3
D
D1
D2
D3
D4

DIN 476

The standard paper formats (DIN 476) were defined in the twenties of the last century by the German Institute for Standardization (Deutsches Institut für Normung), to which they also owe their abbreviation. The internal logic of the format canon always consists of the same aspect ratios, namely 1:1.414 (this corresponds to the ratio of the side edges according to the Pythagorean theorem). The largest format is called A0 and has an area of one square meter. The indication of the paper weight refers to this. In addition to the DIN A series, the DIN C series is important for graphic designers. It is used to define the envelope sizes. The aspect ratios of the series are identical. → DIN A4 p. 104, DIN C4 p. 105

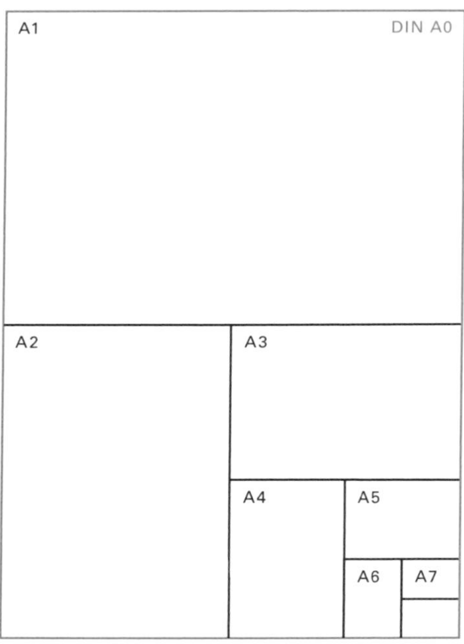

DIN A series (mm)				DIN C series (mm)			
A0	841	×	1189	C0	917	×	1297
A1	594	×	841	C1	648	×	917
A2	420	×	594	C2	458	×	648
A3	297	×	420	C3	324	×	458
A4	210	×	297	C4	229	×	324
A5	148	×	210	C5	162	×	229
A6	105	×	148	C6	114	×	162
A7	74	×	105	C7	81	×	114
A8	52	×	74	C8	57	×	81

E

Engagement time

is an online marketing term, engagement time is the measured time that a visitor spends at a website. → p. 92

F

Fibonacci sequence

The Fibonacci sequence (named after one of the most famous mathematicians of the Middle Ages, Leonardo Fibonacci, Pisa, Italy) consists of an infinite series of numbers: 0, 1, 1, 2, 3, 5, 8, 13, 21, 34, 55, 89, 144, 233 and so on.
The recognizable characteristic of this series is that each number is composed of the sum of its two predecessors (0+1=1, 1+1=2, 1+2=3, 2+3=5, 3+5=8, 5+8=13, 8+13=21...). With this series, Fibonacci described the results of his observations of a rabbit population in the year 1202. In fact, research and observations based on these results showed that the Fibonacci sequence seems to represent a kind of basic pattern of nature, for example in the arrangement of flowers or fruit patterns. Observations of this kind date back to antiquity, but Fibonacci reserved the right to give his name to the series published by him in the book "Liber Abbaci". → p. 18

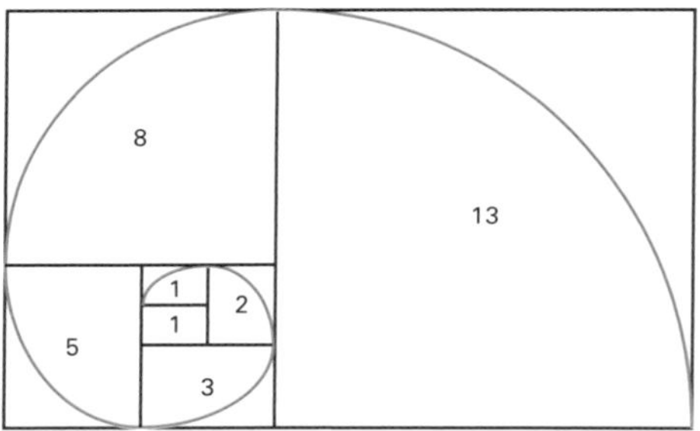

The Fibonacci sequence is closely related to the golden ratio. → Golden ratio

G

Font size

The size of a font in combination with the line spacing (see Line spacing) is responsible for the readability of a text. The font size depends on the reading distance, which in turn depends on the selected medium. The choice of font size also depends on the type of reading (see Reading expectation).
For example, a novel with long texts that is to be read linearly should have a different (and more comfortable) font size than a dictionary that is to be read consultatively and consists of many small portions of text. Here the reader can be expected to accept a smaller font size, since the reading process only refers to a short passage of text. Headlines and sub-headlines are based on the macro-typography overall picture and should be large enough for clear reading guidance.
Caution: Identical sizes appear different from font to font. Therefore, binding size recommendations for the different reading types cannot be given.

Experience with reading texts from media held in the hand when reading (books, magazines) shows, however, that font sizes between 8 and 11 points are well suited for running texts (depending on the selected font, the selected font style and the selected line spacing). Text sizes to be read consultatively, such as captions or marginal texts, range from 5 to 8 points. The difference in size between a running text size and the font size of marginal information should be clear (at least 2 points). → p. 20
→ Marginal note

Format

is the term used to describe the size of a sheet of paper, indicating both the width and the length, e.g. 210 mm × 297 mm. The first number indicates the width.

Golden ratio

Like the numerical sequence of the Fibonacci sequence, the golden ratio is a principle borrowed from nature, which (from an evolutionary perspective) has ideal proportions. In schematic terms, the golden ratio works as follows: Imagine a line C to be divided into the two parts A and B. The golden ratio is given if the greater distance A to the smaller distance B behaves in the same way as the total distance C to the partial distance A. This ratio is approx. 61.8 % to 38.2 %.

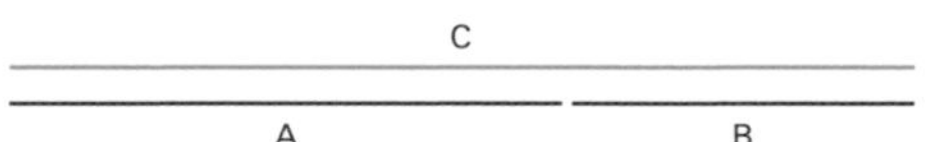

The proportions of the golden ratio appear everywhere in nature, whether it is the ivy leaf, the sunflower, the poplar, the starfish or the honey bee. Also one of the oldest cultural symbols of mankind, the pentagram, reflects the proportions of the golden ratio. Recent research has shown that the schematic representation of the helix of our DNA should be imagined as a pentagram-based construction. The golden ratio has been known since antiquity and had a great influence on the subsequent development of natural sciences and architecture. It is not by chance that human beings – influenced by the omnipresence of this principle – perceive proportions according to the golden ratio as harmonious and coherent. The golden ratio appears in various forms: as a golden rectangle, as a golden triangle, as a golden angle, as a golden spiral, as a golden sequence of numbers. The golden ratio also plays a role in design. In addition to the ideal book format (ratio of width to height = 1:1.618), the golden ratio was often used to construct the type area on a double-page spread.

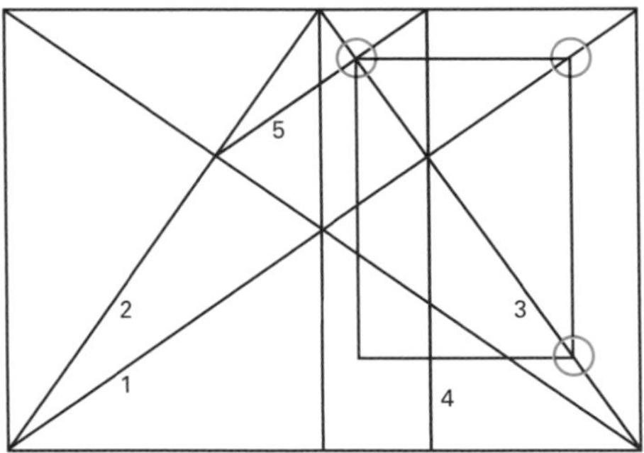

Double-page spread layouts based on the golden ratio are no longer common today, as the lavish white space that accompanies them represents an uneconomical use of space. However, the margins of a layout often refer to the golden ratio, for example when they are laid out in the → Fibonacci sequence 2:3:5:8. → p. 14

H

Hipster

is the name for a subculture of the beginning 21st century. The characteristics of hipsterism lie in the external extravagance with which one hopes to distinguish oneself from the mainstream.
Hipster culture refers to avant-garde movements that played a role in the middle of the 20th century, especially in the USA. Hipsterism has meanwhile arrived in the mainstream. In terms of design, the scene was represented by a typical graphic language whose essential characteristics included extravagance and creative opulence. The design style seemed revolutionary, but had no contextual weight. → p. 143

Humanist Serif

The Humanist Serif is considered to be the first form of the old-style sans serif typeface with lower case letters (minuscules) and upper case letters (majuscules). It is based on the 15th century humanistic shape principle. → p. 130

I

Images

In the graphic sector, an image or format is measured by first specifying the width and then the height in millimeters (for example, 210 × 297 mm for a portrait A4 sheet). In the case of art to be reproduced, for example in catalogs, the situation is different.
If images have to be measured there, the height is mentioned first and then the width. Depending on the size of the artwork, this is done in millimeters or centimeters. → p. 46

Informative reading

→ p. 58 → Reading expectation

Interaction style

describes the way a user uses the website (mouse, track pad, keyboard, touch, controller, etc.). → p. 92

Justified typesetting

Justified text looks like a block: All lines have the same length underneath each other. Justified typesetting is the oldest form of typesetting, already used by the monks of the early Renaissance (15th century). Johannes Gutenberg, the inventor of the movable lead letters (end of the 15th century), took over justified typesetting. It is still a widely used composition style today, for example in books and newspapers. The quality of a justified typesetting can be recognized by the fact that the text is distributed more or less evenly in the line. The (visible) compressions of words or (clearly visible) variances in the spaces between words, which in the worst case appear like "holes", are therefore regarded as quality shortcomings. In order to prevent such errors, it is advisable not to fall below the minimum number of 50 characters per line.
→ p. 20, p. 46 → Types of typesetting

L

Legibility

In terms of legibility, a distinction is made between textual legibility and typographic legibility.
Textual legibility is given when the written text is addressed to the intended reader in an understandable form. Typographical legibility is given when the design makes it possible to grasp the text effortlessly. → p. 79

Letter format

The letter format is used mainly in the USA.
It differs from the DIN A4 format and measures 215.9 × 279.4 mm. → p. 106

Letter top edge

The common line on which all letters stand is called the baseline (G). Letter parts that extend downwards below this line are called descenders (U). The height of the small x is called the x-height (X). The parts of the letters that rise above the x-height are called ascenders (O). The top edges of the ascenders are usually identical to the top edges of the capital letters (V). However, there are also fonts that have higher ascenders than the capital letters for better readability. If dimensioning is necessary, one orients oneself to the capital letters height of a font. → p. 46

Line length

The line length together with the font size and the line spacing is responsible for the legibility of a text. Lines that are too short cause unfavorable word separations. Lines that are too long make it difficult to continue reading in the following line. → p. 20

Line spacing

The line spacing, together with the font size is responsible for the legibility of a text. The size of the line spacing to be chosen depends on many factors, such as the number of lines below each other, the length of the lines, or the font selected. The basic rule is that the line spacing must be chosen so large that the descenders of a font and its ascenders do not touch when two lines are placed over each other. → p. 10, p. 20

Linear reading

→ p. 14 → Reading expectation

M

Macro-typography

Macro-typography refers to all typographical measures relating to the layout. → p. 128

Marginal note

A marginal note is supporting information of the running text and therefore arranged next to it – usually in a marginal column provided for this purpose. Its font size is usually at least 2 pt smaller than the running text.

Margins

→ p. 19

Method

The term is used in various ways in science. In this book, the term describes the fixed nature of a procedure. → p. 140

Micro-typography

Micro-typography refers to all typographical measures that relate to the handling of type. → p. 130

Module

→ p. 32

Morphology

The term "morphology" is found in many sciences. Essentially it is about the doctrine of shapes, forms, organisms and their peculiarities, their developments as well as their laws. → p. 130

N

Native display

A native display is the initial display of a website where all content is given its position and each pixel its size. If the resolution or format of the output device changes, the display must be adjusted accordingly. For example, an online service like the WhatsApp messenger is used by most users on mobile devices, so the native display is the one on the mobile device. The browser version of the messenger is used less often, so it is "less important" and is customized.

A
A1
A2
A3
A4
A5
A6
A7
A8
B
B1
C
C1
C2
C3
D
D1
D2
D3
D4

Another example: The Internet presence of a design office is usually visited via the desktop browser, so the native display is found here. Since the website is visited less often on mobile devices, the presentation is "less important" and is adapted accordingly. → p. 93

O

OFC – OBC (book covers)

The four pages of a book cover are not included in the numbering of the pages. The cover is described as follows:

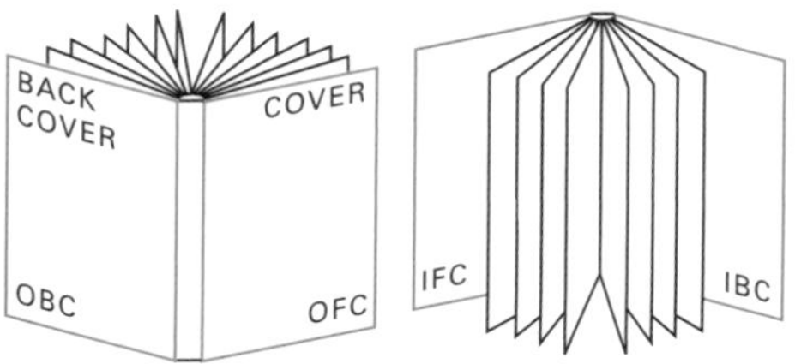

OFC: outside front cover
IFC: inside front cover
IBC: inside back cover
OBC: outside back cover

Orientation system

→ p. 102

P

Page number

→ p. 22

Pagination

→ p. 20

Paper

Paper is divided into "graphic paper", "technical and special paper" and "packaging paper, cartons and boards". The "graphic paper" is subdivided into "coated paper" (picture printing papers, art printing papers, poster paper) and "uncoated paper" (offset paper, colored paper, stationery, bond paper). → p. 14

Personas

is a term from marketing. It denotes "invented and/ or investigated" person profiles, which are exemplarily for persons of a certain target group. They help to put oneself in the position of the respective target group. → p. 92

Pictogram

A pictogram is the simplified graphic representation of information by a single symbol. → p. 128

Poster

→ p. 106

R

Ragged typesetting

Ragged typesetting is called this way because the lines run out unevenly. Flush left is generally used. Here, the lines on the left and below each other form a uniform edge, while the right edge of the sentence is "ragged" (the reverse principle applies to flush right ragged typesetting). In the ideal case, the alignment results in a shorter line being followed by a longer line, according to the principle "short – long – short – long ...".
Ragged typesetting is particularly suitable for narrow columns with a rather small number of letters per line and for shorter texts. For long texts such as those in a novel, for example, ragged typesetting is rather unsuitable. → Types of typesetting

Rational Serif

The Rational Serif has strong line thickness differences, has no curving of the serifs and is characterized by the techniques of copper and steel engraving. → p. 130

Readability

The readability of a text is guaranteed by a series of typographical measures that go beyond the measure of pure legibility. These measures include the balanced relationship between font selection, font size, line length and line spacing. But macro-typographical decisions, such as the organization of texts on a page, also influence the degree of readability. → p. 79

Reading expectation

The expectation of reading is the reaction to the visual promise emanating from a medium. When viewing a book layout, one assumes that one is dealing with a longer reading text that has to be read linearly. Linear means that the meaning of the content can only be grasped after the book has been read completely – i.e. when the book has been read from front to back (linearly). Magazines promise that they can be read in an informative way due to their multi-part structure into various texts and images. The reading expectation here is that texts, images and graphics that stand alone in the layout are placed that allow "jumping" from information to information (i.e. non-linear reading). The reading expectation in relation to a lexicon corresponds to a reading offer that is described as consultative. → p. 14, p. 58

Register

→ p. 32

Responsive web design

→ p. 90

Running title (dead, alive)

→ p. 22

S

Semiotics

is a science that theoretically deals with all kinds of signs and sign processes that are based on both linguistic and visual codes. As part of linguistics, semiotics is an integral part of the humanities, social sciences, economics and cultural studies. → p. 143

Science

The text often refers to "science" or "scientific approach". What the text generally refers to within this context are "objectively measurable" procedures. In fact, the concept of science is interpreted in various ways in the design discourse. The reason for this is the fact that designers have unclear concepts of "science" due to their profession, because as a rule they are not forced to grasp "design as science" either in their studies or in their professional life (except for occasional excursions into "neighboring" fields of knowledge). The representatives of design theory, on the other hand, have been debating for some time how "design as science" should be conceived. The shortcoming of the theorists is their lack of practical experience and the resulting lack of feedback from everyday design life. You should follow the discourse attentively and form your own opinions. But here once again the lexical definition of the term (excerpt): "Science, the epitome of the knowledge of a time, formed, ordered and founded on the basis of research, teaching and literature handed down to us (...) The main characteristic of science is (...) an objectivity based on factual relevance and free of evaluations, feelings and external determinants, which, in addition to the methodic consensus, establishes the capacity to be generalized and general verifiability of scientific statements. (...)" Source: German dtv Lexikon, Volume 20 (own translation).

Chapter C3 also deals casually with the concept of art, which is sometimes confused with design and sometimes with intuition. This may rightly be criticized. The reason for this ambiguous use lies on the one hand in the constantly changing interpretation of the nature of art since the Renaissance. On the other hand, the "artistic" part of the designer's work is in itself ambiguous and dependent on the respective protagonists. In any case, this does not mean that a graphic design idea is already an artistic act. In the chapter text, "the artistic" stands for the free and individual/conceptual use of pictorial means. → p. 140 → Art

Signage

→ p. 102

Source code

Source code is the readable text of a computer program written in a programming language. The term originates from computer science. → p. 86

Symmetry

is an essential feature of book typography. It is in the logic of an evenly comfortable reading offer that the type areas of a novel double-page spread turn symmetrically to the left as well as to the right of the book page. The symmetry in the design gave rise to many ideological debates. Thus it was judged – by many spokespersons of Modernism thought – as a frozen expression of dominant thinking (Tschichold, Bill, Aicher) and to be replaced by asymmetrical design. Far from such debates, symmetry and asymmetry are primarily rhetorical instruments of visual communication and should thus be regarded subjectively.
→ p. 14 → Asymmetry

T

Template

→ p. 90

Text columns

→ p. 12

Top edge of a text

→ Letter top edge

Type area

→ p. 16

Types of typesetting

In addition to ragged typesetting (1), (2) and justified typesetting (3), which are most frequently used, there are also flush left ragged right hand-corrected setting (4), centered typesetting (5) and runaround (6). ↓

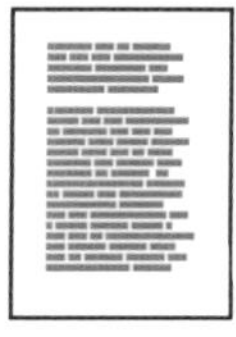

1 2 3

4 5 6

U

User experience (UX)

is the experience of users when using or viewing a website. UX describes all experiences a user has when interacting with a service, website or product. For example, if a website has extremely long loading times or complicated navigation, the user will leave it faster. This is called a "negative user experience". → p. 92

V

Visual rhetoric

This term has a central meaning in visual communication and describes its functionality. In the communication method of "sender – content – receiver", designers must present the content to be visualized adequately and in a manner appropriate to the target group. Various rhetorical instruments are available for this purpose. One of the best known is visual analogy. This term refers to the fact that verbal conceptual paraphrases are given their visual counterpart regarding the desired effect of a content to be achieved. → p. 114

X

XML, XSLT, XSLFO

are programs or programming languages that are used in connection with content management systems. → p. 91

A

A1

A2

A3

A4

A5

A6

A7

A8

B

B1

C

C1

C2

C3

D

D1

D2

D3

D4

This book addresses a variety of topics and facts that should be studied in greater depth. Below I shall present a number of specialized books that are suitable for this purpose.

In addition, I recommend reading "Read + Play – Einführung in die Typografie". This book is a bibliography with comments that will help you gain an overview of around one hundred specialized books on the topic of typography and design.

Further reading

D—2

Continued basic design principles:

Read + Play – Einführung in die Typografie

Voelker, Ulysses
Verlag Hermann Schmidt Mainz
ISBN 978-3-87439-868-8

The book serves as a commented bibliography – around 100 reference books and links about typography and graphic design are sorted according to their content and relevance. In addition, the book offers a historic overview, helps with stylistic classification and provides answers to basic typography questions.

Designing books

Hochuli, Jost, Robin Kinross
Hyphen Press
ISBN 978-0-90725-923-7

The book offers a good entry into book design and answers all relevant questions about typography, design, and production.

Detail in typography

Hochuli, Jost
Édition B42
ISBN 978-291-7855-669

This book presents and discusses many details concerning typography. It is a good entry into the topic.

Signs and symbols

Frutiger, Adrian
Studio Editions
ISBN 9781851704019

In this book, Adrian Frutiger discusses the practical and theoretical principles of designing signs and substantiates his theses with many drawings.

Grid systems in graphic design

Müller-Brockmann, Josef
Niggli Verlag
ISBN 978-3-7212-0145-1
In German and English

The fundamental work of the famous Swiss graphic designer Josef Müller-Brockmann.
Even though it was published in 1961, it is a helpful compendium on the topic of "grids".

typographie

Aicher, Otl
Verlag Hermann Schmidt Mainz
ISBN 978-3-87439-683-7
Reprint. In German and English

The standard work of one of Germany's most influential designers on the topic of typography. It covers a range of topics from the history of script via visual rhetorics or readability up to philosophical and political observations.

A
A1
A2
A3
A4
A5
A6
A7
A8

The anatomy of type

Coles, Stephen
Harper Design
ISBN 978-0-0622-0312-0

The book offers an orientation for selecting typographic tools. It discusses in detail typefaces, their classification and their mixed use.

Design and art:

Design Thinking

Ambrose, Gavin, Paul Harris
Verlag Stiebner
ISBN 978-3830713814

The book discusses the steps that are behind the concept of "design thinking" – question, research, brainstorming, prototyping, selection, implementation, feedback. It is accompanied by many work samples.

Design als Rhetorik. Grundlagen, Positionen, Fallstudien

Joost, Gesche; Arne Scheuermann
Birkhäuser Verlag
ISBN 978-3-7643-8345-9
Only in German

The anthology presents classical rhetoric as a meta-theory of design. It also includes historic positions as well as contemporary controversial discussions. The contributions deal with all design genres, from product design via communication design up to interactive design.

Kunst+Zufall

Janecke, Christian
Verlag für moderne Kunst
ISBN 3-928342-51-7
Only in German

The book discusses the strategies of utilizing coincidences in art.

Designing programmes

Gerstner, Karl
Lars Müller Publishers
ISBN 978-3-03778-093-0

In his book, Gerstner shows that design is based on the systematic application of graphical means. His motto is "Instead of solutions to tasks, programs for solutions."

B
B1
C
C1
C2
C3
D
D1
D2
D3
D4

Rasterfahndung. Das Raster in der Kunst nach 1945

Gross, Ulrike, Schimpf, Simone (eds.)
Wienand Verlag
ISBN 978-3-86832-089-3
Only in German

The catalog for the exhibition of the same name at the Stuttgart art museum is dedicated in various ways to the role of grids in art.

Further theory:

A theory of semiotics

Eco, Umberto
Indiana University Press
ISBN 978-0-253-35955-1

Eco defines with a semiotic viewpoint what constitutes signs and how the interpretation of the term has evolved throughout history. He introduces the various schools of thought and explains the interactive relationship of the concept with other scientific disciplines (philosophy, esthetics, linguistics, mathematics, etc.).

Proust and the squid: the story and science of the reading brain

Wolf, Maryanne
Harper Perennial
ISBN 978-0060933845

The American scientist Maryanne Wolf describes the neuronal activities that take place in the brain during reading and reflects on the social and societal dimensions of written communications.

General communications:

Pragmatics of human communication

Watzlawick, Paul, Janet Beavin Bavelas, Don D. Jackson
W.W. Norton & Company
ISBN 978-0393710595

The book deals with the topic of communication by describing basic effects of human interaction. A good introduction to understanding the social and cultural coexistence within a society.

Six tools for clear communication

Schulz von Thun, Friedemann
Schulz von Thun Institut für Kommunikation

The English version introduces the principles of the general psychology of communication. This introductory text is also compulsive reading for designers even though at first glance it has nothing to do with design.

A

A1

A2

A3

A4

A5

A6

A7

A8

B

B1

C

C1

C2

C3

D

D1

D2

D3

D4

Picture credits

D—3

Intro

p. 2
Photo: Stefanie Pretnar

Graphic Grids in Everyday Design
A

p. 8
Photo: Ulysses Voelker

Introduction
A—1

01 → p. 11
Grün ist die Hoffnung

Scan from:
Boyle, T. C.: Grün ist die Hoffnung (German edition of "Budding Prospects"), Frankfurt am Main, 1990

02 → p. 13
Süddeutsche Zeitung

Scan from:
Süddeutsche Zeitung (2017), no. 43, p. 2–3

Novel
A—2

01_01 → p. 15
Ulysses

Scan from:
Joyce, James: Ulysses, Rhein–Verlag, Zurich, 1956, p. 200–201

01_02 → p. 15
Tropic of Capricorn

Scan from:
Miller, Henry: Tropic of Capricorn, London, 1964, p. 122–123

01_03 → p. 15
Kritik der Macht

Scan from:
Honneth, Axel: Kritik der Macht – Reflexionsstufen einer kritischen Gesellschaftstheorie, suhrkamp verlag, Frankfurt am Main, 2014, p. 152–153

08 → p. 22
Water Music

Scan from:
Boyle, T. C.: Water Music, London, 1998, p. 284–285

10 → p. 25
Detailtypografie

Scan from:
Forssmann, Friedrich, Ralf de Jong: Detailtypografie, Mainz, 2004, p. 402–403

01 → p. 27
Ulysses

Scan from:
Joyce, James: Ulysses, Rhein–Verlag, Zurich, 1956, p. 200–201

02 → p. 27
Water Music

Scan from:
Boyle, T. C.: Water Music, London, 1998, p. 284–285

03 → p. 28
Tropic of Capricorn

Scan from:
Miller, Henry: Tropic of Capricorn, London, 1964, p. 122–123

04 → p. 28
Kritik der Macht

Scan from:
Honneth, Axel: Kritik der Macht – Reflexionsstufen einer kritischen Gesellschaftstheorie, suhrkamp verlag, Frankfurt am Main, 2014, p. 152–153

05 → p. 29
Der Krieg mit den Molchen

Scan from:
Capek, Karel:
Der Krieg mit den Molchen, Frankfurt, 2016, p. 102–103

06 → p. 29
Finnegans Wake

Scan from:
Joyce, James: Finnegans Wehg (the German translation of "Finnegans Wake"), author of the English edition: James Joyce; translation by the publisher, 1993, p. 331–332

07 → p. 30
Die neuen Leiden des jungen W.

Scan from:
Plenzdorf, Ullrich:
Die neuen Leiden des jungen W., Frankfurt, 1983, p. 162–163

08 → p. 30
Das hündische Herz

Scan from:
Bulgakow, Michail: Das hündische Herz, Büchergilde Gutenberg, Frankfurt, 2016, p. 122–123

Non-fiction book
A—3

01 → p. 33
Alvar Aaalto

Scan from:
Aalto, Alvar and Karl Fleig: Alvar Aalto, Verlag für Architektur Artemis, Zurich, 1991, p. 88–89

01 → p. 39
Klassiker des Produktdesigns

Scan from:
Eisele, Petra: Klassiker des Produktdesigns, Reclam Verlag, Ditzingen, 2014, p. 282–283

02 → p. 39
Israel – Mit dem Westjordanland

Scan from:
Teifer, Hermann: Israel – Mit dem Westjordanland, Artemis Verlag, Zurich, 1981, U2f

03 → p. 40
Nieuw Handwoordenboek der Nederlandse Taal

Scan from:
Nieuw Handwoordenboek der Nederlandse Taal, Van Dale, 1968, p. 650–651

04 → p. 40
Das Mysterium der Zahl

Scan from:
Endres, Franz Carl, Annemarie Schimmel: Das Mysterium der Zahl, Diederichs, Munich, 1996, p. 248–249

05 → p. 41
Black Transparency. The right to know in the age of mass surveillance

Scan from:
Metahaven: Black Transparency. The right to know in the age of mass surveillance, Sternberg Press, 2015, p. 78–79

06 → p. 41
Grundbau

Scan from:
Arz, Schmidt, Seitz, Semprich: Grundbau, Ernst & Sohn Verlag für Architektur und technische Wissenschaften GmbH, Berlin, 1994, p. 114–115

07 → p. 42
Die schönsten deutschen Bücher, The best German book design 2013

Scan from:
Sender, Alexandra: Die schönsten deutschen Bücher, The best German book design 2013, Stiftung Buchkunst, Frankfurt, 2013, p. 298–299

08 → p. 42
Urbane Interventionen Istanbul

Scan from:
Von Borries, Friedrich, Moritz Ahlert, Jens-Uwe Fischer: Urbane Interventionen Istanbul, Merve Verlag, Berlin, 2014, p. 60–61

09 → p. 43
Zeichensysteme der visuellen Kommunikation

Scan from:
Otl Aicher, Martin Krampen: Zeichensysteme der visuellen Kommunikation: Handbuch für Designer, Architekten, Planer, Organisatoren, Stuttgart, 1977, p. 90–91

10 → p. 43
Zeichensysteme der visuellen Kommunikation

Scan from:
Otl Aicher, Martin Krampen: Zeichensysteme der visuellen Kommunikation: Handbuch für Designer, Architekten, Planer, Organisatoren, Stuttgart, 1977, p. 46–47

11 → p. 44
Konstruktion einfacher Möbel

Scan from:
Schneck, Adolf G.: Konstruktion einfacher Möbel, Julius Hoffmann Verlag, Stuttgart, 1948, p. 26–27

12 → p. 44
Grundlagen der Straßen-Verkehrstechnik und der Verkehrsplanung

Scan from:
Schnabel, Werner, Dieter Lohse: Grundlagen der Straßen-Verkehrstechnik und der Verkehrsplanung, vol. 2, Verlag für Bauwesen, Berlin, 1997, p. 194–195

Art catalog
A—4

01_01 → p. 47
Jean-Michel Basquiat

Scan from:
Emmerling, Leonhard: Jean-Michel Basquiat, TASCHEN Verlag, Cologne, 2007, p. 90–91

01_02 → p. 47
Local Wind, Aroch. Catalogs and books published by Israeli artists in the 70s and 80s

Scan from:
Yonatan Vinitsky, Ellie Armon Azoulay, Assaf Cohen, Johanna Asseraf (eds.): Local Wind, Aroch. Catalogs and books published by Israeli artists in the 70s and 80s, Public School Editions, Tel Aviv, 2014, p. 34–35

01_03 → p. 47
Die schönsten deutschen Bücher, The best German book design 2013

Scan from:
Sender, Alexandra: Die schönsten deutschen Bücher, The best German book design 2013, Stiftung Buchkunst, Frankfurt, 2013, p. 166–167

01 → p. 53
Thomas Klefisch – 60 Monate, 60 Bilder

Scan from:
Bruno Kehrein – Thomas Klefisch – 60 Monate, 60 Bilder, Grupello Verlag, 1st edition, 2017, p. 32–33

02 → p. 53
10+1 Talents Messe Frankfurt

Scan from:
Hansjerg Maier–Aichen: 10+1 Talents Messe Frankfurt, av edition, Ludwigsburg, 2011, p. 38–39

03 → p. 54
Vivace

Scan from:
Hanne van der Woude, Vivace, 2016, FW:Books, 2nd edition, p. 48–49

04 → p. 54
Laurie Anderson Tisha Brown Gordon Matta-Clark

Scan from:
Laurie Anderson Tisha Brown Gordon Matta-Clark – Pioneers of the Downtown Scene New York 1970s, Prestel Verlag, Munich, 2011, p. 118–119

05 → p. 55
Der Maler Peter Weiss. Bilder Zeichnungen Collagen Filme

Scan from:
Der Maler Peter Weiss. Bilder Zeichnungen Collagen Filme, Verlag Frölich&Kaufmann, Berlin, 1982, p. 102–103

06 → p. 55
Pink Wave Hunter Part 1

Scan from:
Wekua, Andro: Pink Wave Hunter Part 1, Verlag der Buchhandlung Walter König, Cologne, 2011, p. 40–41

07 → p. 56
Kunste zur Text, Michael Riedel

Scan from:
Kunste zur Text, Michael Riedel, Ed.: Matthias Ulrich and Max Hollein, 2012, Verlag der Buchhandlung Walther König, Cologne, p. 114

08 → p. 56
The Städel Paintings, John Baldessari

Scan from:
John Baldessari. The Städel Paintings, Martin Engel (ed.), Hirmer Verlag, 2015, p. 28–29

Magazine
A—5

01 → p. 59
Der Spiegel

Scan from:
Der Spiegel (2017), no. 18, p. 32–33

02_01 → p. 61
Der Spiegel

Scan from:
Der Spiegel (2016), no. 02, p. 10–11

02_02 → p. 61
Der Spiegel

Scan from:
Der Spiegel (2017), no. 18, p. 22–23

02_03 → p. 61
Der Spiegel

Scan from:
Der Spiegel (2017), no. 18, p. 48–49

03_01 → p. 62
Unnamed Fanzine

Scan from:
Fanzine (2012), p. 12–14

03_02 → p. 62
Unnamed Fanzine

Scan from:
Fanzine (2012), p. 8–9

01 → p. 67
The Gentlewoman

Scan from:
The Gentlewoman (2015), no. 11, p. 96–97

02 → p. 67
form

Scan from:
form (2017), no. 267, p. 44–45

03 → p. 68
The Weekender

Scan from:
The Weekender (2016), no. 23, p. 20–21

04 → p. 68
Freimodekultur. POPGender, Mode, Fotografie und Texte

Scan from:
Dünhölter, Kai: Freimodekultur: POPGender, Mode, Fotografie und Texte, Textem Verlag, Hamburg, 2015, p. 2–3

05 → p. 69
West–End: Neue Zeitschrift für Sozialforschung

Scan from:
West–End: Neue Zeitschrift für Sozialforschung (2015), no. 1, p. 144–145

06 → p. 69
Lodown Magazine

Scan from:
Lodown Magazine (2008), no. 60, p. 100–101

07 → p. 70
Slanted

Scan from:
Slanted (2011), no. 16, p. 28–29

08 → p. 70
_Nieuwe Culturele Netwerken/
_New Cultural Networks

Scan from:
_Nieuwe Culturele Netwerken/
_New Cultural Networks,
Stichting All Media, Amsterdam,
2008, p. 6–7

09 → p. 71
11 Freunde

Scan from:
11 Freunde (2007), no. 63,
p. 45–46

10 → p. 71
Back Cover

Scan from:
Back Cover (2013), no. 05,
p. 44–45

11 → p. 72
Adbusters

Scan from:
Adbusters (2016), no. 128

12 → p. 72
Fanzine

Scan from:
Fanzine, p. 19–20

Newspaper
A—6

01_01 → p. 75
Süddeutsche Zeitung

Scan from:
Süddeutsche Zeitung (2017),
no. 101, p. 4–5

01_02 → p. 75
Süddeutsche Zeitung

Scan from:
Süddeutsche Zeitung (2017),
no. 102, p. 4–5

01_03 → p. 75
Süddeutsche Zeitung

Scan from:
Süddeutsche Zeitung (2017),
no. 103, p. 4–5

02_01 → p. 76
Süddeutsche Zeitung

Scan from:
Süddeutsche Zeitung (2017),
no. 43, p. 1

02_02 → p. 77
Frankfurter Allgemeine Zeitung

Scan from:
Frankfurter Allgemeine Zeitung
(2017), no. 44, p. 1

01 → p. 81
Die Zeit

Scan from:
DIE ZEIT (2017), no. 12, p. 6–7

02 → p. 81
The Guardian

Scan from:
The Guardian (2017), May 10,
2017, p. 14–15

03 → p. 82
Frankfurter Rundschau

Scan from:
Frankfurter Rundschau (2017),
no. 102, p. 4–5

04 → p. 82
The New York Times

Scan from:
The New York Times
International Edition (2017),
no. 41.774, p. 6–7

05 → p. 83
Corrierre della sera

Scan from:
Corrierre della sera (2017),
no. 26, p. 2–3

06 → p. 83
Le Monde

Scan from:
Le Monde (2017), May 9, 2017,
p. 2–3

07 → p. 84
Haaretz

Scan from:
Haaretz (2016), August 26, 2016,
p. 13–14

08 → p. 84
De Volkskrant

Scan from:
de Volkskrant (2017), no. 28.347,
p. 10–11

Web design
A—7

05_01 → p. 93
arte

Screenshot:
<https://www.arte.tv>, Feb. 25,
2018, 14:28

05_02 → p. 93
arte

Screenshot:
<https://www.arte.tv>, Feb. 25,
2018, 14:28

05_03 → p. 93
arte

Screenshot:
<https://www.arte.tv>, Feb. 25,
2018, 14:28

05_04 → p. 93
arte

Screenshot:
<https://www.arte.tv>, Feb. 25,
2018, 14:28

01_01 → p. 95
faz.net

Screenshot:
<https://www.faz.net>, Feb. 25, 2018, 14:28

01_02 → p. 95
faz.net

Screenshot:
<https://www.faz.net>, June 11, 2017, 14:28

01_03 → p. 95
faz.net

Screenshot:
<https://www.faz.net>, June 11, 2017, 14:28

02_01 → p. 95
stedelijk.nl

Screenshot:
<https://www.stedelijk.nl>, Feb. 11, 2018, 12:03

02_02 → p. 95
stedelijk.nl

Screenshot:
<https://www.stedelijk.nl>, Feb. 11, 2018, 12:03

02_03 → p. 95
stedelijk.nl

Screenshot:
<https://www.stedelijk.nl>, Feb. 11, 2018, 12:03

03_01 → p. 96
tm-research-archive.ch

Screenshot:
<https://www.tm-research-archive.ch>, Jan. 10, 2018, 12:05

03_02 → p. 96
tm-research-archive.ch

Screenshot:
<https://www.tm-research-archive.ch>, Jan. 10, 2018, 12:05

03_03 → p. 96
tm-research-archive.ch

Screenshot:
<https://www.tm-research-archive.ch>, Jan. 10, 2018, 12:05

04_01 → p. 96
typotheque.com

Screenshot:
<typotheque.com/blog/new_typeface_gordon>, Feb. 26, 2018, 12:07

04_02 → p. 96
typotheque.com

Screenshot:
<typotheque.com/blog/new_typeface_gordon>, Feb. 26, 2018, 12:07

04_03 → p. 96
typotheque.com

Screenshot:
<typotheque.com/blog/new_typeface_gordon>, Feb. 26, 2018, 12:07

05_01 → p. 97
brutalistframework.com

Screenshot:
<http://brutalistframework.com>, Jan. 28, 2018, 22:50

05_02 → p. 97
brutalistframework.com

Screenshot:
<http://brutalistframework.com>, Jan. 28, 2018, 22:50

05_03 → p. 97
brutalistframework.com

Screenshot:
<http://brutalistframework.com>, Jan. 28, 2018, 22:50

06_01 → p. 97
opensource.london

Screenshot:
<https://opensource.london>, Jan. 28, 2018, 17:15

06_02 → p. 97
opensource.london

Screenshot:
<https://opensource.london>, Jan. 28, 2018, 17:15

06_03 → p. 97
opensource.london

Screenshot:
<https://opensource.london>, Jan. 28, 2018, 17:15

07_01 → p. 98
letteror.com

Screenshot:
<http://letteror.com/dev/mathshapes/>, Jan. 28, 2018, 23:10

07_02 → p. 98
letteror.com

Screenshot:
<http://letteror.com/dev/mathshapes/>, Jan. 28, 2018, 23:10

07_03 → p. 98
letteror.com

Screenshot:
<http://letteror.com/dev/mathshapes/>, Jan. 28, 2018, 23:10

08_01 → p. 98
manifestoproject.it

Screenshot:
<https://manifestoproject.it/>, Feb. 25, 2018, 17:16

08_02 → p. 98
manifestoproject.it

Screenshot:
<https://manifestoproject.it/>, Feb. 25, 2018, 17:17

08_03 → p. 98
manifestoproject.it

Screenshot:
<https://manifestoproject.it/>, Feb. 25, 2018, 17:24

09_01 → p. 99
ikob.be

Screenshot:
<https://www.ikob.be/>, Aug. 30, 2018, 01:06

09_02 → p. 99
ikob.be

Screenshot:
<https://www.ikob.be/>, Aug. 30, 2018, 01:06

09_03 → p. 99
ikob.be

Screenshot:
<https://www.ikob.be/>, Aug. 30, 2018, 01:09

10_01 → p. 99
89plus.com

Screenshot:
<https://www.89plus.com/>, Aug. 30, 2018, 01:12

10_02 → p. 99
89plus.com

Screenshot:
<https://www.89plus.com/>, Aug. 30, 2018, 01:13

10_03 → p. 99
89plus.com

Screenshot:
<https://www.89plus.com/>, Aug. 30, 2018, 01:15

11_01 → p. 100
random-wikipedia.com

Screenshot:
<https://www.random-wikipedia.com/index.html#info>, Aug. 30, 2018, 00:53

11_02 → p. 100
random-wikipedia.com

Screenshot:
<https://www.random-wikipedia.com/index.html#info>, Aug. 30, 2018, 00:53

11_03 → p. 100
random-wikipedia.com

Screenshot:
<https://www.random-wikipedia.com/index.html#info>, Aug. 30, 2018, 00:54

12_01 → p. 100
balenciaga.com

Screenshot:
<https://www.balenciaga.com/de>, Aug. 30, 2018, 00:48

12_02 → p. 100
balenciaga.com

Screenshot:
<https://www.balenciaga.com/de>, Aug. 30, 2018, 00:48

12_03 → p. 100
balenciaga.com

Screenshot:
<https://www.balenciaga.com/de>, Aug. 30, 2018, 00:49

Design Process – First Steps
B

p. 110
Photo: Ulysses Voelker

Idea and sketch
B—1

01–07 → p. 116–119
Sketches: Ulysses Voelker

Background Information
C

p. 122
Photo: Stefanie Pretnar

Humans need order
C—1

01_01 → p. 125
Wardrobe

Screenshot:
<https://upload.wikimedia.org/wikipedia/commons/a/a7/Walk_In_Closet_-_Expandable_Closet_Rod_and_Shelf.jpg>, July 5, 2017, 14:24

01_02 → p. 125
Bookcase

Screenshot:
<https://upload.wikimedia.org/wikipedia/commons/1/18/Two_bookshelves_full_of_books_belonging_to_Unitedmissionary_%28 2919%29.jpg>, Jan. 12, 2018, 23:44

01_03 → p. 125
Road situation

Screenshot:
<https://www.pexelS. com/photo/bird–s–eye–view–cars–crossing–crossroad–5486/>, July 5, 2017, 14:26

02 → p. 127
Field irrigation (Nebraska)

Screenshot:
<https://eoimageS.gsfc.nasa.gov/images/imagerecords/5000/5772/kansas_AST_2001175_lrg.jpg>, July 5, 2017, 14:28

03 → p. 127
Dices

Screenshot:
<https://upload.wikimedia.org/wikipedia/commons/9/99/Dice_-_1-2-4-5-6.jpg>, Jan. 15, 2018, 02:26

04 → p. 129
Das Ringelnatz Lesebuch

Scan from:
Das Ringelnatz Lesebuch, Diogenes Verlag, Zurich, 1994, p. 236

05 → p. 129
Sumerian board

Screenshot:
<http://historiaproject.altervista.org/wp-content/uploads/2015/03/akkadian-cuneiform.jpg>, July 05, 2017, 04:42

Intuition and method in design
C—3

01 → p. 145
"Number 32", Jackson Pollock, 1950

Scan from:
Janke, Christian. Kunst+Zufall: Analyse und Bedeutung. [Ed. by the Institut für Moderne Kunst Nürnberg]. Verlag für moderne Kunst. Nuremberg, p. 159

02 → p. 147
"La mort du patriarche", Niki de Saint Phalle, 1962

Scan from:
Hulten, Pontus. Niki de Saint Phalle. [Ed. by the Kunst- & Ausstellungshalle der Bundesrepublik Deutschland GmbH]. Verlag Gerd Hatje. Bonn, 1994, p. 213

03 → p. 147
"collage V67–30 randomised distribution", Herman de Vries, 1967

Scan from:
Janke, Christian. Kunst+Zufall: Analyse und Bedeutung. [Ed. by the Institut für Moderne Kunst Nürnberg]. Verlag für moderne Kunst. Nuremberg, p. 115

Appendix
D

p. 150
Photo: Stefanie Pretnar

Outro

p. 175
Photo: Stefanie Pretnar

A

A1

A2

A3

A4

A5

A6

A7

A8

B

B1

C

C1

C2

C3

D

D1

D2

D3

D4

172—173

Imprint

D—4

Structuring Design

Author
Ulysses Voelker

Visual concept, design
Michael Schmitz & Ulysses Voelker

Translation
Editorial office van Uffelen

Editing
Cosima Talhouni

Proofreading
Sophie Steybe

Paper
Pergraphica Natural Rough 120 g/m²

Cover
MGP 1.8 mm

Typefaces
Antwerp (A2-TYPE)
Univers (Linotype)

The Deutsche Nationalbibliothek lists this publication in the Deutsche Nationalbibliografie; detailed bibliographic data are available on the Internet at http://dnb.dnb.de

ISBN 978-3-7212-0994-5

www.niggli.ch

2nd edition 2020